Maple Talk

Maple Talk

Steven G. Adams

Prentice Hall, Upper Saddle River, NJ 07458

Library of Congress Cataloging-in-Publication Data

Adams, Steven G.
   Maple talk / Steven G. Adams.
      p.   cm.
    Includes bibliographical references (p. -) and index.
    ISBN 0-13-237306-8
     1. Maple (Computer file) 2. Mathematics—Data processing.
  I. Title.
  QA76.95.A28   1997
  510'.285'53—dc20   96-27154
                                   CIP

Acquisitions Editor: Tom Robbins
Production Editor: Joseph Scordato
Director Prod. & Mfg.: David Riccardi
Production Manager: Bayani Mendoza DeLeon
Cover Designer: Bruce Kenselaar
Copy Editor: Peter J. Zurita
Buyer: Donna Sullivan
Editorial Assistant : Nancy Garcia

©1997 by Prentice-Hall, Inc.
Simon & Schuster/A Viacom Company
Upper Saddle River, NJ 07458

The author and publisher of this book have used their best efforts in preparing this book. These efforts
include the development, research, and testing of the theories and programs to determine their effectiveness.
The author and publisher make no warranty of any kind, expressed or implied, with regard to these programs
or the documentation contained in this book. The author and publisher shall not be liable in any event for
incidental or consequential damages in connection with, or arising out of, the furnishing, performance, or use
of these programs.

Printed in the United States of America

10 9 8 7 6 5 4 3 2 1

ISBN 0-13-237306-8

Prentice-Hall International (UK) Limited, London
Prentice-Hall of Australia Pty. Limited, Sydney
Prentice-Hall Canada Inc., Toronto
Prentice-Hall Hispanoamericana, S.A., Mexico
Prentice-Hall of India Private Limited, New Delhi
Prentice-Hall of Japan, Inc., Tokyo
Simon & Schuster Asia Pte. Ltd., Singapore
Editora Prentice-Hall do Brasil, Ltda., Rio de Janeiro

For those that are here: my wife Fiona, our daughter Sophie, my mother-in-law Glenys Campbell and my father Geoffrey Adams and in memory of those who are not: my mother Valerie and my father-in-law Angus.

Preface

During the five or so years that I spent working for companies directly involved with computer algebra systems I had the chance to view many good books explaining how best to use one system or another. Almost without exception the books take the same approach; a symbolic algebra system means a system used by mathematicians. Therefore the books discuss using the particular computer algebra system related to some branch of mathematics. Maple Talk is for all of the other users out there who are not mathematicians as well as those who are.

Maple Talk, as an idea, started while I was working for Waterloo Maple Software. Maple Talk, as a project, started soon after Tom Robbins moved to Prentice Hall. Fortunately this coincided with a time when I was living and consulting in Boston MA and so I could devote the necessary time to it. A little over 18 months later here it is, Maple Talk.

Why Read It?

Maple Talk does not explain Maple by simply listing every function and procedure available to the user. Instead I have tried to introduce the elements of the Maple system through examples. This means that some of the 2500 or so functions and procedures are never discussed. I have also tried to avoid going into so much detail that the text becomes tedious, forcing you to give up and go and do something else. This means that you may have to do some exploration of your own. Most importantly I have tried to make you feel comfortable enough that finding help on any Maple function is never a cause for concern. In short I have tried to introduce Maple in such a way that you have the understanding, the tools, and the desire to explore Maple beyond the topics covered in this book.

Layout

A great deal of effort has been spent in making the important things the most prominent, so the layout of Maple Talk is a little different to the norm. Instead of finding the table of contents at the beginning of the book you will find the index, and where the index is normally found you will find an index of frequently asked questions. The table of contents is on the back cover.

Every chapter of Maple Talk is built-up in the same way: a general discussion incorporating examples, pointers to FAQs and additional information, a list of the new functions introduced, followed by an answers to the FAQs section. Chapter 0 outlines the book and introduces you to the basic idea of a computer algebra system, Chapter 1 gives you an informal introduction to Maple, Chapter 2 takes a more formal look at the Maple system, Chapter 3 introduces you to Maple programs, Chapter 4 deals with how Maple interfaces with external data files, Chapter 5 shows how Maple can be used as a problem solving tool and Chapter 6 takes a look at using Maple to provide symbolic capabilities as part of a third party tool.

Thanks Go To ...

Grateful thanks go to Kate Atherley for making working for Waterloo Maple such an enjoyable experience, which in turn meant that I learned far more about the Maple system than is, maybe, healthy, and to Fiona, my wife, for allowing me to stop consulting in order to write Maple Talk. In addition, I would like to both acknowledge and thank, in no particular order, the following people for taking the time to review earlier versions of Maple Talk: Professor William J. Eccles, Dept. of Electrical and Computer Engineering Rose-Hulman Institute of Technology, Professor William C. Bauldry, Department of Mathematical Sciences Appalachian State University and Professor Robert J. Lopez, Department of Mathematics Rose-Hulman Institute of Technology. Although I cannot say that I agreed with all of their comments and suggestions I sincerely hope that I have produced a better book because of them. Finally, I must thank Tom Robbins for allowing me the opportunity to fulfill a long standing ambition of mine - to write a book.

Steve Adams

West Worthing, England

Index

Symbols

A

Introduction

Who Should Read This Book?

Although Maple is a sophisticated software tool for doing mathematics quickly and accurately on a computer, it is not solely a tool used by mathematicians. On the contrary, it has been designed to be used by scientists, engineers, financial analysts, research, teaching staff, and students as well as mathematicians. In fact, anyone who uses mathematics can gain from using Maple.

This book should be read by anyone who uses mathematics professionally but does not want to become a mathematician. Of course you can also use this book if you just want to investigate mathematics in a fun and interactive way. If you are a mathematician, you are more than welcome to use Maple and this text. By encouraging the reader to use Maple as a problem-solving aid, it is not the author's intent to get them to stop thinking about the mathematics underpinning the problem; on the contrary the reverse is true. When using Maple you only have to recognize when a mathematical operation has to take place; you do not have to remember the exact mechanism to apply. For example, an expression needs to be integrated but the method of integration could be direct integration, integration by parts, integration by substitution, and so on. As far as you are concerned, you just want the integral and, in most cases, are not concerned which method is used. In all probability Maple "knows" more methods than you and is capable of selecting the appropriate one faster than you. So let Maple do the grunt work for you! This is like saying, "I need to bake a cake, but I don't remember the exact recipe, so I will ask a cook to do it for me." Using Maple allows you to do the mathematics without having to recall the exact theory every time. This lets you concentrate on the problem without getting bogged down in the mechanics of the mathematics.

Why Read This Book?

A common approach taken when introducing a software tool is to take the reader through every function available in it. This is not the case with this book. The approach taken is to introduce enough of Maple's functionality so that Maple becomes a tool that is useful to the reader. Many functions are not described formally but are introduced in examples that have been chosen as a way both to introduce useful techniques and to show how Maple can be applied in a given subject area. Scattered throughout the text are pointers to additional information, complimentary functions, frequently asked questions (FAQs), and potential pitfalls (Beware). To get something from this book and Maple you do not have to be a mathematician, engineer, financial analyst, and so forth; all that is needed is a willingness to explore a problem using Maple.

Finally, the only assumption made about the reader is that he or she has some exposure to computer programming. It is not assumed that the reader has a strong mathematics background and that he or she will immediately recognize every example used.

How to Use This Book

The layout of this book is a little different from the norm. The important things have been made the most prominent. So, instead of finding the table of contents at the beginning, you will see the index, and where the index is normally found you will find an index of frequently asked questions. The table of contents is on the back cover.

Every chapter is built up in the same way: general discussion incorporating examples, pointers to FAQs and additional information, a list of the new functions introduced, and the answers to the FAQs. Additional information can be found in sidebars throughout the text. The FAQ pointer is the large question mark found in the margin (see left). The number following the question mark is the question index. This means that there is at least one frequently asked question associated with the subject of the text. This book is primarily concerned with Maple Vr4 and as such the syntax used is valid for this version of the product. Where the syntax differs from that used in Maple Vr3 and before, it is indicated with the large exclamation mark in the margin. It is used in the same way as the FAQ pointer. In this case, however, it points to the Beware section at the end of each chapter. Finally, it is recommended that you have Maple running as you work through the book. You only really learn when you have to do it yourself!

A typographic note: Maple keywords such as function names and procedure options appear in the text in `courier`. All Maple input lines begin with the prompt >. This should not be entered as part of the command line, as it is machine-generated.

Outline of the Book

It is not the goal of this book to introduce the reader to every Maple function and procedure. Instead, where possible, functions and procedures from all of the main groups of Maple are introduced by example. It is the aim, however, to give the reader a good feel for Maple, its structure, objects, and syntax. More importantly the reader should feel comfortable enough that finding help on any Maple function should never be a cause for concern.

Chapter 0 outlines the book and introduces the reader to the basic idea of a computer algebra system, or CAS.

Chapter 1 gives the reader an informal introduction to Maple, its origins, the system, and its place in the market. You are taken on a whistle-stop tour of Maple's functionality and features. In this chapter we do not dwell on the basic syntax, the idea of expressions, function calls, or how to keep track of calculations.

Chapter 2 takes a more formal look at the Maple system: starting and stopping, initialization files, interacting with the operating system, and getting help are all covered. Additionally, you are introduced to doing arithmetic with Maple, Maple objects, and plotting.

Chapter 3 introduces the reader to Maple programs, which may be as simple as grouping a set of functions and procedures together to automate a task, or as complex as extending Maple's functionality into areas not yet supported. The Maple language allows programs to be written using functional, procedural, or rule-based paradigms.

Chapter 4 deals with how Maple interfaces with external data files. The standard input/output procedures will be discussed along with how to interface Maple to the data files of other scientific packages.

Chapter 5 shows how Maple can be used as a problem-solving tool applicable to many disciplines. Tutorials introduce additional Maple functionality as well as demonstrating how Maple can be applied in different problem areas.

Chapter 6 takes a look at using Maple, to provide symbolic capabilities, as part of a third-party tool, in this case MATLAB.

Computer Algebra

Research into computer-based systems capable of doing symbolic mathematics began in the 1960s. In the late 1960s, early 1970s MACSYMA and REDUCE were released. These early computer algebra systems were LISP-based and tended to be very resource-hungry in terms of storage and CPU time. In the early 1980s, a new generation of CASs made their debut: MuMath (later to become Derive), Maple, *Mathematica*, and Theorist. These were far more efficient than their predecessors as they used the C programming language instead of LISP, which resulted in smaller, portable systems that ran faster in less memory. Notably, Theorist runs in less than one megabyte of RAM and Derive is available on a hand-held calculator.

The Maple project started in November 1980 and produced its first results in December of the same year. Its rapid development was due in part to its being coded in C and partly to its incorporating only the most efficient algorithms into the fledgling CAS. In the intervening years Maple has grown into a comprehensive CAS capable of performing symbolic, numeric, and graphical computations on many different types of computer systems. Maple comes with over 2,500 functions and a Worksheet or command-line-style interface. It is now available on over 30 hardware platforms from Macintosh to Alpha.

Why Use Computer Algebra?

Today's computer-aided design and analysis tools fall broadly into one of two camps: numerical or symbolic. Despite their immense power, the numerical tools have two serious failings: finite accuracy and an inability to deal with algebraic or symbolic quantities. This means that certain types of problems cannot be tackled either literally or with any degree of confidence. In general these tools are not suited to dealing with problems that involve the manipulation of either unknown (symbolic) quantities or very large or very small numbers. In most cases (unfortunately there are still some problems that we do not know how to deal with), an answer will be found using a tool from the second group.

The Word-Length Problem

Numerical tools only produce floating-point solutions that have been computed using either floating-point hardware or a software emulation of the hardware. This means that these tools rely exclusively on a floating-point model that has a fixed word length and data definition.

Although the the word length associated with these floating-point models has increased steadily from 16 to 32 to 64 bits and hence increased their ability to store and manipulate numbers, they are still restricted. The larger the word length, the bigger or smaller the number that can be stored and manipulated accurately. For example, if a floating-point data definition only allows for a word length of one then only two quantities can be stored and manipulated: one and zero. If the word length is doubled, four quantities can be dealt with, and so on.

MORE BITS MEANS BETTER ACCURACY	Here π is represented as a floating-point number. Each iteration uses a word length capable of supporting one more significant digit than the previous. With each iteration the accuracy with which π is represented improves.	3. 3.1 3.14 3.142 3.1416 3.14159 3.141593 3.1415927 3.14159265 3.141592654

If at any time during a calculation a number becomes either so large or so small that the number of bits needed to store and manipulate it accurately exceeds the available word length, errors will creep into the answer. These errors are known as roundoff errors. Of course not everybody is concerned with eliminating these errors. In the banking world, however, roundoff errors, appearing as fractions of a cent, can quickly accumulate. If these fractions of a cent can be siphoned off into another account, millions of dollars can be made. Unfortunately this is illegal.

ERRORS DUE TO FINITE WORD LENGTH	Here the result of $1/7$ times 7 is computed as a floating-point number using a calculator. The number of significant digits used is increased by one with each iteration. It is quite apparent that all of the answers are erroneous, the size of the error being inversely proportional to the word length.	.7 .98 1.001 1.0003 1.00002 .999999 .9999997 .99999998 1.000000001 1.0000000003

ERRORS DUE TO FINITE WORD LENGTH We now convert ten billion pounds sterling to U.S. dollars at an exchange rate of 1.569 dollars to the pound. We do this operation twice: first using a calculator with only ten digits of accuracy and then using one with 15.

1st transaction: $10^{10}/1.569 = \$ 6.373486297 \ 10^9$

2nd transaction: $10^{10}/1.569 = \$ 6.37348629700446 \ 10^9$

What is the difference between the two numbers? This does not seem like a big deal. However, repeat this operation 100,000 times a day keeping the difference and you will be \$466.00 richer.

The difference per transaction: \$ 0.00446

Therefore, numerical tools should be viewed as machines that are capable of making millions of approximations per second. How approximate any result will be is dependent on the floating-point arithmetic model used and its word length.

Most CASs do not suffer from the limitations imposed by floating-point models and their implementation and therefore are capable of representing floating-point numbers to any arbitrary level of accuracy chosen by the user. By selecting the word length for a calculation and hence the number of significant digits used, the user is setting the level of error acceptable. In fact, by changing the number of significant digits used in consecutive calculations, a qualitative measure of how good a calculation is can be gauged. Another consequence of being able to control word length is that exact integer arithmetic is now possible.

UNLIMITED BY WORD LENGTH By using Maple the result of dividing 1356669 by 10989019 will be determined to a given number of significant digits. Unlike the preceding answers, the final calculation contains no roundoff errors.

```
> for n from 1 to 10 by 1 do
    evalf(1356669/10989019,n)
  od;
```

$$.1$$
$$.12$$
$$.123$$
$$.1235$$
$$.12346$$
$$.123457$$
$$.1234568$$
$$.12345679$$
$$.123456789$$
$$.1234567890$$

UNLIMITED ACCURACY Similarly, we can use Maple to calculate the floating-point approximations of any mathematical constant to any level of accuracy. Here we calculate π to 25 places, e to 40 places—and the popular approximation to π, 22/7 to 35 places. Then we calculate the error between π and its approximation to 35 places.

```
> evalf(Pi,25);
```

$$3.141592653589793238462643$$

```
> evalf(exp(1),40);
```

$$2.718281828459045235360287471352662497757$$

```
> evalf(22/7,35);
```

$$3.14285714285714285714285714285714285714285714285714429$$

```
> evalf((22/7)-Pi, 35);
```

$$.0012644892673496186802137595776400$$

```
> 2^100;
```

$$1267650600228229401496703205376$$

Here we get Maple to calculate and display the exact value of 2^{100} and 100! When Maple does exact integer arithmetic, it automatically selects the appropriate word length for the calculation. This is an important difference separating floating-point calculations and integer arithmetic.

```
> 100!;
```

$$93326215443944152681699238856266700490715968264381621468592963895217599993229915608941463976156518286253697920827223758251185210916864000000000000000000000000$$

Finally, a sobering thought—even Maple has limits, as this computation reveals.

```
> 20.34^(10^10);
```

```
Error, (in evalf/power) argument too large
```

Not Everything Is a Number

The following are examples of algebraic quantities: $1/7$, π, x, $\sqrt{(1 + a)}$, $\sqrt{5}$, $\sin y$, and $ax^2 + bx + c = 0$. Numerical tools are unable to manipulate them in their natural state. This is not a problem to a CAS. It is obvious why a numerical tool will be unable to manipulate x, $\sqrt{(1 + a)}$, $\sin y$, and $ax^2 + bx + c = 0$ as the expressions all contain symbolic quantities that have no numerical value. But what is the problem with $1/7$, π, and $\sqrt{5}$? It is true that a floating-point approximation can be obtained for each expression, but in that lies the problem! We are now using approximations to the previously stated exact values. Consider the following example where we calculate the area of a circle using a conventional 10-digit calculator.

| FINDING THE AREA OF A CIRCLE | The area of a circle is given by the formula πr^2. | $\text{area} = \pi\, r^2$ |
| | First, all of the algebraic quantities have to be transformed into floating-point numbers. Then these values are substituted into the formula. | $\pi = 3.141592654$ $r = .5641895835$ $\text{area} = 0.9999999999$ |

In order for an answer to be calculated, all the parts of the problem must have a corresponding numerical value. Sometimes this is not possible, as in the next example.

| FINDING THE ROOTS OF A QUADRATIC | The roots of a quadratic can be found using a formula. | $x = \dfrac{-b \pm \sqrt{(b^2 - 4\,ac)}}{2a}$ |
| | If variables a, b and c are known, then the roots can be calculated. If however they are not, no further computation can take place. It should be noted that $b^2 \geq 4ac$ is an additional constraint. | $a = 1,\ b = 3.4,\ c = -2$ $x = 0.5113 \text{ or } x = -3.9113$ $a = 1,\ b = B,\ c = -2$ $x = ? \text{ or } x = ?$ |

The great power of a CAS is its ability to manipulate algebraic quantities, symbols (or unknowns) as well as numbers. Being able to perform calculations on expressions containing algebraic quantities means that exact solutions can be obtained. If we take another look at the area-of-a-circle problem with Maple we can see the difference.

| FINDING THE AREA OF A CIRCLE WITH MAPLE | The area of a circle is given by the formula πr^2. | ```> area:=Pi*radius^2;``` $\text{area} := \pi\, \text{radius}^2$ |
| | If the radius r is $1/\sqrt{\pi}$, then by substitution the area is unity. | ```> radius:=1/sqrt(Pi);``` $\text{radius} := \dfrac{1}{\sqrt{\pi}}$ ```> area;``` 1 |

$\boxed{?_2}$

With Maple, we are not restricted to just manipulating algebraic and numeric quantities; on the contrary, we are able to manipulate expressions containing unknown quantities represented as symbols. This means that we can now compute a problem's general solution, assuming that one exists, as a function of its unknown quantities, something mathematicians, scientists, and engineers have been doing for centuries by hand. The advantage of using a general solution is self-evident as we do not have to start from scratch every time the input parameters change. For example, we can find an expression for the interest payments on a loan as a function of time and interest rate that can be used time and time again as the input parameters change without having to resort to first principles every time. Let us now take a second look at the roots-of-a-quadratic example, but this time using Maple to deal with the unknowns.

FINDING THE ROOTS OF A QUADRATIC WITH MAPLE

The roots of a quadratic can be found using the formula expressed in Maple at the right.

```
> ROOTS:=[ (-b + sqrt(b^2-4*a*c))/(2*a), (-
  b - sqrt(b^2 - 4*a*c))/(2*a)]:
```

If the variables have numeric values, then the roots can be calculated.

```
> values := a = 1, b = 3.4, c = -2:
```

Here are the calculated roots.

```
> subs(values, ROOTS);
```

$$[.511334438749600, -3.91133443874960]$$

If, however, all or some of the variables do not have corresponding numeric values, then the roots can only be calculated as a function of the unknowns.

```
> values:=a=1, b=B, c=-2:
> subs(values, ROOTS);
```

$$[-(1/2)\,B + (1/2)\,(B^2 + 8)^{1/2}, -(1/2)\,B - (1/2)\,(B^2 + 8)^{1/2}]$$

NEW **FUNCTIONS** **AT A GLANCE**	`expr!`	Return the factorial of `expr`.
	`name:=expr`	Assign the value of `expr` to `name`.
	`evalf( expr )` `evalf( expr, digits )`	Evaluate as a floating-point number. The number of digits can be specified by setting `digits`.

$\boxed{?2}$

	`exp( 1 )`	The exponential constant e.
	`for var from start to stop by inc do body od`	Evaluate `body` repeatedly with `var` as the loop count. `Var` is initialized to `start` and is incremented by `inc` until the end condition `stop` is reached.
	`Pi`	Symbolic π.
	`sqrt( expr )`	Calculate the squareroot of `expr`.
	`subs( eqn`$_1$`, eqn`$_2$`, .., eqn`$_n$`, expr )`	Substitute the values given in equations `eqn`$_i$ into `expr`.

FAQs

1: What does the large question mark in the margin mean?

This tells the reader that there is a corresponding entry in the FAQs list related to this section.

2: Why is entering the variable name sufficient to get an answer?

As you have assigned values to variable names, Maple has automatically substituted them into the expression. By entering the variable name you are asking Maple to return its current value.

BEWARE

1: This indicates that there has been a change in either the syntax or the name from release three to release four.

2: In Vr3,[1] E can be used to represent `exp(1)`. In Vr4,[2] E has no special meaning.

---

[1] Vr3 is shorthand for Maple V Release 3.

[2] Vr4 is shorthand for Maple V Release 4.

Maple Is a CAS

Maple V can be thought of as a sophisticated desktop calculator that can be used by physicists, biologists, chemists, social scientists, graphic artists, engineers, mathematicians, financial analysts, research and teaching staff, and students to performing numeric and symbolic mathematical operations quickly and accurately. It is interactive and can be easily applied to a wide range of problems by providing the user with over 2,500 standard functions. It is also a comprehensive visualization tool capable of plotting scientific data in both two and three dimensions. Extra dimensions can be effectively added through the use of animations and color functions.

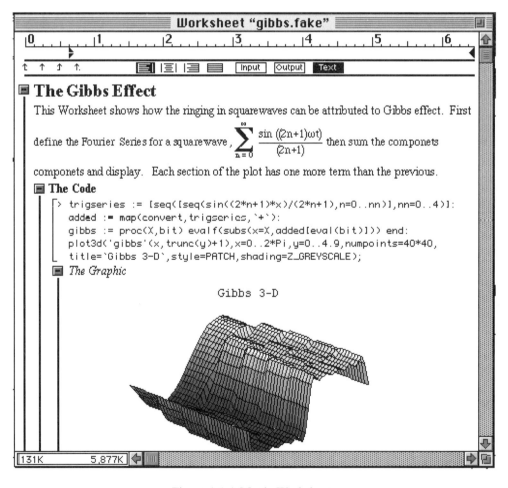

Figure 1.1 A Maple Worksheet

Over 95% of all users interact with Maple via the Worksheet GUI, an example of which is shown on the previous page. The GUI allows the user to integrate live mathematical expressions, text, and interactive graphics into a single document. Alternatively, Maple can be integrated into existing software tools, such as word processors, through MathOffice, the C callable version, or via an intermediate file. Standard formats such as L^{A}T$_E$X, HPGL, Postscript, C, and FORTRAN are supported.

Last but not least, Maple is its own programming language that is ideally suited to the manipulation of mathematical expressions. Through a variety of programming techniques, new functionality can be quickly added or existing functions customized. Customization of standard functions is possible as Maple is an open system allowing the user access to all but the functions that comprise the kernel.

A Brief History

The first Maple system was tested in December 1980 with first public demonstration taking place in 1982. A year later in 1983 that design criteria was presented at the EUROCAL Conference.[1] By the end of 1983, approximately 50 institutions were using the software in research and teaching activities. In 1984 the first commercial form of the system was shipped. The number of installations using Maple continued to grow, reaching approximately 300 by 1987. Later in the same year Waterloo Maple Software was incorporated and took on the marketing, distributing, and support activities. The installed base continued to grow, reaching 2,000 in 1989–90, and now stands at approximately 5,000 worldwide (a single site can be an individual, an academic or commercial institution).

What Is Maple?

Maple consists of three distinct parts: the kernel, the user interface or *Worksheet,* and the libraries.

The Kernel

The Maple kernel is now implemented in C although a large part of the original code was written in B and later ported over. Selecting C meant a system that would be compact, efficient, and inherently portable could be coded. The kernel contains approximately 130 core functions and accounts for approximately 5% of the total Maple system. The kernel functions are the only ones that cannot be viewed and altered by the user.

These functions can be divided into four major groups: evaluators, algebraic functions, algebraic service functions, and general service functions. The evaluators, such as `evalf`,

---

[1] B.W. Char, K.O. Geddes, W.M. Gentleman, and G.H. Gonnet, "The Design of Maple: A Compact, Portable, and Powerful Computer Algebra System, Computer Algebra", Proceedings of EUROCAL '83, J.A. Van Hulzen (ed.), Lecture Notes in Computer Science, No. 162, Springer-Verlag, Berlin, 1983 pp.101–115.

eval, evaln, and evalb, are the main functions controlling evaluation of expressions within Maple. The algebraic functions cover the basic functions such as diff, divide, op, and expand. The algebraic service functions cannot be explicitly called by the user but provide the means by which Maple performs many arithmetic operations such as integer, rational, and floating-point arithmetic, arbitrary precision arithmetic, simplification, and set operations. The final group covers such diverse functions as error handling, garbage collection, and general input and output.

The Interface

The Worksheet interface allows mathematics, text, and graphics to be combined in one document and is common to all platforms (the Macintosh version has a few cosmetic differences). A common interface across platforms means that the user's adjustment time is minimal and that work is easily transferable.

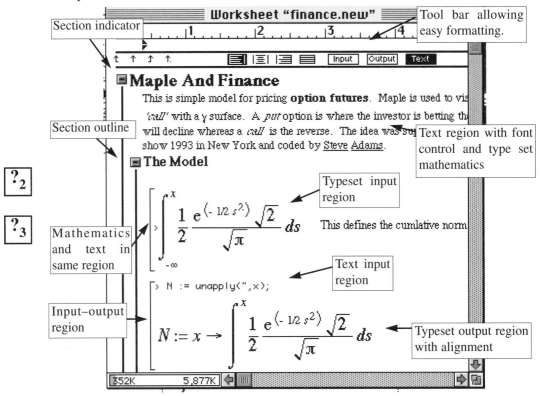

Figure 1.2 Regions of a Worksheet

The comfortable appearance of the Worksheet makes it easy for the user to interact with the computational power of Maple. Interactive documents containing live mathematics, typeset output, explanatory text, and powerful graphics can be developed quickly using the Worksheet paradigm. Models and ideas can be implemented and tested interactively resulting in prototypes that can be debugged efficiently, all within the Worksheet. The ability to display both mathematical input and output in a typeset form not only helps to reduce transcription errors in formulas but also helps to reduce code repetition. All of these attributes make the Worksheet a powerful ally in reducing the standard development cycle and providing fast delivery of results to the end users for model testing and verification. The interactive nature of the interface means that the current state of a model (test data, parameters, and state) can be obtained; functions, expressions as well as model definitions can also be edited and rerun without fuss at any time. Routine or repetitive tasks therefore can be performed quickly and without error. In addition, the interface gives the user, through the inclusion of a comprehensive set of menu items, access to the features of the resident operating system in a standard nonplatform-specific way. Finally, the Maple on-line help system can be easily browsed using the GUI.

Connecting to the Kernel

The interface can be linked to the kernel in one of three ways: direct mode (default), shared mode, and parallel mode. In the direct mode, the kernel and interface are bound together as a single process. In the shared mode, multiple interfaces can be linked to a single kernel resulting in a multitasking environment. The mathematical context, however, is the same for all the active interfaces. That is, an assignment made to a variable via one interface is automatically made in all of the others. Finally, if the parallel mode is used, a new kernel is started for each interface opened. In every case, the new kernel is linked to only one interface.

The Libraries

Approximately 95% of the Maple system is made up of libraries. All of the library routines are user-readable and customizable, being written in Maple's own programming language. The library functions are divided into three basic categories: demand loaded, miscellaneous, and packages. The demand-loaded functions are defined using unevaluated `readlib` functions. When the function is called by name, say, `sin(x)`, a `readlib` is automatically evaluated so that the function becomes known to the system. The groups of related functions have been placed together into packages, all or part of a which is loaded using `with.`, whereas functions in the second category must each be loaded explicitly using `readlib`.

STANDARD		
	`combinat`	Combinatorial functions
PACKAGES	`combstruct`	Combinatorial structures
	`DEtools`	Differential equation tools
	`difforms`	Differential forms
	`Domains`	Create domains of computation
	`finance`	Financial functions

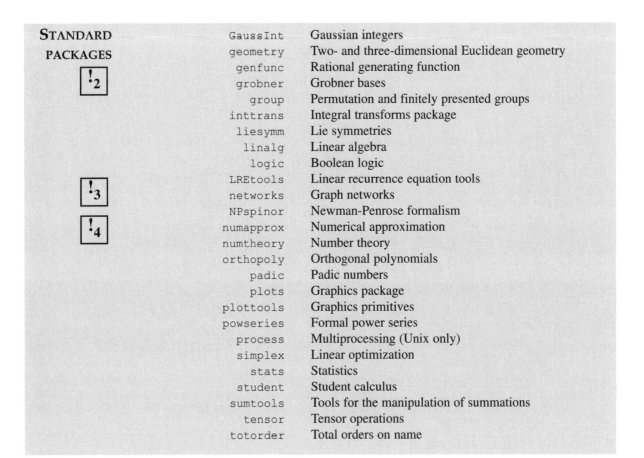

STANDARD	`GaussInt`	Gaussian integers
PACKAGES	`geometry`	Two- and three-dimensional Euclidean geometry
!2	`genfunc`	Rational generating function
	`grobner`	Grobner bases
	`group`	Permutation and finitely presented groups
	`inttrans`	Integral transforms package
	`liesymm`	Lie symmetries
	`linalg`	Linear algebra
	`logic`	Boolean logic
	`LREtools`	Linear recurrence equation tools
!3	`networks`	Graph networks
	`NPspinor`	Newman-Penrose formalism
!4	`numapprox`	Numerical approximation
	`numtheory`	Number theory
	`orthopoly`	Orthogonal polynomials
	`padic`	Padic numbers
	`plots`	Graphics package
	`plottools`	Graphics primitives
	`powseries`	Formal power series
	`process`	Multiprocessing (Unix only)
	`simplex`	Linear optimization
	`stats`	Statistics
	`student`	Student calculus
	`sumtools`	Tools for the manipulation of summations
	`tensor`	Tensor operations
	`totorder`	Total orders on name

A Brief Tour

NUMERICS Using Maple is as simple as using a calculator.

```
> 1 + 2 + 3 + 4 + 5 + 6 + 7 + 8 + 9;
```

$$45$$

Unlike a calculator, Maple can give exact results.

```
> 1/2 - 3/4 + 5/6 - 7/8 + 9*10;
```

$$\frac{2153}{24}$$

By using `evalf`, Maple can also give approximate numerical results. Here we compute the previous result to ten significant digits.

```
> evalf(");
```

$$89.70833333$$

Maple also works in the complex plane. In Maple, `I` stands for the complex constant $\sqrt{-1}$.

```
> (1 + 7*I)/((2 + I)*(3 - 5*I));
```

$$-\frac{19}{85} + \frac{42}{85} I$$

```
> big_number:=5!*5^15;
```

$$big\_number := 3662109375000$$

Maple can manipulate integers of any size exactly. Here a big number is calculated.

This number is easily tested to see if it is prime.

```
> isprime(big_number);
```

$$false$$

As it is not, Maple can calculate the integer factors.

```
> ifactor(big_number);
```

$$(2)^3 (3) (5)^{16}$$

Floating-point numbers can be calculated to any degree of precision. In this example, 20 digits are used.

```
> evalf(log(big_number), 20);
```

$$28.929060429293551613$$

Standard mathematical functions can be evaluated using Maple. Here the error function `erf(0.5)` and the Airy wave function

```
> erf(0.5); evalf(Ai(2.5));
```

$$.5204998778$$

$$.01572592338$$

SYMBOLICS Maple can also be a symbolic calculator.

```
> normal(1/a + 1/b + 1/c);
```

$$\frac{b\,c + a\,c + a\,b}{abc}$$

Here Maple is being used to expand an algebraic expression.

```
> expand((x - 3*y^(-3))^5);
```

$$x^5 - \frac{15x^4}{y^3} + \frac{90x^3}{y^6} - \frac{270x^2}{y^9} + \frac{405x}{y^{12}} - \frac{243}{y^{15}}$$

The inverse of expand is factorization.

```
> factor(");
```

$$\frac{(xy^3 - 3)^5}{y^{15}}$$

Maple can generate power-series expansions, in this case about the point $x = h$. Three terms are computed.

```
> series(g(x), x=h, 3);
```

$$g(h) + D(g)(h)(x - h) + (1/2)\,D^{(2)}(g)(h)(x - h)^2$$
$$+ O((x - h)^3)$$

This generates the first three terms of the Γ function about $x = 0$.

```
> series(GAMMA(x), x=0, 3);
```

$$x^{-1} - \gamma + (1/12\,\pi^2 + 1/2\,\gamma^2)\,x +$$
$$(-1/3\,\zeta(3) - 1/12\,\pi^2\,\gamma - 1/6\,\gamma^3)\,x^2 + O(x^3)$$

Maple can perform both definite and indefinite integration. This is the indefinite integral $\int 1/(1-x^3)\,dx$

```
> int(1/(1-x^3), x);
```

$$-1/3\,\ln(x - 1) + 1/6\,\ln(x^2 + x + 1) +$$
$$1/3\,\sqrt{3}\,\arctan(1/3\,(2\,x + 1)\,\sqrt{3})$$

Symbolic differentiation is also supported. The derivative of the preceding integral will give a different form of the original expression.

```
> diff(", x);
```

$$-\frac{1}{3(x - 1)} + 1/6\,\frac{2x + 1}{x^2 + x + 1} + \frac{2}{3\,[1 + (1/3)\,(2x + 1)^2]}$$

This can be manipulated further using `simplify`.

```
> simplify(");
```

$$-\frac{1}{(x - 1)\,(x^2 + x + 1)}$$

SYMBOLICS Definite and indefinite summations can be calculated.

```
> sum(1/(1-n)^x, x=1..4);
```

$$\frac{1}{1-n} + \frac{1}{(1-n)^2} + \frac{1}{(1-n)^3} + \frac{1}{(1-n)^4}$$

This is the indefinite product $(1-n)^x/(x+1)$.

```
> product((1-n)^x/(x+1), x);
```

$$\frac{(1-n)^{((1/2)x(x-1))}}{\Gamma(x+1)}$$

Here are two algebraic equations describing a circle and a straight line.

```
> circle:=x^2 + y^2=r^2;
```

$$circle := x^2 + y^2 = r^2$$

```
> line:=y=a*x;
```

$$line := y = ax$$

This finds the points of intersection.

```
> pts:=allvalues([solve({circle, line},
  {x, y})], d);
```

$$pts := \left[\left\{ y = \frac{a\,r}{\sqrt{(1+a^2)}}, \; x = \frac{r}{\sqrt{(1+a^2)}} \right\} \right],$$

$$\left[\left\{ x = \frac{-r}{\sqrt{(1+a^2)}}, \; y = \frac{-a\,r}{\sqrt{(1+a^2)}} \right\} \right]$$

By using `fsolve`, equations can be solved numerically.

```
> fsolve(cos(x)=x^2, {x});
```

$$\{x = .8241323123\}$$

By using `fsolve`, the roots of the seventh-order equation $x^7 - 2x + 1.7 = 0$ can be found.

```
> Digits:=3:
  fsolve(x^7 - 2*x + 1.7=0, {x}, complex);
```

$$\{x = -1.23\}, \{x = -.669 - .999\,I\}, \{x = -.669 +$$
$$.999\,I\}, \{x = .430 - 1.04\,I\}, \{x = .430 + 1.04\,I\},$$
$$\{x = .851 - .193\,I\}, \{x = .851 + .193\,I\}$$

Maple can be used to find solutions to differential equations. This describes the motion of a particle in an E-B field.

```
> System:={diff(Y(t), t$2) =
  1 - diff(X(t), t), diff(X(t),
  t$2)=diff(Y(t), t)}:
```

SYMBOLICS The particle is injected at (1, 0) with velocity (-1, 0), giving rise to the initial conditions shown. `D(X)(0)` denotes the first derivative of `X(t)` at $t = 0$, and so on.

```
> ics:={ X(0)=1,  Y(0)=0,
    D(X)(0)=-1,  D(Y)(0)=0} :
```

By using `dsolve`, the exact solution can be found.

```
> dsolve(System union ics, {Y(t), X(t)});
```

$$\{Y(t) = 2 - 2\cos(t),\ X(t) = 1 + t - 2\sin(t)\}$$

Numerical solutions to differential equations can be found by setting the optional argument `type=numeric`.

```
> nsol:=dsolve({ diff(y(t), t, t) +
    0.01*diff(y(t), t) + y(t)+sin(t)*t^3=
    cos(t)^2, y(0)=-100, D(y)(0)=0}, y(t),
    type=numeric);
```

Maple returns a procedure.

```
nsol := proc(rkf45_x) ... end
```

Now $y(t)$ and $y'(t)$ can be calculated for any t.

```
> nsol(1);
```

$$\left[t = 1,\ y(t) = -53.8,\ \frac{d}{dt}y(t) = 84.1 \right]$$

Expressions can be altered through substitution. Here a sequential substitution is made.

```
> subs( x=y, y=Pi, [ sin(x), cos(y),
    tan(x*y)] );
```

$$[\sin(\pi),\ \cos(\pi),\ \tan(\pi^2)\ ]$$

Substitutions also can be made in parallel, as this example demonstrates.

```
> subs({ x=y, y=Pi}, [ sin(x), cos(y),
    tan(x*y)] );
```

$$[\sin(y),\ \cos(\pi),\ \tan(y\pi)]$$

Specific operands also can be manipulated. Here the second element in the list is removed by setting it to NULL.

```
> subsop(2=NULL, [ one, two, three] );
```

$$[one,\ three]$$

The zeroth operand is the head of an expression. Here we change the function name.

```
> subsop(0=g, f(x, x));
```

$$g(x, x)$$

Simplify can be coerced into performing substitutions of our choosing through side relations.

```
> simplify(b*a - b*a^3, { (1 - a^2)=h} );
```

$$bah$$

GRAPHICS Maple is a powerful visualization tool. Here is a plot of the function $\sin 2t \exp[-(t/5)^2]$

```
> plot(sin(2*t)*exp(-(t/5)^2), t=-10..10);
```

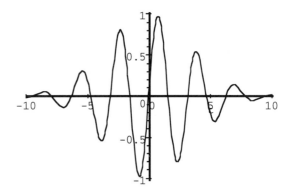

Maple supports different coordinate axes. Other plot attributes are also user-selectable.

```
> plot([ cos(4*x), x, x=0..2*Pi],
    coords=polar, style=point,
    symbol=circle);
```

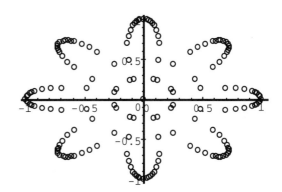

GRAPHICS Here we create a line and a contour plot and store the results.

```
> p1:=plot(sin(x)/x, x=-10..10, axes=NONE):
> p2:= plots[ contourplot] (1/(sqrt(sin(x)^2
  + cos(y)^2) + .25), x=-3..3, y=-3..3,
  axes=NONE):
```

> [?7]

We can now display them as an array of graphics.

```
> plots[ display] (array([[ p1], [ p2]]));
```

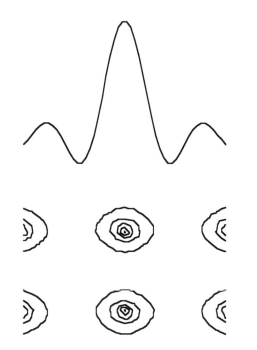

GRAPHICS Here is a plot of the differential equation solved earlier. The `subs` command is used to select the right-hand side of expressions having the form $y(t) = \ldots$.

```
> plot('subs(nsol(x), y(t))', x=0..10);
```

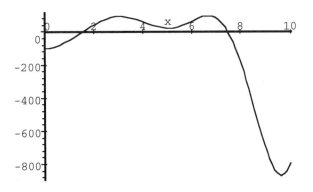

Maple supports three-dimensional plots. This plot uses the default settings for the plot options.

```
> plot3d(x*y*sin(2*x)*cos(3*y), x=0..2*Pi,
    y=0..Pi);
```

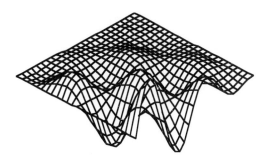

GRAPHICS Plot attributes can be modified and plots rerendered. Here the long name `plots[ display3d]` is used to access `display3d` stored in the plots package.

```
> plots[ display3d] (", axes=FRAMED,
    style=PATCHCONTOUR);
```

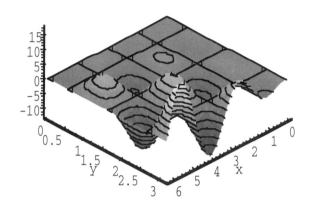

Variable end points for plot ranges are supported, as this example demonstrates.

```
> plot3d(x* y* sin(2* x)* cos(3* y), x=0..2* Pi,
    y=-sin(x)..sin(x));
```

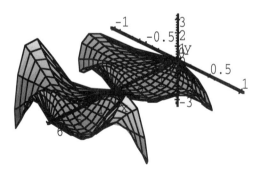

GRAPHICS Here is a parametric plot showing the Boolean intersection of two half cylinders. The open look of the cylinders is obtained by the appropriate choice of the plot range of `t`.

```
> plot3d({[ l, 3*cos(t), 3*sin(t)],
  [ 3*sin(t), 3*cos(t), l]}, l=-4..4,
  t=-Pi/2..Pi/2, scaling=CONSTRAINED,
  orientation=[ -110, 75] );
```

Implicit equations can be solved graphically, as this final example shows.

```
> plots[ implicitplot3d] (x^3 + y^3 + z^3 +
  1= x + y + z + 1)^3, x=-2..2, y=-2..2,
  z=-2..2, grid=[ 13, 13, 13] );
```

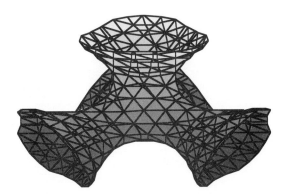

DATA TYPES Maple supports a variety of special data types. These tend to reflect mathematical data types. Here is a two-by-two array.

```
> A:=array(1..2, 1..2, [[1, x],
  [x^2, x^3]]);
```

$$A := \begin{bmatrix} 1 & x \\ x^2 & x^3 \end{bmatrix}$$

This is the element $\mathbf{A}_{2,2}$.

```
> A[2, 2];
```

$$x^3$$

Matrices differ from arrays in that the lower bound on a dimension must be one. Here is a two-by-two symbolic matrix.

```
> M:=linalg[matrix](2, 2, [a, b, c, d]);
```

$$M := \begin{bmatrix} a & b \\ c & d \end{bmatrix}$$

Matrix algebra can be applied to both matrices and arrays. By using the non-commutative multiply operator &* , M and A are multiplied together.

```
> evalm(M &* A);
```

$$M := \begin{bmatrix} 2bx & a + 3bx^2 \\ 2dx & c + 3dx^2 \end{bmatrix}$$

By using the long function name, V is assigned to a four-element vector. Vectors can have any number of elements.

```
> V:=linalg[vector](4, [1, 4, 9, 16]);
```

$$V := [1\ 4\ 9\ 16]$$

Sets can be defined and manipulated using Maple. A set is denoted using curly braces { ... }.

```
> {1, 2, 3, 4} union {a, b, c, d};
```

$$\{1, 2, 3, 4, c, b, a, d\}$$

Lists of expressions, on the other hand are grouped together using square brackets [...].

```
> trig_functions:=[sin, cos, tan];
```

$$trig\_functions := [\sin, \cos, \tan]$$

Here three new entries are appended to the list `trig_functions`.

```
> new_trig:= [op(trig_functions), sec,
  cosec, cot];
```

$$new\_trig := [\sin, \cos, \tan, \sec, \csc, \cot]$$

DATA TYPES Maple supports the concept of tables. A table is a group of entries tagged with unique indices. In this example, a weekly calendar is built.

```
> calendar:=table([ mon=book, tue=squash,
  wed=gym, thur=soccer, fri=SCUBA] ):
```

On Thursday, the author has a soccer match.

```
> calendar[ thur] ;
```

$$soccer$$

Table entries can be quickly changed by making a simple assignment.

```
> calendar[ wed] :=weights:
```

Using `eval`, we are able to view the table structure.

```
> eval(calendar);
```

$$
\begin{aligned}
\text{table([} \\
thur &= soccer \\
mon &= book \\
tue &= squash \\
wed &= weights \\
fri &= SCUBA \\
])
\end{aligned}
$$

Placeholders, such as `RootOf`, are also supported. Placeholders are used to simplify output, argument passing, and storage. Here the eigenvectors of the matrix M are calculated.

```
> linalg[ eigenvects] (M);
```

$$
\left[\text{RootOf}(\_Z^2 + (-d - a)\,\_Z - bc + ad), 1, \right.
$$
$$
\left. \left\{ \left[-\frac{-\text{RootOf}(\_Z^2 + (-d - a)\,\_Z - bc + ad) + d}{c}, 1 \right] \right\} \right]
$$

ADDING TO THE MAPLE SYSTEM

We can extend Maple by defining new functions. Here is a function to return a quadratic in x: $f(a, b, c) = ax^2 + bx + c$.

```
> f:=(a, b, c)->a*x^2 + b*x + c;
```

$$f := (a,b,c) \rightarrow ax^2 + bx + c$$

Try it out with coefficients 2, -3, and 4.

```
> f(2, -3, 4);
```

$$2x^2 - 3x + 4$$

Here is a simple program, using the for loop, to calculate the factorials of the integers 1 through 4.

```
> for n to 5 do n! od;
```

$$1$$
$$2$$
$$6$$
$$24$$

This can also be achieved with the sequence function seq.

```
> seq(n!, n=1..4);
```

$$1, 2, 6, 24$$

Here we use procedural programming to extend the previous quadratic function. The two parameters are the degree of the polynomial and a coefficient list.

```
> ff:=proc(a, l) local x, n, temp;
    temp:=[ seq(x^n, n=0..a)];
    temp:=zip((x, y)->x*y, temp, l);
    convert(temp, `+`);
  end:
```

Here we produce a cubic in x with coefficients 1, 2, 3, and 4.

```
> ff(3,[ 1, 2, 3, 4]);
```

$$1 + 2x + 3x^2 + 4x^3$$

Rule-based programming is also supported. Here we define a new function a_log to perform simple logarithmic arithmetic using rules. Note the use of the two pairs of hold evaluation quotes '' ... ''.

```
> rule1:=forall(`*`(x),
  ''a_log(x)=map(a_log, convert(x,`+`))''):
> rule2:=forall([ x, y],
  ''a_log(x^y)=y*a_log(x)''):
```

Define the new function.

```
> define(a_log, rule1, rule2);
```

And try it.

```
> a_log(a^y*f);
```

$$ya\_log(a) + a\_log(f)$$

PACKAGES Packages are collections of functions possessing a common theme. Here we load the `plots` package.

```
> with(plots):
```

Using tubeplot, we can produce interesting three-dimensional plots with relative ease.

```
> tubeplot([ t, 2*sin(t), 0],
  t=-3*Pi/2..3*Pi/2, radius=abs(0.5*t),
  tubepoints=30, orientation=[ 60, 60],
  style=PATCHNOGRID, color=ZHUE,
  projection=FISHEYE);
```

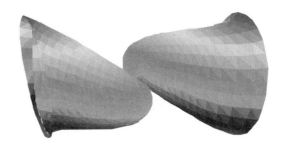

The single biggest grouping of functions forms the `linalg` package. Here, though, we only load a single function.

```
> with(linalg, [ charpoly] ):
```

Here the characteristic polynomial is calculated for a three-by-three matrix.

```
> charpoly(matrix(3, 3,
  [ 1, 2, 3, 1, 2, 3, 1, 5, 6] ), x);
```

$$x^3 - 9x^2$$

This loads the statistical package. Notice that the `random` function defined in the `stats` package has replaced the default one.

```
> with(stats):
```

```
Warning: new definition for    random
```

Enter two data sets.

```
> data1:=[ 1, 2, 3, 4, 5] :
  data2:=[ 0, 5, -6, 1, 1] :
```

PACKAGES Using the `describe` subpackage, we can calculate the data's correlation. These data sets have a low correlation. The use of subpackages is currently limited to the statistics package.

```
> evalf(describe[ linearcorrelation] (data1,
  data2));
```

$$-.07980868848$$

The logic package enables Boolean expressions to be manipulated.

```
> with(logic):
```

Here we check for a tautology within an expression.

```
> tautology(&and(a ,b) &or  (&not a) &or
  (&not b));
```

$$\textit{true}$$

Load the networks package. It should be noticed that the current definitions for the functions `charpoly` and `rank` have been overwritten.

```
> with(networks):
```

```
Warning: new definition for    charpoly
Warning: new definition for    rank
```

Now draw the Petersen graph.

```
> draw(petersen());
```

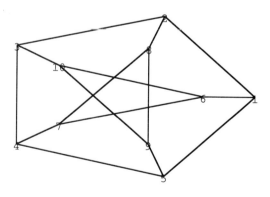

PACKAGES This "loads" the graphics primitives package `plottools`.

```
> with(plottools):
```

This plots faces of an icosahedron.

```
> display3d(cutin( icosahedron(), 1/2 ) );
```

We can combine graphics primitives to create compound graphics. Here we plot a cube with a cone on top.

```
> display([ cuboid([ 0, 0, 0], [ 1, 1, 1]),
cone([ .5, .5, 1] )],
orientation=[ -50, 60] );
```

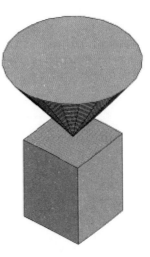

NEW FUNCTIONS AT A GLANCE		
	`&*`	Noncommutative multiply.
	`&and`	Found in the `logic` package, this is the inert form of the logical *and*.
	`&or`	Found in the `logic` package, this is the inert form of the logical or.
	`` ` ``	Shorthand for previous non-NULL output.
	`args -> expr`	Function definition with formal parameters `args` and function body `expr`.
	`Ai( expr )`	The Airy wave function Ai(expr).

!·6

`allvalues( expr, dependent )`
`allvalues( expr )`   Evaluate all values of `expr`. Commonly used if `expr` contains `RootOf`s. If the first form is used, `RootOf`s of the same equation have the same value.

`array( index, range`$_1$`, range`$_2$`, [ elems] )`
`array( range`$_1$`, range`$_2$`, [ elems] )`

Create an array with dimensions `range`$_1$ by `range`$_2$ and entries given by the list `elems`. Index is optional and specifies how the array is indexed, for example, `symmetric`.

`charpoly( mat, var )`   Calculate the characteristic polynomial of the matrix `mat` in the variable `var`.

`convert( expr, type, opts )`

Convert `expr` to Maple type `type`. Optional arguments are type-specific.

`define( name, attrib, rules )`
`define( name, rules )`   Create the procedure `name` using the rule sequence `rules`. The procedure can have attributes, such as linear, specified by `attrib`.

`diff( expr, var )`   Differentiate `expr` with respect to `var`.

`Digits`   Global variable setting number of digits used in floating-point calculations. The default is 10.

New	`display3d( {graphics}, opts )`	
FUNCTIONS		Display the threedimensional graphics with the options specified.
AT A GLANCE		
	`draw( graph )`	Draw the graph.
	`dsolve( eqns, vars, opts )`	Solve the differential equation or system of equations `eqns` in the variables `var` with the options `opts`.
	`eigenvects( mat )`	Calculate the eigenvectors of a matrix.
	`erf( expr )`	Calculate the error function erf(expr).
	`eval( expr )`	Force evaluation of `expr`.
	`evalb( expr )`	Evaluate as a Boolean expression.
	`evalm( expr )`	Evaluate `expr` as a matrix.
	`evaln( expr )`	Evaluate `expr` as a name.
	`exp( expr )`	Calculate the exponential e^{expr}.
	`expand( expr )`	Force the expansion of products and powers in `expr`.
	`factor( expr )`	Factor the multivariate polynomial `expr`.
	`forall( vars, eqn )`	Create transformation rules to be used by `define`.
	`fsolve( eqns, vars, opts )`	Solve algebraic equations using numerical methods for the variables `var`.
	`GAMMA( expr )`	Calculate the Gamma function Γ(expr).
	`ifactor( expr )`36	Calculate the integer factors of `expr`.
	`implicitplot3d( eqn, range_1, range_2, range_3, opts )`	Plot the three-dimensional solution to the implicit equation over the ranges $range_1$, $range_2$, and $range_3$ with the specified options.
	`int( expr, range )` `int( expr, var )`	Find the definite or indefinite integral of expression if possible.

`isprime( expr )`	Test `expr` to determine if it is a prime number.
`linearcorrelation( list`$_1$`, list`$_2$` )`	Determine the linear correlation between two data lists.
`log( expr )`	Calculate the natural logarithm of `expr`.
`map( func, expr, opts)`	Map `func` on to `expr`. The function `func` can take additional arguments specified by `opts`.
`matrix( dim`$_1$`, dim`$_2$`, [ elems] )`	Create a `dim`$_1$-by-`dim`$_2$ matrix of elements.
`normal( expr )`	Attempt to normalize the rational expression `expr`.
`op( expr )` `op( var, expr )`	Return the operands of `expr`. If `var` is present, then the operand specified by `var` is returned.
`petersen()`	Construct the Petersen graph.
`plot( expr, range, opts )` `plot( expr )`	Create a two-dimensional graph of `expr` over `range` with the specified options. In the second case, default settings supplied by Maple are used.
`plot3d( expr, range`$_1$`, range`$_2$`, opts )`	Create a three-dimensional graph of `expr` over `range`$_1$ and `range`$_2$ with the specified options.
`proc( args ) body end`	Definition of a procedure taking formal parameters `args` and returning `body`.
`product( expr, range )` `product( expr, var )`	Find the definite and indefinite product of `expr`.
`readlib( name )`	Load an individual readlib-defined function into the current Maple session.
`RootOf( eqn )`	A placeholder representing all of the roots of `expr`.
`seq( expr, range )`	Produce a sequence by applying `expr` to each element in `range`.

NEW FUNCTIONS AT A GLANCE	`series( expr, var, opts )`	Generate the series form of `expr` about the point given by `var` that can be a name or an equation. The number of terms (default is six) can be set by `opts`.
	`simplify( expr, { siderels } )` `simplify( expr )`	Simplify `expr` using the side relationships `siderels` if present.
	`sin( expr )`	Return the sine sin(*expr*).
	`subs( { eqn`$_1$`, eqn`$_2$`, .., eqn`$_n$` }, expr )`	Make substitutions according to `eqn`$_i$ in `expr` simultaneously.
	`subsop( eqn, expr )`	Substitute for a given operand, specified by `eqn`, in `expr`.
	`sum( expr, range )` `sum( expr, var )`	Find the definite and indefinite sum of `expr`.
	`table( [eqns] )`	Create a Maple table with entries specified by `eqns`.
	`tautology( expr )`	Test `expr` for a tautology.
	`tubeplot( expr, range`$_1$`, range`$_2$`, opts )`	Create a tube plot in three dimensions over the range `range`$_1$ and `range`$_2$.
	`set`$_1$ `` `union` `` `set`$_2$	Form the union of `set`$_1$ and `set`$_2$.
	`vector( len, [elems] )`	Create a vector of length `len` and entries `elems`.
	`with( package, [ func`$_1$`, func`$_2$`, .., func`$_n$` ] )` `with( package )`	Replace the function long names (`package[ function]`) with the short version. The first form allows the functions `func`$_i$ only to be loaded individually.
	`zip( oper, expr`$_1$`, expr`$_2$` )`	Produce a new list by applying `oper` to each element pair of `expr`$_1$ and `expr`$_2$.

FAQs 1: What programming paradigms does Maple V support?

Procedural, functional, and rule-based programming paradigms are supported.

2: What format is a Worksheet stored in?

Worksheets are stored as flat ASCII text and can be transmitted via the Internet. However, graphics are lost during this process and any other interplatform transfer.

3: Are all GUIs the same?

In general, yes. The menu and toolbar layouts will differ slightly. Windows- and X/Motif-based systems look and feel the same. There are, however, minor differences between these and the Macintosh systems.

4: Why is the GUI only talked about?

Less than 5% of all users use the command-line interface. It was therefore not considered worthwhile to explore this interface in this edition.

5: Which platforms support multitasking?

This is not really a hardware problem but an operating system problem. For instance, Windows 95-, OS/2-, MacOS-, and UNIX-based computers support this feature. For more information, see the Maple installation notes.

6: How do I get a list of the functions in a package?

Use the help system by typing either `?package_name` or `?package` to get a list of the packages.

7: What is special about names of the form `package[function]` and why are they used?

Long names are Maple's equivalent of a directory path name. It is the function's exact location in the Maple library and is used to avoid loading packages. Their use also prevents program errors due to name clashes and should be used when programming.

8: How do I operate upon all of the elements of an array, matrix, vector, list, and so on?

Use the `map` function.

BEWARE 1: The package `Domains` was called `Gauss` in previous versions.

2: The `geometry` package contains the Vr3 packages `geom3d` and `projgeom`.

3: The `NPspinor` package supercedes the Vr3 package `np`.

4: The `numapprox` package supercedes the Vr3 package `approx`.

5: In Release 4, assignments can be made to lists directly, so elements can be removed by assigning NULL to an element, for example, `old_list[ 2] :=`NULL.

6: The keyword `dependent` is just `d` in Vr3.

A REVIEW OF SOME OTHER CASs

REDUCE

First available the late 1960s, REDUCE is considered by many as the first general CAS. It was targeted at large formal problems in applied mathematics, physics, and engineering.

MACSYMA

MACSYMA was first released in the 1960s. Now a commercial product, it started as a research project at MIT. MACSYMA has strong traditions in algebraic and trigonometric simplification, integration, transforms, and symbolic ordinary and partial differential equations.

Derive

Derive was first presented to the general public at the Joint Mathematical Society meeting in January 1989. It is a DOS-based CAS capable of performing numerical and symbolic computations. It can support data visualization in both two and three dimensions.

Mathematica

Mathematica is a general-purpose CAS that first shipped in 1988. It combines symbolic, numeric, and graphical computation in an interactive system. Its main claim is its comprehensive support of rule-based programming.

Theorist

Theorist started as a small independent CAS produced by Prescience and first shipped in 1989. Theorist has a GUI that allows the user to integrate typeset mathematical expressions, text, and graphics in a single document. Notably, it supports drag and drop manipulation of expressions.

AXIOM

AXIOM was started by IBM in the 1980s and was finally released commercially in 1992. Due to its mathematical rigor, AXIOM is well suited to the prototyping and development of advanced symbolic algorithms.

Maple Basics

Installation

It is during installation that Maple is at its most inconsistent across platforms. Although the process of installation itself is the same (taking files from the distribution medium and installing them on your computer), the way in which it is done differs across platforms.

Macintosh

The Maple distribution kit contains the following components: base distribution files, floating-point-compatible application (FPU), nonfloating-point-compatible application (non-FPU), PowerPC-compatible application (PPC), and the share library. First, you need to decide on which application is appropriate to your particular computer and use the FPU, non-FPU, or PPC application accordingly. Next, you must decide if you require the share library. Depending upon the configuration you choose, between 12 and 20 megabytes of hard-disk space will be required. Now you are ready to begin the installation.

Place disk 1 in your machine and double click on the installer icon. A splash screen is displayed that is removed with a mouse click. You will then be asked to select the location for the about-to-be-created Maple system folder. Once you are happy with this, begin the installation procedure by clicking OK. This will install the Maple library along with some utilities. Once this is complete, the relevant application is installed in the same way. Although it is possible to have the Maple application and libraries in different folders, it is good practice to keep them together. Now the share library, if required, can be installed. The share library is a self- contained module, and if you choose not to install it now, it can be installed later without any fuss.

PCs

The Maple distribution kit for PCs contains the following components: base distribution files, DOS-compatible application, Windows-compatible application, and the share library. First, you need to decide on which application is appropriate to your particular computer and use the DOS or Windows application accordingly. Next, you must decide if you require the share library. Depending on the configuration you choose, between 15 and 25 megabytes of hard-disk space will be required. Now you are ready to begin the installation.

Place the first disk in your machine and either type A:/DOSINST followed by a RETURN if in DOS or navigate to the A drive and double click on INSTALL.EXE if in Windows. Both installation programs behave in basically the same way: You choose the required configuration of the Maple system to be installed. Unlike the Macintosh installation procedure, you must select whether you want the share library installed at this point. Of course, if you choose not to, it is easy to rerun the installation and only select the share library at a later date. It is at this point that the location of the Maple directory is set. Once you are happy with the configuration, begin the installation procedure by clicking CONTINUE. This will install the Maple system on your computer.

Passwords

Maple is password-protected; the password supplied with the license agreement will have to be entered the first time that you run Maple. For more information on entering the password, you should refer to the release notes supplied with the software.

Starting and Stopping

The three basic operations that you must be able to accomplish are: starting the Maple system, starting a calculation, and stopping either a calculation or the system.

The Maple system can be started in one of two ways: double click on either the application icon (or executable from the Windows file manager) or on an existing Worksheet. Assuming that Maple has been started using the first method, you will now be looking at a new Worksheet. It is now time to enter a calculation.

OTHER OSs	Workstations	Type XMAPLE at the prompt.
	DOS	Type MAPLE at the prompt.

At the prompt, enter the Maple input terminated by a semicolon and press either ENTER or SHIFT-ENTER if you are using a Macintosh, or ENTER if you are using a PC or workstation. This causes the input that you have just typed to be sent to the kernel for evaluation. Once the evaluation process has been completed, the kernel sends the answer back to the Worksheet where it is displayed. A before-and-after view of a Worksheet is shown in Figure 2.1.

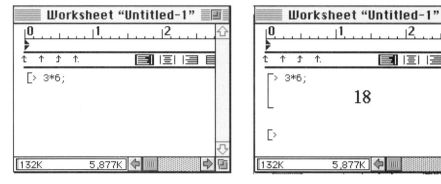

Figure 2.1 Using a Worksheet

Note: Throughout the remainder of this book, only ENTER will be used to indicate that the Maple input has been sent to the kernel for evaluation.

INSTEAD OF ENTER	Windows and Workstations	Place the cursor in the input region and double click.

Maple allows a single input to be spread over more than one line, as shown in Figure 2.2. The parser will only send a correctly terminated expression (one ending with either a colon or semicolon) to be evaluated. This means that if you press ENTER before the Maple input is complete another prompt is issued. Maple is allowing you to finish the command.

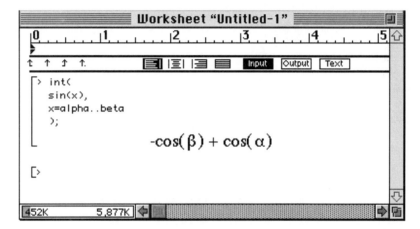

Figure 2.2 Maple Input Over Multiple Lines

During a Maple session, you may find it necessary to abort a long calculation gracefully. This is done easily by pressing COMMAND-. (COMMAND-period) if you are using a Macintosh or by pressing either the STOP BUTTON or CTRL-BREAK if you are using a PC or a workstation.

OTHER OSs	UNIX	CTRL-C or the interrupt key
	DOS	CTRL-C or CTRL-B

Finally, the last task that you have to perform in any Maple session is to quit. This can be done either from within the Worksheet itself or from the FILE menu. If you want to quit Maple from the Worksheet, simply type `stop`, `quit`, or `done`, and then press ENTER.

QUITTING SHORTCUTS	Macintosh	COMMAND-Q
	Windows	ALT-F4
	DOS	F3

Menus

Before we continue, let us take a brief look at some of the items in the menu bar. The items available are essentially the same across platforms and are by and large self-explanatory. For example, the FILE menu contains items for loading and saving Worksheets. The EDIT menu holds the cut, paste, and copy functions and the FORMAT and OPTIONS/SETTINGS menus contain functions that let you customize the look and feel of your Worksheet. It is through the use of the menus and the tool bars that you set worksheet regions, fonts, prompts, styles, replacement mode, and ultimately the layout of a worksheet.

DIFFERENCES IN MENUS	The Macintosh	
	The FILE menu has IMPORT and EXPORT items	
		Worksheets can be exported and text to be imported.
	Windows	
	A tool bar	Buttons for manipulating graphics, inserting regions, setting region type, and so forth, are grouped together in the tool bar.

 ## Getting Help

Maple comes with a comprehensive user-friendly on-line help system containing over eight megabytes of searchable data that cover both the user interface and mathematical functionality. Help on the interface is delivered via a balloon help mechanism that once activated automatically displays help on the portion of the interface currently being pointed to, whereas help on a particular function or group of functions is supplied via a help page mechanism. A help page is reminiscent of the UNIX *man* page and contains information on calling sequence, parameters, synopsis, examples, and further reading and related functions. In the current release, the help pages are displayed as Maple Worksheets containing in-line typeset mathematics and hypertext links. The Worksheet help page, although not active and editable, can be copied either in part or its entireity, in making it easy to transfer and use the information contained within it. The examples section, for instance, can be copied and pasted into an active Worksheet, where they can be run in one of two ways: the conventional highlight-copy-and-paste process or by using the menu item EDIT: COPY EXAMPLES which copies the examples only to the clipboard

The easiest way to get help on Maple and its standard functions is interactively from within a Worksheet by typing `? keyword`, `?? keyword` or `??? keyword` followed by ENTER. The keyword does not have to be complete; if it is incomplete, a list of close matches is returned. Alternatively, help can be obtained via the help dialogs found under the HELP menu. Using these, we can quickly perform both keyword and full text searches on Maple's help database. Once a help topic has been found in this manner, its help page is viewed by either double-clicking on the function name or by selecting it and pressing ENTER.

GETTING HELP

This will return a list of all the functions known to Maple beginning with *eva*.

```
> ?eva

Try one of the following topics:

{eval, evalb, evalf, evalhf, evaln, evala,
 evalc, evalm, Eval, evalfint, evalp,
 evalpow, evalr, evalapply, evalgf}
```

This returns the help page on the Fresnel Sine Integral.

```
> ?FresnelS
```

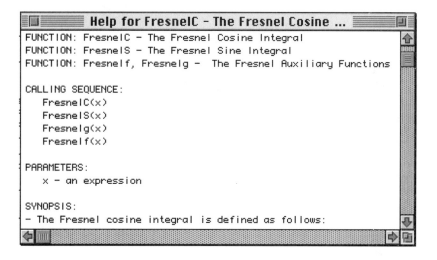

This accesses the calling sequence information for The *Riemann-Zeta* function.

```
> ??Zeta

CALLING SEQUENCE:
    Zeta(s)
    Zeta(n, s)
    Zeta(n, s, q)

PARAMETERS:
    s - an expression
    n - an expression, understood to be a
    non-negative integer
    q - an expression, understood to be a
    positive real number
```

GETTING HELP The topics related to the function `limit` are obtained by using `related(limit)`.

```
> related(limit);

SEE ALSO: limit[ dirs] , limit[ return] ,
     series, signum
```

Using `???BesselJ` will return the examples section for the function `BesselJ`.

```
> ???BesselJ
```

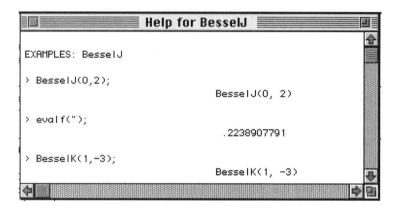

Maple's help system is full of useful information for both beginner and the experienced user alike. The following list gives some good starting points.

MORE HELP		
	`?constants`	Initially known constants
	`examples( name )`	Return the examples section of a help page
	`?index`	A general index
	`?index[ packages]`	An index of the standard packages
	`?inifcn`	A list of initially known functions
	`?ininames`	A list of initially known names
	`?introduction`	An on-line introduction to Maple
	`?help`	Help on help
	`?type`	A list of standard Maple types
	`?tutorial`	An on-line tutorial introduction to Maple
	`?update`	A list of new release updates

A good and dynamic source of information and help on Maple is the Internet. The following is short list of what is available.

SOME MAPLE ON THE INTERNET Here is a partial list of WWW and the Internet sites where Maple information can be found.

http://www2.ncsu.edu/math/Projects/MapleArchive/MapleArchive.html
http://www.maplesoft.com/MathOffice/
http://www.maplesoft.com/Maple/share.html
http://www.maplesoft.comhttp
http://web.mit.edu/afs/athena.mit.edu/software/maple/www/teaching.html
http://archives.math.utk.edu/maple.html
http://daisy.uwaterloo.ca
http://www.sm.luth.se/math/
http://web.mit.edu/afs/athena.mit.edu/software/maple/www/home.html
http://www2.ncsu.edu/math/NewStuff.html
http://rchs1.chemie.uni-regensburg.de/maple_software.html
The Maple User Group (MUG)

Basic Syntax

Due to historical reasons, Maple suffers with some syntactical idiosyncrasies. Despite this it does conform to some basic rules.

The first rule: Maple is case-sensitive. Maple names can include any alphanumeric character and can be up to 498 characters in length. If the name includes any "special" characters, for example, ", [,], {, }, or /, care must be taken to make the name a string by enclosing it in string quotes ``. The underscore, although not a "special" character, should also be used with care as names starting with one could clash with either variables internal to Maple or machine - generated names.

MAPLE NAMES Names are case-sensitive so these are distinct.

```
> evalb(a_variable=A_Variable);
```
$$false$$

Here is a funny name.

```
> `a_funny_name{['"/`:
```

Here is a long name.

```
> `type\myutils\mytest\checksum`:
```

This name contains white spaces.

```
> `This is answer 1`:
```

This is an internal underscored variable. Any variable beginning with _Env is considered as an environment variable.

```
> _Env:
```

MAPLE NAMES This is a machine-generated name representing the constant of integration.

```
> op(2, rhs(dsolve(diff(y(t), t)=y(t),
    y(t)))));
```

$$\_C1$$

The second rule: Every complete input expression must be terminated with either a semicolon or a colon. A colon will suppress the Maple output. More than one expression can be entered on a single input line provided that each one is properly terminated.

DELIMITERS The semicolon is the most common delimiter, and causes the result to be echoed to the screen.

```
> numtheory[divisors](12);
```

$$\{1, 2, 3, 4, 6, 12\}$$

Using a colon as the delimiter allows long output to be suppressed. Here a five-by-five Hilbert matrix is assigned to the variable mat without the intermediate output being displayed.

```
> mat:=linalg[hilbert](5, 2 - g):
```

Evaluate two expressions in sequence and display the final result.

```
> binomial(x, 4): expand(");
```

$$\frac{1}{24}(x-3)(x-2)(x-1)x$$

The third rule: Wherever possible, Maple tries to copy standard mathematical notation. However, white spaces are just that and not taken to mean the multiplication operation. The expression 2 multiplied by x is represented in Maple as 2*x and not 2 x.

The fourth rule: Use parentheses to influence evaluation order. The precedence of evaluation is the same as in standard mathematics: power, multiply, divide, addition, and subtraction. The evaluation order can be altered by the inclusion of parentheses.

ORDERING This means $(zx^2) + y$ and not $z(x^2 + y)$.

```
> z*x^2 + y;
```

$$zx^2 + y$$

This means $z(x^2 + y)$.

```
> z*(x^2 + y);
```

$$zx^2 + zy$$

The fifth rule: There is only one type of assignment available in Maple: immediate assignment. Values can be assigned to a tag or variable by using the function assign or its infix form :=.

Clearing variables is just a special form of assignment. You clear a variable by assigning it an unevaluated copy of itself. Alternatively unassign can be used. A drastic method is to use `restart`, which will reset the current Maple session, clearing all variables and effectively unloading any packages and readlib defined functions that are loaded.

ASSIGNING AND CLEARING

By using :=, the variable `big_num` is assigned the value 10^{10}.

```
> big_num:=10^10;
```

$$big\_num := 10000000000$$

Here `assign` is used to set the variable `small_num`.

```
> assign(small_num, 0.000000001);
```

Here `assign` is used to make multiple assignments.

```
> assign(2French=table([ one=une,
  two=deux] ), Entries=2);
```

A variable can be cleared by assigning it the unevaluated form of itself.

```
> big_num:='big_num';
```

$$big\_num := big\_num$$

This loads `unassign`.

```
> readlib(unassign);
```

$$proc() \ldots end$$

This clears the table `2French` using `unassign`.

```
> unassign(`2French`):
```

This resets the Maple session.

```
> restart;
```

Functions

Both active and inert functions are available to the Maple user. A call to an inert function will cause the formation of a Maple object without any evaluation taking place. Inert functions start with a capital letter. Evaluation of an inert function can be forced by using `value` or `eval` or `evalf`.

INERT AND ACTIVE FUNCTIONS

Find the limit lim $1/x$ from the right using the inert function.

```
> Limit(1/x, x=0, right);
```

$$\lim_{x \to 0^+} 1/x$$

Evaluation is forced using `value`.

```
> value(");
```

$$\infty$$

INERT AND Get a list of inert functions.   `> ?inert`
ACTIVE
FUNCTIONS

```
┌─────────────────────────────────────────────────────────────┐
│ ▣▤▤  Help for Index of descriptions for iner... ▤▤▤  ▣ │
├─────────────────────────────────────────────────────────────┤
│    AFactor    AFactors    Ai       Berlekamp   Bi        Co │
│    Det        Diff        Discrim   DistDeg     Divide    Ei │
│    Eval       Expand      Factor    Factors     Gausselim Ga │
│    Gcd        Gcdex       GetAlgExt Hermite     Indep     In │
│    Interp     Irreduc     Limit     Norm        Normal    Nu │
│    Power      Powmod      Prem      Prime       Primfield Pr │
│    Primpart   Product     ProbSplit Quo         Randpoly  Ra │
│    Rem        Resultant   RootOf    Roots       Smith     Sp │
│    Sqrfree    Subres      Sum       Svd         Trace        │
│                                                              │
└─────────────────────────────────────────────────────────────┘
```

Function Application

Functions can be applied to arguments using prefix, infix, or postfix notation. In the prefix form, the function name appears before its arguments; it is the most common method of evoking a function. In infix notation, the function name appears between the arguments. Finally, in postfix notation, the function name follows the arguments on which it operates. Maple has very few operators that fall into this final category.

FUNCTION By using `map`, the cotangent of
STYLES every entry in the list is obtained. The arguments to `map` are `cot` and `[1., 2, 3., 4]`.

```
> map(cot,[1., 2, 3., 4]);
```

$$[.6420926159, \cot(2), -7.015252551, \cot(4)]$$

Prefixed functions can be nested. Here the complementary error function `erfc(2.3)` is calculated to five significant digits.

```
> evalf(erfc(2.3), 5);
```

$$.0011432$$

The arithmetic operations are all infix.

```
> 2 + 6;
```

$$8$$

The concatenation operator is also infix.

```
> `Join this to ` . `that`;
```

$$\text{Join this to that}$$

Factorial is the postfix form of the prefix function `factorial`.

```
> 10!;
```

$$3628800$$

Numerical Calculations in Maple

Maple is capable of doing exact and approximate arithmetic using integer, rational, irrational, floating-point, and complex numbers. You will soon find that doing numerical calculations with Maple is as easy as using any electronic calculator. There is, however, one important point to remember: When manipulating expressions containing floating-point numbers, Maple will cast, wherever possible, all numbers into their floating-point approximations. You should be careful — floats tend to be contagious! The exception to this rule is "exact" mathematical objects such as unevaluated roots. These objects remain unaltered due to their internal representation; they are stored as functions and not numbers. An explicit `evalf`, however, will force their evaluation to floating-point numbers.

SIMPLE ARITHMETIC

This returns an exact result.

```
> (3*4/5000)^3;
```

$$\frac{27}{1953125000}$$

This returns an approximate numerical result. Note that only the power is a float.

```
> (3*4/5)^3.;
```

$$13.82400000$$

This returns the largest integer less than the previous result.

```
> floor(");
```

$$13$$

This performs floating-point normalization. Zero is returned if the argument is less than 10^{-6}.

```
> fnormal(27/1953125000, 6);
```

$$0$$

INTEGER ARITHMETIC

Here the integer approximation to $\sqrt{10002}$ is computed.

```
> isqrt(10002);
```

$$100$$

This computes the integer quotient of 100 divided by 7.

```
> iquo(100, 7);
```

$$14$$

Here the 55th prime number is returned.

```
> ithprime(55);
```

$$257$$

INTEGER ARITHMETIC This calculates the greatest common divisor of the integers 2^5 and $5^2 + 3$.

```
> igcd(2^5, 5^2 + 3);
```

$$4$$

Using Maple, you can do both integer and floating-point arithmetic. You should remember, however, that functions optimized for floating-point operations do not always perform optimally over the integers. It is prudent therefore to search out those functions provided specifically for integer arithmetic if you are only working over the integers.

If an exact solution cannot be found, it is possible, in most cases, to calculate a floating-point approximation. In most instances, `evalf` is simply applied to the stubborn problem. If you are reduced to using `evalf` on a function, take some time to see if an inert form of the function exists; by applying `evalf` directly to the inert form of the function, the time of computation is often reduced. If, on the other hand, machine-precision answers are acceptable, then the floating-point hardware can be accessed directly using `evalhf`. If `evalhf` is used, two simple rules need to be followed: The arguments must be representable as floats and arrays must be passed by value using the `var` construct as shown in what follows.

HARD ARITHMETIC Here the inert form of integrate is used with `evalf` to calculate a numeric integral.

```
> evalf(Int(abs(BesselJ(0, x)), x=0..10));
```

$$3.072233814$$

Here data arrays x and y are defined.

```
> x:= array([ 7., 5, 6, 9]):
> y:=array([ 0, 0, 0, 0]):
```

By using `readlib`, the Fast Fourier Transform function is loaded.

```
> readlib(FFT):
```

By calling the floating-point hardware with `evalhf`, the FFT of the data arrays x and y is calculated.

```
> evalhf(FFT(2, var(x), var(y))):
```

Use `print` to view the real and imaginary components.

```
> print(x, y);
```

$$[27., 1.000000000000000, -1., 1.000000000000000],$$
$$[0, 4., 0, -4.]$$

The wrapper `var` is only necessary when functions with array arguments are passed to `evalhf` and its use causes the wrapped arrayt to be passed by value and not by reference. This means that the array elements and not the array name are passed to `evalhf`, where they are converted to machine-precision floats before the function is evaluated further. Once evaluation is complete, the results are automatically converted back to arrays that overwrite the originals.

When you ask Maple to calculate a numerical result, it will return an answer with a fixed number of digits. Because the number of digits is fixed, roundoff errors tend to creep into any numerical calculation if you are not careful. The number of digits used, unless otherwise specified, is set by the global variable `Digits`. By setting `Digits`, the user sets the degree of precision that Maple will use. Maple is capable of representing numbers in excess of 500,000 digits instead of the 10 used by a common calculator. In general, as the level of precision used increases, the size of the roundoff errors will decrease. Because Maple only works at the level of precision set by the user, care should always be exercised when doing numerical calculations to ensure that the answers obtained are valid.

ARBITRARY PRECISION

Here the "exact" result to log10(4.7) is returned

```
> a:=log10(4.7);
```

$$a := \log 10(4.7)$$

Here the floating-point approximation is calculated.

```
> b:=evalf(a);
```

$$b := .6720978579$$

The difference is computed.

```
> c:=a - b;
```

$$c := \log 10(4.7) - .6720978579$$

Here the difference between the "exact" and approximate results is calculated as the precision is increased from 10 to 16 digits.

```
> seq(evalf(c), Digits=10..16); Digits:=10:
```

$$0, .4 \ 10^{-10}, .36 \ 10^{-10}, .357 \ 10^{-10}, .3572 \ 10^{-10},$$
$$.35717 \ 10^{-10}, .357175 \ 10^{-10}$$

Maple is capable of doing calculations in the complex domain. The complex constant √-1 is denoted in Maple by `I`.

COMPLEX ARITHMETIC

The complex constant `I` is equal to √-1.

```
> sqrt(-1);
```

$$I$$

The argument of the complex number sinπ/4 + i cosπ/4 is 1/4 π.

```
> argument(sin(Pi/4) + I*cos(Pi/4));
```

$$\frac{1}{4\pi}$$

The imaginary part of the *Riemann-Zeta* function at the point 0.3 + i5 is calculated.

```
> Im(Zeta(.3 + I*5));
```

$$.2541447866$$

Although it is common to do arithmetic in base 10, it is not always convenient to do so. Maple permits the user to change numbers from one base to another using `convert`. However, once the base has been changed to something other than base 10, the arithmetic operations that are possible are severely limited.

OTHER BASES Maple can do calculations in bases other than decimal. Here 35 is represented in hexadecimal, binary, and octal.

```
> for n in [ hex, binary, octal] do
    convert(35, n)
  od;
```

$$23$$
$$100011$$
$$43$$

Other, more unusual number bases can be used.

```
> convert(35, base, 3);
```

$$[2, 2, 0, 1]$$

Data Types

List and Sets

Lists and sets are linear data structures that can be used to store and manipulating data. True to the mathematical object, a set in Maple maintains no order information about its contents. Data stored in a list, however, will preserve their order. Both lists and sets can contain any valid Maple expressions; they can be nested and include null lists and sets.

LISTS AND SETS Here a list is entered. Note the square-bracket notation.

```
> a_list:=[ 1, 2, a/3, 3, c, sin(x),
    1/cos(x), x->x^2 + 1] ;
```

$$a\_list :=$$
$$\left[1, 2, \frac{1}{3}\,a, 3, c, \sin(x), \frac{1}{\cos(x)}, x \rightarrow x + 1\right]$$

Sets are denoted using curly braces. Here a three-element set is entered.

```
> a_set := { 1, {}, `this is a set`};
```

$$a\_set := \{\{\}, 1, \mathit{this\ is\ a\ set}\}$$

Membership in a set can be determined quickly.

```
> member(3/5, a_list);
```

$$\mathit{false}$$

LISTS AND SETS Here each element in a list is doubled.

```
> map((x, y)->x*y, [1, sin(x), a], 2);
```

$$[2, 2\sin(x), 2a]$$

!2 Here it is established that the null set {} belongs to the set *a_set*.

```
> member({}, a_set);
```

true

Set elements can be removed.

```
> a_set minus {1};
```

$$\{\{\}, \textit{this is a set}\}$$

Here the intersection of two sets is determined.

```
> a_set intersect {1, c, `this is a set`};
```

$$\{1, \textit{this is a set}\}$$

Specific elements or groups of elements can be selected and manipulated in a variety of ways.

PARTS OF LISTS AND SETS By using a square bracket to mean an indexed variable, the sixth element of *a_list* is returned.

```
> a_list[6];
```

$$\sin(x)$$

Indexing operates over sets as well as lists.

```
> a_set[3];
```

$$1$$

!3 If the index is a range, a sequence of terms is returned. Here elements 3 through 5 are returned.

?10

```
> a_list[3..5]
```

$$[1/3\, a, 3, c]$$

Elements of lists can be removed using subsop. Here the eighth entry in the list is replaced with NULL and so is removed from the list.

```
> new_list:=subsop(8=NULL, a_list)
```

$$new\_list := \left[1, 2, \frac{1}{3}a, 3, c, \sin(x), \frac{1}{\cos(x)}\right]$$

!4 Elements of lists can be changed. If the element is set to NULL, it will be removed form the list.

```
> new_list[7]:=new_one:
> new_list;
```

$$\left[1, 2, \frac{1}{3}a, 3, c, \sin(x), new\_one\right]$$

PARTS OF LISTS AND SETS The function `select` is useful for manipulating both sets and lists. Here all elements of `a_list` that are algebraic numbers are returned.

```
> select(type, a_list, algnum);
```

$$[1, 2, 3]$$

Tables, Arrays, Vectors, and Matrices

Multidimensional data structures are defined in Maple using `table`, `array`, and `matrix`. The structures `array` and `table` are automatically available, whereas `matrix` and the corresponding matrix algebra functions, including some special matrices, are grouped together in the `linalg` package, which must be accessed explicitly.

Maple tables are very useful structures, as they can be created either explicitly or implicitly; they are dynamic, which means that their size can be altered implicitly; and their indices or keys can take any value. In addition, their access time is directly proportional to their size. Linear access time is achieved by using a hash table that is added to every time a new entry is made. If a clash occurs, the entire hash table is rebuilt so removing the clash.

TABLES By assigning to an indexed variable, a table is implicitly created

```
> imperial_2_SI[ inch] :=.0254*m:
> imperial_2_SI[ lb] :=.454*kg:
> imperial_2_SI[ pint[ English]] :=.568*l:
```

The entries are retrieved by giving the table name and the index.

```
> imperial_2_SI[ lb] * 2;
```

$$.908 \text{ kg}$$

Table entries can be tables, lists, sets and so forth. Here a table containing tables holding currency exchange information is defined explicitly.

```
> exchange:=table([ Dollar=table([ CND=1/1.3,
    Sterling=1.5, DMark=1/1.6] ),
    Sterling=table([ CND=2, Dollar=1/1.5,
    FF =8] )] ):
```

Here the table entries are returned using `entries`.

```
> entries(exchange);
```

[table([ ]	[table([ ]
FF = 8	*DMark* = .6250000000
CND = 2	*CND* = .7692307692
Dollar = .6666666667	*Sterling* = 1.5
])	])]

By using `indices`, the table index can be displayed.

```
> indices(exchange);
```

$$[Sterling], [Dollar]$$

TABLES The subtables can also be accessed.

```
> indices(exchange[ sterling] );
```

$$[FF], [CND], [Dollar]$$

Here the exchange rate from sterling to the Canadian dollar is returned.

```
> exchange[ sterling][ CND] ;
```

$$2$$

Arrays and matrices are very similar in Maple. The main differences are: the rows and columns of a matrix are indexed from 1, whereas an array's index can start from any integer and arrays support indexing functions and matrices do not. Both arrays and matrixes are limited to being two-dimensional. Each element within a two-dimensional array or matrix can itself be a matrix or array. In this way *n*-dimensional structures can be approximated.

ARRAYS AND MATRICES

This "loads" the `linalg` package.

```
> with(linalg):
```

```
Warning: new definition for     norm
Warning: new definition for     trace
```

This is how an array with unknown elements is defined. Note how an array with row and column indices starting at 1 is returned.

```
> mat:=array(1..2, 1..2, [] );
```

$$mat := array(1 .. 2, 1 .. 2, [])$$

Here element $mat_{2,2}$ is set to the value `non_zero`.

```
> mat[ 2,  2] :=non_zero;
```

$$mat[2, 2] := non\_zero$$

We can look at the array using `eval(mat)`.

```
> eval(mat);
```

$$A := \begin{bmatrix} ?_{[1, 1]} & ?_{[1, 2]} \\ ?_{[2, 1]} & non\_zero \end{bmatrix}$$

A system of linear simultaneous equations can be easily defined and manipulated using matrix algebra. A matrix can also be defined using a list of lists, for example, `matrix([ [ x] , [ y]] )`.

```
> the_eqn:=array([[ 1,  2] , [ 3,  4]] ) &*
  matrix(2, 1, [ x,  y] ) =
  array([[ 0] , [ 0]] ):
```

ARRAYS AND MATRICES We can ask Maple to print the equation.

```
> evalm(the_eqn);
```

$$\begin{bmatrix} x + 2y \\ 3x + 4y \end{bmatrix} = \begin{bmatrix} 0 \\ 0 \end{bmatrix}$$

This returns the row dimension of the matrix on the right-hand side of the equation.

```
> rowdim(rhs("));
```

$$2$$

The elements of a matrix can be operated on directly by using functions like map and zip.

```
> map(x->x*3*f, matrix([[1, r],[t, 4]]));
```

$$A := \begin{bmatrix} 3f & 3fr \\ 3ft & 12f \end{bmatrix}$$

The final structure in this group is the vector, which can be defined in one of five ways as shown in what follows. Maple treats a vector as a mathematical object that can be either represented as a row or a column and the formt that is used is determined by the operation that we wish to perform; for example, if we multiply the vector **A** by the vector **B,** Maple will treat vector **A** as a row vector and vector **B** as a column vector. If the order is reversed, then vector **B** would be assumed to be a row vector and vector **A** would be treated as a column vector.

VECTORS This is the easiest way to define a vector.

```
> vector([a, b, c]);
```

$$[a\ b\ c]$$

Vectors can contain unknown elements. Here we define a four-element vector with two unknown entries, which are flagged.

```
> vector(4, [1, 2]);
```

$$[1\ 2\ ?_1\ ?_2]$$

If no second argument is given in the vector definition, unknown entries are assumed, as shown in this example, where an unknown vector of length 2 is defined.

```
> vector(2);
```

$$[?_1\ ?_2]$$

A function can be specified in the definition that is used to calculate the vector's elements.

```
> vector(5, x->dialog(x));
```

$$[dialog(1)\ dialog(2)\ dialog(3)\ dialog(4)\ dialog(5)]$$

VECTORS Vectors can also be defined as a one-dimensional array.

```
> array(1..4, [ 0.5, sin(x), A, x->x^2] );
```

$$[0.5, \sin(x), A, x \rightarrow x^2]$$

?12 Here a two-element vector is defined, which is then multiplied by itself.

```
> a:= vector([ 1, aa] ):
  evalm(a &* a);
```

$$[1 + aa^2]$$

?13 A vector can also be multiplied by a scalar.

```
> evalm(a * 4);
```

$$[4, 4aa]$$

MORE HELP

Clearing entries	Entries of tables, arrays, matrices, and vectors can be cleared in the usual way.
Indexing functions	Tables and arrays can take indexing functions. For more information, see ? indexfcn.
Map across entries	Elements can be manipulated using map. For example: map(diff, array(1..2, 1..2, [[n, n^2], [n^3, n^4]]), n);
Special evaluation rules	Tables and arrays fall victim to last name evaluation. If a table or array is assigned to a tag, only the tag is returned unless full evaluation is forced using eval.

Type Checking

Maple is a strongly typed system, and in the previous section, some of the more common data types were introduced. Standard Maple knows in excess of 80 individual data types. The concept of types is a powerful one that enables the user to ensure that functions are applied correctly to valid expressions. For example, Fibonacci numbers are only valid for positive integers, an expression can only be said to be constant if all parts of it are constant, and so on. These and other tests are easy to do using Maple's types and type-checking functions

DATA TYPES

!	*	..	=	TEXT
&*	**	<	PLOT	algebraic
&+	+	<=	PLOT3D	algext
^	.	<>	RootOf	algfun

DATA TYPES	algnum	evenfunc	logical	primeint	scalar
	algnumext	evenodd	mathfunc	procedure	series
	and	expanded	matrix	protected	set
	anyfunc	facint	monomial	quadratic	specfunc
	anything	factorial	name	quartic	sqrt
	arctrig	float	negative	radext	square
	argcheck	fraction	nonneg	radfun	string
	arithop	function	not	radfunext	structure
	array	identical	nothing	radical	surface
	boolean	indexed	numeric	radnum	table
	complex	infinity	operator or	radnumext	taylor
	constant	integer	point	range	trig
	cubic	laurent	polynom	rational	type
	defn	linear	positive	ratpoly	uneval
	dot	list	posneg	realcons	union
	equation	listlist	posnegint	relation	vector

TYPE CHECKING

The function `whattype` is an interactive way of finding out the type of an object.

```
> whattype(40);
```

$$integer$$

Here the type of an object is tested to see if it is a negative integer. The function `type` is designed to be used in programming applications.

```
> type(40, negint);
```

$$false$$

This assigns an array to the tag `a`.

```
> a:=array(0..2, 1..3);
```

$$a := \text{array}(0 \,..\, 2, 1 \,..\, 3, [])$$

Is it a matrix? No. The first dimension definition is not valid for a matrix.

```
> type(a, matrix);
```

$$false$$

Here a complex expression is assigned to the tag `expr`.

```
> expr:=sin(Pi/7)^exp(GAMMA(1)*24/10):
```

This shows that `expr` is of type power.

```
> whattype(expr);
```

$$\wedge$$

TYPE CHECKING By using the `map` function, a slightly more intuitive view of the expression is obtained.

```
> map(whattype, expr);
```

$$function^{function}$$

Objects can be tested to see if they contain given expressions. Here `expr` is tested to see if it contains π.

```
> has(expr, Pi);
```

$$true$$

Here it can be seen that `series` by default generates Taylor series.

```
> type(series(GAMMA(x), x=a + h), taylor);
```

$$true$$

By using `dismantle`, an object's data structure can be viewed. The function is readlib-defined.

```
> readlib(dismantle)(sin(x^4));

FUNCTION(3)
   NAME(4): sin
   EXPSEQ(2)
      PROD(3)
         NAME(4): X
         INTPOS(2): 4
```

MORE HELP		
	`?type[ structured]`	Help page for nested data types such as `list(name=range)`. This will match `[ a=1..2]`.
	`?index[ data types]`	Help page giving an index of descriptions for Maple data types. This is a subset of the list given in the type help page.
	`?type[ data type]`	Help page for a specific data type, for example, `?type[ polynorm]`.
	select	The `select` function provides an easy way to retrieve elements from lists, and so on, based on their type.
	indets	By using `indets`, the indeterminates of an expression that match a given type can be determined.
	ispoly	Test to determine if an expression is a polynomial.
	attributes	Maple objects can now be assigned attributes.

Keeping Track

In a Maple session, there are a number of things of which you need to keep track.. The most obvious of these are the states of computations, models, and objects. Less obvious is the state of the system resources.

Resource Usage

The level of resource usage can be seen at a glance via the simple status bar found at the bottom of the Worksheet.

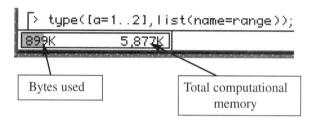

Figure 2.3 Simple Status Bar

A comprehensive status report can always be displayed using the WINDOWS menu item STATUS.

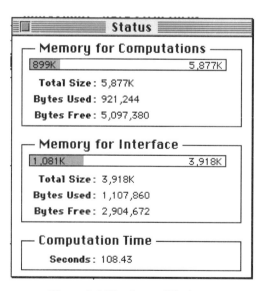

Figure 2.4 The Status Window

Finally, you can get all of the preceding data and additional information by accessing the kernel options data structure from within the Worksheet. This data structure holds the kernel version, the Maple data structure word size, the current print level, the total number of bytes allocated, the number of bytes used, amongst other data.

KERNELOPTS   This returns the number of bytes used in the session.

```
> kernelopts(byteused);
```

$$3855148$$

This sets the print level to 10. Note how `printlevel` is passed using delay evaluation quotes.

```
> kernelopts('printlevel'=10);
```

$$1$$

Here we check the print level at the top level.

```
> printlevel;
```

$$10$$

This shows the version information for the kernel.

```
> kernelopts(version)
```

Maple V, Release 4, IBM INTEL WIN, Jun 13 1995, Unserialized

Here we see how much CPU time we have used in this session

```
> kernelopts(cputime);
```

$$48.000$$

MORE HELP   `?status`   Return the help page for the global table `status`. The contents of the table are returned with `status;`.

    `?kernelopts`   Return the help page for `kernelopts`. All of the names recognized by `kernelopts` are listed.

Calculations

Previous outputs can be referenced with the ditto character ". Using this method, you can quickly review output or use it in the next calculation. Up to three previous outputs are always stored in a three-level stack that can be accessed using ","" ,and """ to retrieve the last, the one before last, and the second before last, respectively. It should be noted that the output stack only stores output expressions, which means that an expression that prints an output, for example, but returns NULL will be ignored. This behavior can lead to unexpected results if you are not careful. The use of the ditto command is limited, and when you do use it, it should be used with care and should never be used in functions or procedures.

USING "S   This places e^x on the stack.   `> exp(x):`

This calculates the first three terms in the Taylor series of e^x.   `> series(", x, 3);`

$$1 + x^2 + \frac{1}{2}x^3 + O(x)$$

This computes the definite integral of e^x.   `> int("", x=a..b);`

$$e^b - e^a$$

This takes the first derivative of e^x.   `> diff(""", x);`

$$e^x$$

ANOTHER WAY: SHOWTIME   `Showtime` and `history` are readlib-defined functions that, when used, automatically assign a unique name to every output expression starting with **O1** (capital oh-one) and continuing **O2**, **O3**, ... The machine-generated tags can be used just like any other Maple name.

This loads `showtime`.   `> readlib(showtime):`

This enables the function. The first tag is **O1**.   `> on;`

This assigns $x^2 + 1$ to the tag. The function also provides time and words used data.   `> O1:=x^2 - 1;`

$$x^2 - 1$$

```
time     0.23     words     876
```

The output of `factor(O1)` is automatically assigned to the tag **O2**.   `> O2:=factor(O1);`

$$(x - 1)(x + 1)$$

```
time     2.95     words     5829
```

The showtime function is disabled.   `> O3:=off;`

If either `showtime` or `history` are used, the stack-based method of recalling previous output is temporarily disabled.

The most risk-free method of keeping track of your calculations, and so on, is to assign any output of a calculation, a data structure or a definition to a unique variable name explicitly.

Anames and Unames

The functions `anames` and `unames` can be used to obtain lists of all of the names, functions, strings, and variables known to the current Maple session. The function `anames` will return a set containing all of the current names to which a valid Maple expression has been assigned. Similarly, unames returns a set of all names that are known but as yet remain unassigned. The amount of data returned by either function can be restricted by specifying the type desired.

ASSIGNED OR NOT ASSIGNED This returns all of the assigned names of type *constant*.

```
> anames(`constant`);
```

property/NameCount, expr, Digits, discont/count, print-level, Order, factor/icontsign/global

By using `unames` in conjunction with `select`, all of the single-letter unassigned names can be found.

```
> select(x->length(x)=1, {unames()});
```

{E, O, +, *, ^, =, !, ., <, I, k, l, L, A, c, P, M, m, N, r, S, U, u, n, Q, q, R, f, /, T, p, b, i, j, x, t, s, y, J, K, V, e, o, X, Y, Z, z, B, C, F, w, d, G, g, H, h, v, ~, }

Customizing Your Sessions

Customizing the look and feel of your sessions is done using the menu options to set such attributes as style and size of output, input font, separator lines, and so forth. You can also make adjustments by setting system options that let you set page size, type of prompt, and the level of error reporting. System options are accessed for either review or setting by using `interface`.

INTERFACE OPTIONS This sets the prompt to the string `` `#>> ` ``.

```
> interface(prompt=`#>>   `);
```

This returns the echo level. It is 1, the default value.

```
#>>   interface(echo);
```

1

INTERFACE OPTIONS Maple will simplify expressions automatically by removing and labeling common terms.

```
#>>    test:=sum((a+1)^s, s=0..5);
```

$$test := 2 + a + \%1^2 + \%1^3 + \%1^4 + \%1^5$$
$$\%1 := a + 1$$

This forces common terms to be removed if they are longer than five characters.

```
#>>    interface(labelwidth=5);
```

We can now see the expression as a whole.

```
#>>    test;
```

$$2 + a + (a + 1)^2 + (a + 1)^3 + (a + 1)^4 + (a + 1)^5$$

If you had to set the internal options manually every time you used Maple, it would soon become tedious. By using an initialization file, option settings can be set automatically every time you use Maple. An initialization file is also a convenient way of automatically loading frequently used functions and packages. The file is a plain ASCII text file stored in either the Maple application directory (Macintosh and PC) or the user's home directory (Workstations) and must be named mapleinit. When Maple is launched it reads the file and interprets each line as a Maple command. A sample initialization file is shown below.

MAPLEINIT FILES

Set a new prompt.

```
interface(prompt=`Vr4 > `);
```

Read a utilities package from the directory:
`steve's work:maple.`

```
read(``.`steve's work:maple`.`:utils.m`):
```

Read the FFT, Fourier, and Laplace functions into the session.

```
readlib(FFT);
with(inttrans, [laplace, fourier]);
```

Load the linalg package.

```
with(linalg);
```

Echo a message to the user.

```
lprint(`functions have been loaded`);
```

NEW FUNCTIONS AT A GLANCE	`expression sequence:`	No echo terminator for input expressions.
	`tag := expr`	The infix form of assign.
	`expression sequence;`	Normal terminator for input expressions.
	$expr_1 = expr_2$	The equality operator.
	`abs( expr )`	Calculate the absolute value of `expr`.
	`anames( pattern )`	Return the assigned names matching pattern.
	`argument( expr )`	Calculate the argument of the complex number `expr`.
	`array( [ elems ] )`	Create an array with entries `elems`.
	`assign( eqns )`	Assign the values to variables. The relationships are determined by `eqns`.
	`BesselJ( expr )`	Calculate the Bessel function of the first kind.
	`binomial( n, r )`	Return the binomial coefficient $(n!\ (n-r)!)/r!$.
	`cos( expr )`	Calculate the cosine cos(*expr*).
	`cot( expr )`	Calculate the cotangent cot(*expr*).
	`divisors( expr )`	Calculate integer divisors of `expr`.
	`dismantle( expr )`	Show the structure of the Maple data structure used to store `expr`.
	`echo`	Interface variable setting the echo level taking a value between 0 and 4. The default is 1.
	`entries( table )`	Return the entries of `table`.
	`erfc( expr )`	Calculate the complimentary error function erfc(*expr*).
	`examples( name )`	Return the examples section from the help page of `name`.
	$FFT(\ expr,\ array_1,\ array_2\ )$	Calculate the *Fast Fourier Transform* of the sampled function stored in $array_1$ and $array_2$.

NEW FUNCTIONS AT A GLANCE	floor(expr)	Truncate `expr` to an integer.
	fnormal(expr)	Will return zero if $expr \leq 10$ - `Digits`.
	for count in expr do .. od	Evaluate the body of the for loop once for every element in `expr`. The loop counter takes the value of the current element.
	has(expr, pattern)	Test for pattern in `expr`.
	hilbert(size, opts)	Return the Hilbert matrix of dimension `size`. The optional parameter, if present, is used in the calculation of each element.
	igcd($expr_1$, $expr_2$, .., $expr_n$)	Calculate the greatest common divisor of the integers $expr_1$, $expr_2$, .., $expr_n$.
	Im(expr)	Take the imaginary part of `expr`.
	indices(table)	Return the indices of `table`.
	Int(expr, range)	The inert form of the integration function.
	interface(var = value) interface(var)	View or set the interface variable `var`.
	set_1 intersect set_2	Calculate the integer quotient of $expr_1$, $expr_2$.
	iquo($expr_1$, $expr_2$)	Compute the intersection set_1 and set_2.
	isqrt(expr)	Compute the approximate integer square root of `expr`.
	ithprime(n)	Return the nth prime number.
	kernelopts($expr_1$, $expr_2$ .., $expr_n$)	Read or set the kernel options given by $expr_i$. An expression can be a name or an equation.
	labelwidth	The interface variable setting the minimum width a common subexpression must be before it is replaced with a machine-generated label.

NEW FUNCTIONS AT A GLANCE		
	`length( expr )`	Calculate the length of `expr`.
	`Limit( expr, var, dir )`	The inert form of `limit`.
	`limit( expr, eqn, dir )`	Calculate the limit given by eqn of `expr`. If `dir` is present, then a directional limit is calculated.
	`log10( expr )`	Calculate the logarithm to the base 10 of `expr`.
	`member( expr, set)`	Test to see if `expr` is a member of `set`.
	set_1 `minus` set_2	Remove the elements of set_2 from set_1.
	`NULL`	The NULL expression.
	`print( `$expr_1$`, `$expr_2$`, .., `$expr_n$` )`	Print $expr_1$, $expr_2$, .., $expr_n$ to the current stream.
	`prompt`	The interface variable setting the prompt.
	`related( name )`	Return the "See Also" section from the help page of `name`.
	`reset`	Reset the current Maple session.
	`rhs( expr )`	Return the right-hand side of `expr`.
	`rowdim( mat )`	Return the row dimension of the matrix **mat**.
	`select( oper, expr, opts )`	Select the elements of `expr` that satisfy the Boolean-valued operation `oper`. The optional arguments are passed to oper as additional parameters.
	`showtime`	A readlib-defined function used to keep track of session output automatically.
	`type( expr, type)`	Test `expr` to see if it is of type `type`.
	`unames( )`	Return the currently unassigned names within the Maple system.
	`unassign( name )`	Clear the variable `name`.
	`value( expr )`	Force evaluation of the inert function `expr`.

NEW	`var( expr )`	Pass/retrieve `expr` by value. Used with `evalfh`.
FUNCTIONS	`verboseproc`	Interface variable, taking values 0 through 2, determining how much of a procedure is printed. The default value is 1.
AT A GLANCE		
	`whattype( expr )`	Return the type of `expr`.
		Calculate the *Riemann-Zeta* function $\zeta(expr)$
	`Zeta( expr )`	
	`[ expr_1, expr_2 .., expr_n ]`	List and index brackets.
	`{ expr_1, expr_2 .., expr_n }`	Set brackets.

FAQs

1: What is the share library?

The share library is a collection of Maple functions and Worksheets produced by Maple users.

2: An existing Worksheet will not launch Windows-Maple. Why not?

Windows, unlike the Macintosh, does not save resource information as part of the Worksheet file. There is therefore no record of which application created the file, so the user must tell Windows which file extensions launch which applications. The *mws* (*ms* in Vr3) extension must be associated with Maple

3: Can RETURN be used instead of ENTER when using a Macintosh?

Yes, check the EXECUTE INPUT WITH RETURN KEY option in the SETTINGS — PREFERENCES dialog box.

4: ENTER has been pressed by mistake, the cursor has been placed in the previous input region, and the statement has been completed. On pressing ENTER again a syntax error is flagged. Why?

The Maple parser has accepted the first portion of the input statement including the ENTER. When you complete the statement with the second ENTER, it is parsed by Maple. It is invalid as it now contains two ENTER characters. To correct this, just place the cursor in the input region and press ENTER again.

5: I am using Vr3 on a Macintosh and I want to transfer a Worksheet onto an other platform. How do I do this?

The Worksheet must be saved using the SAVE COPY IN ... command in the FILE menu. The SAVE IN STANDARD FORMAT option must be checked in the dialog box before the file is saved.

6: Why use inert functions?

An inert function can be used if typeset output is required, an expression is to be evaluated numerically, or if an expression, say, a limit, is used as a mathematical object. In the second case, using an inert function inhibits any symbolic operations, and the third allows for manipulation of objects without full evaluation.

FAQs   7: Why does `evalhf(Int(abs(BesselJ (0, x)),x=0..10));` not work?

The `evalhf` function expects arguments that are or can be transformed into floats. The result of this integral is symbolic and hence cannot be represented as a float.

8: Why does `2^100 - evalf(2^100);` equal zero?

This is a good example of floats being contageous. Maple will convert the exact 2^{100} to its approximate floating-point representation using the default value of `Digits` prior to the subtraction taking place. So, both values are identical and the result is zero.

9: Can I use different number bases in calculations?

Not really, `convert` only returns strings when converting to binary, octal, or hexadecimal. When converting to any other base, a list of integers is returned.

10: How are lists joined?

Lists can be joined by using `op` as follows: `[ op(list_1), op(list_2)]`.

11: How can I define an *n*-dimensional array?

n-dimensional arrays are defined using `table`. A two-by-two-by-two array would be created as follows.

```
a[1, 1, 1]:=1:
a[1, 1, 2]:=2:
a[1, 2, 1]:=3:
...
a[2, 2, 1]:=7:
a[2, 2, 2]:=8:
```

Be careful—the matrix algebra routines will not work with tables.

12: Why do I need to use `eval` or `evalm` to display the contents of an array or table?

Maple uses *last name evaluation*. If, for example, an array is assigned to a name, say, `an_arr`, then unless full evaluation is forced with `eval` or `evalm`, only the name `an_arr` will be returned because it was the last name to be evaluated and not the contents of the array. This is done to save the amount of display area used each time an array, or similar, operation is performed.

FAQs 13: I have defined a row vector but it can be used as a column vector. Why?

The data structures used to hold a column and a row vector are essentially the same. During a vector calculation, Maple does not use all of the data structure and can interchange them. This means that vectors are context-sensitive. This means that if a column vector is needed to perform a certain operation, Maple will treat the vector as a column. If for another operation a row vector is needed, then the same vector will be treated as if it were a row. You should be careful when using vectors to avoid unpredictable results.

14: After customizing a session, how do I make the settings the defaults?

The session settings are saved as the defaults by using the SAVE AS DEFAULTS button in the FORMAT menu item FORMATS ... dialog.

BEWARE 1: The five-level browser shown is a Vr3 feature that lets you interrogate the help system by subject or keyword. The browser is started using the HELP menu item. Once in the browser, navigation is simple using either point and click or keywords. Once a function has been selected, its help page is viewed by either double-clicking on the function name or by pressing ENTER.

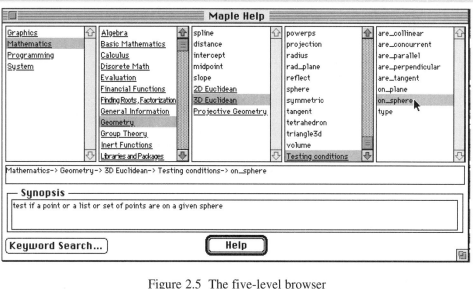

Figure 2.5 The five-level browser

BEWARE 2: Elements of matrices, vectors, sets, and lists cannot be operated on directly; functions like `map` or `zip` have to be used.

3: In releases Vr3 and older, portions of lists and sets are returned as expression sequences and not lists and sets.

4: For a list element to be modified in older releases, `subsop` had to be used.

5: Versions older than V4r used `status` to return resource usage information. Now `kernelopts` is used to access these data.

Programming with Maple

Maple is a programming language that is ideally suited to the manipulation of mathematical expressions. Like any other programming language, Maple is made up of built-in functions, for example, `Ci(x)`, `difforms[scalarpart](y)`, `rand()` and `product(f(x), x=0, 4)`. By combining these standard functions, either sequentially or by nesting, Maple gives us the ability to construct powerful programs very quickly. This means that if Maple does not already have a function capable of performing a needed operation, a new one can be defined. Once a user function has been defined, it can be used in exactly the same way as the built-in ones. Maple supports functional, procedural, and rule-based programming styles.

MAPLE PROGRAMS Here is a simple program to generate a three-by-three Vandermonde matrix.

```
> convert([ seq([ seq(x^y, x=1..3)],
  y=0..2)], matrix ):
```

This is a simple Maple program to return an identity matrix. It takes a single input parameter.

```
> identity_mat:=
  n -> linalg[block](n, [ 1]):
```

Here is a simple procedure to plot the roots of a polynomial.

```
> root_plot:=proc(poly, var)
    local sols, pts;
    sols:=[ solve(poly, var)];
    pts:=map(x->[ Re(x), Im(x)], sols);
    plot(pts, style=POINT, symbol=CROSS);
  end:
```

Functional Programming

In mathematics, the sciences, and engineering, expressions and data are often manipulated by applying functions. We can think of a function as a transformation rule that operates on some data and returns a result. So if we want the absolute value of an expression, we would simply apply the function *abs* to it, for example, *abs(-x)*, *abs([-1, 2, 3])*, *abs(-2 + i3)*. Functional programming is more concerned with the result than how that result is obtained. A function in Maple consists of a single expression and not a series of expressions carried out in sequence with intermediate results propagating through. A function, however, can be built up from nested expressions.

In general, a function will have a name, will take a sequence of arguments, do some manipulation, and return a result. It has a name, sometimes referred to as the head of the function, so that we can invoke it easily. It has an argument sequence, sometimes referred to as the formal parameters, so that it can be used easily time and time again without any recoding. Finally, it has a body that does the manipulation of the parameters passed into it. The function syntax is given in what follows. The function name is represented by the tag *function_name* and the argument sequence is denoted by the sequence arg_1, arg_2, .., arg_n. The formal parameter names appearing on the left-hand side of the arrow (->) in the definition match with corresponding variables in the body of the function. The body is a Maple expression that yields the value of the function when the arguments passed into it replace their corresponding parameter names in the body.

FUNCTION SYNTAX

```
function_name:= (arg₁, arg₂, .., argₙ) -> body
```
Function definition using the arrow operator.

```
function_name(arguments)
```
The method of function application.

The easiest way to see how functional programming is used to solve a problem is through an example. Suppose we want to compute the inverse of a matrix. First, we need to define a set of functional operations that will perform the task. We want to define the functions in such a way that the result returned by one can be immediately used as the input to another. One possible set of functions is calculate the determinants, calculate the adjoint, and compute the inverse. The compute function simply expands each element of the new matrix formed when the adjoint matrix is divided by the determinant.

AN EXAMPLE

```
compute(adjoint(mat)/determinant(mat))
```
Find the inverse of the matrix **mat** using functional programming.

MAPLE FUNCTIONS

The function $t(x) = x^2$ is defined using the arrow operator.

```
> t:=x->x^2:
```

This calculates the square of 3.6 using the new function.

```
> t(3.6);
```

$$12.96$$

Here the function $h(x, y)$, a function of two variables, is defined.

```
> h:=(x, y) -> (x + y)/(x*y):
```

MAPLE
FUNCTIONS

The function h is differentiated.

```
> diff(h(a, log(b)), b);
```

$$\frac{1}{b\, a\, \ln(b)} - \frac{a + \ln(b)}{a\, \ln(b)^2\, b}$$

Here a simple apply function is defined.

```
> simple_apply:=
  (h, b)->map(h, [op(b)]):
```

Here function t is applied to a list of integers.

```
> simple_apply(t, [1, 2, 3]);
```

$$[1, 4, 9]$$

Anonymous Functions

A function does not need a name associated with it in order that it can be used. A function without a name is known as an anonymous or pure function. A pure function can be used in situations where it is only used once or where it is not necessary to call it by name. It can be used either on its own or, more commonly, in conjunction with other functions such as `zip` and `map`. Because anonymous functions have no name assigned to them, they do not clutter the Maple name space.

PURE-
FUNCTION
SYNTAX

```
(arg₁, arg₂, .., argₙ) -> body
```

Pure- or anonymous-function definition using the arrow operator.

As with a named function, the variable list defines the formal parameters and the body defines the operation.

PURE
FUNCTIONS

Here is an anonymous function that returns the real and imaginary parts of an expression.

```
> x -> [Re(x), Im(x)]:
```

$\boxed{?_2}$ Because the function has no name, it can only be called using ditto (`"`).

```
> "(a+I*b);
```

$$[\Re(a) - \Im(b),\ \Im(a) + \Re(b)]$$

An anonymous function can be called directly from within another function. Here the pure function is $(x) \rightarrow x + 1$.

```
> sin(x->x+1(z));
```

$$\sin(z + 1)$$

PURE FUNCTIONS By using `map` and a pure function, each pair in the list is transformed to an equation.

```
> map(x->x[1]=x[2], [[a, 1], [b, 2],
  [c, 3], [d, 4]]);
```

$$[a = 1, b = 2, c = 3, d = 4]$$

MORE HELP All of these functions can use pure functions to manipulate the elements of Maple's data objects.

zip
```
> zip( (x, y)->diff(x, y), [sin(t)^2,
  tan(u*exp(r))], [t, r]);
```

$$[2\ sin(t)\ cos(t), (1 + tan(u\ exp(r))^2)\ u\ exp(r)]$$

```
> zip((a, b)->a + b, [1, 2, 3], [a, b],
  `no entry`);
```

$$[1 + a, 2 + b, 3 + no\ entry]$$

map2
```
> map2(ff, a, [a, b, c]);
```

$$\textit{ff}(a, a), \textit{ff}(a, b), \textit{ff}(a, c)$$

The following functions are found in the `transform` subpackage of the `stats` package.

multiapply
```
> multiapply[ (x, y)->x^(y^2)]([[1, 2],
  [y, z]]);
```

$$\left[1, 2^{z^2}\right]$$

apply
```
> apply[ (x,y)->
  simplify(surd(x, 3))]([1, -1, 8, -8]);
```

$$[1, -1, 2, -2]$$

Manipulating Functions

Functions can be manipulated arithmetically, applied to other functions: $f(g(x))$, differentiated, integrated, and so on. In addition to these common forms of manipulation, Maple provides us with a set of advanced function manipulation tools.

Unapply

Using `unapply` functions can be quickly produced directly from existing Maple output expressions. How `unapply` is used is best demonstrated with an example. We wish to investigate how the rate of change of the surface area of the container shown in Figure 3.1 affects its volume. First, we use Maple to derive an expression relating the rate of change of the object's surface area to its volume. Then we form our new function from this expression using `unapply`.

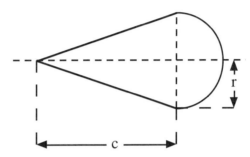

Figure 3.1 The Volume Is Formed by Rotating This Object About Its Long Axis.

USING UNAPPLY First, define the volume in terms of cone height c and the radius of the hemisphere r.

```
> total_vol:=Pi*r^2*c/3+4/3*Pi*r^3;
```

$$total\_vol := \frac{1}{3}\pi r^2 c + \frac{4}{3}\pi r^3$$

Similarly, express the surface area is in terms of c and r.

```
> total_area := Pi*r*(sqrt(c^2 + r^2)) +
  4*Pi*r^2;
```

$$total\_area := \pi r(c^2 + r^2)^{1/2} + 4\pi r^2$$

Now the rate of change of the ratio of the volume to the surface area with respect to the radius is computed.

```
> ans:=diff(total_vol/total_area,r):
```

USING UNAPPLY The solution obtained in the previous step is transformed to function notation using `unapply`. The new function takes arguments c and r.

```
> test:=unapply(ans, c, r);
```

$$test := (c,r) \rightarrow \frac{2/3\,\pi rc + 4\,\pi r^2}{\pi\,r\,(c^2 + r^2)^{1/2} + 4\,\pi\,r^2}$$

$$- \frac{(1/3\,\pi r^2\,c + 4/3\,\pi r^3)\left[\pi(c^2 + r^2)^{1/2} + \dfrac{\pi r}{(c^2 + r^2)^{1/2}} + 8\pi r\right]}{(\pi r\,(c^2 + r^2)^{1/2} + 4\pi\,r^2)^2}$$

By using `plot3d`, a surface is plotted.

```
> plot3d(test(c,r), c=1..15, r=1..15,
  axes=FRAMED, title=`Ratio of volume:
  surface area`, orientation=[-212,65],
  style=PATCHCONTOUR);
```

Ratio of volume:surface area

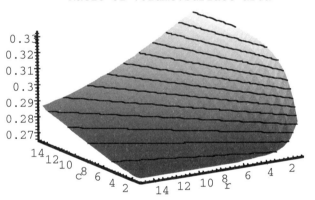

@ and @@

The infix operators @ and @@ are also known as the composition and repeated composition operator, respectively. By using composition, functions can be applied to other functions with or without initial conditions or starting points.

THE @ AND @@ OPERATORS	
`(function1 @ function2)(argument)`	This is shorthand for: $function_1(function_2(argument))$
`(function @@ n)(argument)`	This will apply `function` n times. The first time `function` is applied to `argument`. The second iteration uses the result of the first application as its input argument, the third iteration uses the result of the second iteration and so on. For example: $function(function(\,..\,(function(argument))\,..\,))$.

@ AND @@ The composition operator provides a concise syntax for applying functions to functions.

```
> (sqrt@tan@Bi)(x);
```

$$sqrt(tan(Bi(x)))$$

The repeated function composition operator gives us a convenient way of applying a function repeatedly.

```
> expand(exp@@3)(x))
```

$$e^{e^{e^x}}$$

It should be noted that if a function is applied zero times, the argument is returned.

```
> (sin@@0)(x);
```

$$x$$

In the following example, an aerofoil is generated from a circle using a nonlinear complex mapping technique. The process is as follows: Each point on the circle (x, y) is mapped to a new point given by $(\mathcal{R}(X + 1/X), \mathcal{I}(X + 1/X))$, where $X = x + iy$. The position of the center of the circle dictates the shape of the aerofoil produced.

THE AEROFOIL The first step is to define a mapping for the circle point onto the complex plane.

```
> to_complex:=x->x[1] + I*x[2]:
```

Now the nonlinear mapping $x \rightarrow x + 1/x$ can be defined.

```
> mapping:=x->evalc(x + 1/x):
```

Finally, the resulting complex number must be mapped back into Cartesian coordinates.

```
> get_parts:=x->[Re(x), Im(x)]:
```

This applies the maps to a test point in sequence using the @ operator.

```
> (get_parts@mapping@to_complex)([1.5, 0]);
```

$$[2.166666667, 0]$$

Here a circle of radius 1.25 and with center (0.25, 0) is defined as a list of points.

```
> pts:=[seq([1.25*cos(x*Pi/36) + .25,
  1.25*sin(x*Pi/36)], x=0..72)]:
```

By using `map`, each point is manipulated using the mapping defined before.

```
> map((get_parts@mapping@to_complex), pts):
```

THE   The aerofoil can now be plotted.

AEROFOIL

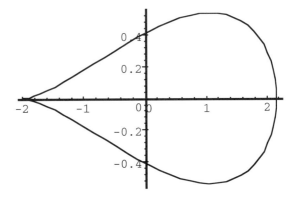

In the second example, we develop a function for root finding using Newton's method. The function is designed in such a way as to allow the use of the repeated composition operator `@@`. Newton's method takes an initial guess and calculates a new one as follows: *new = old - f(old)/f'(old)*. The new guess is then used to find the next guess and so on.

| **NEWTON'S METHOD** Define the function `newtons_method` to calculate the next guess. Note that `@@` only takes a single argument, so a two-element list is used to pass in the function and the guess. | ```
> newtons_method:=(data)->[ data[ 1] ,
  lhs (data[ 2] )=rhs (data[ 2] ) -
  subs (data[ 2] , data[ 1] /diff (data[ 1] ,
  lhs (data[ 2] )))] :
``` |

Here the next guess is calculated for an initial guess of $x = a$.

```
> newtons_method([ sin(x), x=a ])[ 2] ;
```

$$x = a - \frac{sin(a)}{cos(a)}$$

Now the function is applied twice using the initial guess and the calculated guess.

```
> (newtons_method@@2)([ sin(x), x=a ])[ 2] ;
```

$$x = a - \frac{sin(a)}{cos(a)} - \frac{sin\left(a - \frac{sin(a)}{cos(a)}\right)}{cos\left(a - \frac{sin(a)}{cos(a)}\right)}$$
```

NEWTON'S METHOD By using five iterations, one of the roots of sin(x)-x+1⁄4 is calculated for an initial guess of x = 1.5.

```
> evalf((newtons_method@@5)([ 2*sin(x)  - x
  + 1/4,  x=1.5] )[ 2] );
```

$$x = 2.036769500$$

Inverse Functions

The argument following the @@ can be a negative integer, for example, sin@@(-1). This causes the corresponding inverse function, in this case arcsin, to be retuned. All of the inverse functions known to Maple as standard are held in the table invfunc. This table is either loaded implicitly with a call to @@ with a negative argument or explicitly using readlib. The inverse function table is user-editable, so that new inverse relationships can be added.

INVERSE FUNCTIONS This returns a list of the inverse functions initially known to Maple.

```
> [ op(op(readlib(invfunc)))];
```

[ln = exp, sech = arcsech, sinh = arcsinh, tanh = arctanh, conjugate = conjugate, sec = arcsec, sin = arcsin, tan = arctan, W = x → x e^x, cos = arccos, cot = arccot, csc = arccsc, arccos = cos, arccosh = cosh, arccot = cot, arccoth = coth, arccsc = csc, arccsch = csch, cosh = arccosh, arcsec = sec, coth = arccoth, arcsech = sech, csch = arccsch, arcsin = sin, arcsinh = sinh, arctan = tan, arctanh = tanh, exp = ln]

This will add a user-defined inverse relationship to the table.

```
> invfunc[ g] :=1/g^2:
```

The inverse function table is unidirectional, so an entry of the form invfunc[g] = h, will not lead Maple to make the assumption h@@ (-1) =g.

Procedural Programming

The most common style of programming is procedural. It is therefore not surprising that most popular programming languages and tools, such as BASIC, FORTRAN, C, and PASCAL, support it. By using procedural programming, the problem is first broken down into smaller manageable chunks. These chunks or procedures are then coded and called in sequence. The primary differences between this and functional programming is in the style of application and what goes into making up a procedure.

A procedure will commonly take more than just a single argument and will quite often return a sequence of results, which is in contrast to the functional approach. The body of a procedure, in general, will also differ in that it will contain multiple statements, intermediate local variables, conditional statements, and looping constructs.

THE IF STATEMENT Maple supports control structures to govern the flow of evaluation. The conditional or if construct is the most commonly used.

```
if test then t else f fi
        if test then t fi
```

The conditional statement `test` is evaluated as a Boolean expression. If it evaluates to true `t` is returned else `f` is returned. The expression sequence `else f` can be omitted, in which case NULL is returned if `test` evaluates to false.

Example:
```
if 2<x then print(2) fi;
if sin(x)<>cos(x) then sin(x) else cos(x)
fi;
```

```
if test₁ then t₁
   elif test₂ then t₂
   elif test₃ then t₃
   ...
   ...
   else all tests false
fi
```

Nested if statements are constructed using the `elif` statement. If the first `test` evaluates to true then t_1 is returned, if not $test_2$ will be evaluated. Depending on the outcome either t_2 will be returned or $test_3$ will be evaluated and so on. If all the `tests` fail then the statement sequence following `else` will be returned. As before the `else` construct is optional.

Example:
```
if x=1 then sin(x)
   elif x=2 then cos(x)
   elif x=3 then tan(x)
   else print(`Input is invalid`)
fi;
```

A procedure will have a name, will take arguments, do some manipulation, and return a result. The name is sometimes referred to as the head of the procedure and is used to invoke it. The argument sequence, sometimes referred to as the formal parameters, match names in the body of the procedure and is used to pass values into it. Finally, the body of the procedure is where the input parameters are manipulated. The formal parameter names appearing in the body of the procedure match those in the procedure argument sequence and can be considered as just placeholders, their real values to be supplied when the procedure is called. It is only when the procedure is called that actual values are substituted into the procedure body so that computation can take place. The basic syntax of a Maple procedure follows. The procedure name is represented by the tag `procedure_name` and the argument sequence is denoted by the sequence arg_1, arg_2, .., arg_n.

PROCEDURE SYNTAX	`procedure_name := proc( arg₁, arg₂, .., argₙ ) body end;`
	This defines the procedure `procedure_name` with formal parameters arg_1, arg_2, .., arg_n.

If no formal parameters are specified, then the procedure will accept an unlimited number of arguments.

PROCEDURES Our first procedure calculates the resultant force and its point of action on a bar of unit length. It takes two inputs, each a list, and returns a list. The format of each input list is [*force, position*].

```
> `1st_try` := proc(a, b)
   [ a[ 1] +b[ 1] ,
     (a[ 1] * a[ 2]  + b[ 1] * b[ 2] )/(a[ 1]  + b[ 1] )]
   end:
```

This calls the procedure.

```
> `1st_try`([ -2, 0.5], [ -5.6, .9] );
```

$$[-7.6, .7947368421]$$

Maple does some parameter checking automatically, as this example demonstrates. Only one parameter is supplied but two are expected.

```
> `1st_try`([ -21, 0.75] );
```

```
Error, (in 1st_try) 1st_proc uses a 2nd
argument, b, which is missing
```

Args and Nargs

Our first example is limited because it can only operate on two forces. Maple gives us the flexibility to pass any number of parameters into a procedure. During the procedure definition, the formal parameter list is simply left blank. The actual parameters passed into the procedure are then held in the global variable `args` and the number of arguments is stored in `nargs`.

ARGS AND NARGS By using `nargs`, it is possible to determine the number of arguments passed into a procedure, the actual arguments being held in `args`. Our next procedure demonstrates how both are used.

```
> test_args := proc()
   print( cat( `The proc was called with,
   nargs, ` arguments`));
   print(cat(`The parameters are `,
   convert([ args] , string )));
   end:
```

The procedure is called with the following argument sequence: 1, 2, {*a, s*},*cos y*.

```
> test_args(1, 2, {a, s} , cos(y));
```

The proc was called with 4 arguments
The parameters are [1, 2, {*a, s*}, cos(*y*)]

ARGS AND NARGS Using `args`, we modify the procedure `1st_try` so that it can accept an arbitrary number of force-position pairs. The pairs are manipulated using a combination of `map` and pure functions. By converting the resulting lists to type `+`, their elements are summed.

```
>  `2nd_try`:=proc()
     [ convert(map(x->x[ 1], [ args]), `+`),
       convert(map(x->x[ 1]*x[ 2], [ args]),`+`)/
       convert(map(x->x[ 1], [ args]), `+`)]
   end:
```

Here we try the modified procedure.

```
>  `2nd_try`([ -2, 0.5], [ -5.6, .9],
     [ -1, 1], [ -2, 0]);
```

$$[-10.6, .6641509434]$$

Local and Global Variables

Take a closer look at the previous example. We see that the `convert( map( x->x[ 1], [ args]), `+` )` operation is performed twice. It would be far more efficient to do the calculation only once and store the result. If we use variables to store intermediate results, it is good practice to ensure that the variable names appear only in the name space of the procedure, that is to say, make them local variables. This is not only good programming practice, but a wise precaution that ensures that any other data remain undisturbed.

LOCAL VARIABLES

?
4

```
         procedure_name :=
proc(arg₁, arg₂, .., argₙ) local var₁, var₂, .., varₙ; body end;
```
Local variables are defined using the option local. The names var_1, var_2, .., var_n are the local variables.

USING LOCAL VARIABLES The third version of our procedure uses three local variables, one to avoid a repeat calculation, a second for the loop count, and a third to make the procedure easier to read.

```
>  `3rd_try`:=proc()
     local total_force, location, n;
     total_force:=0: location:=0:
     for n in [ args]  do
       total_force:=total_force+n[ 1];
       location:= location + n[ 1]*n[ 2];
     od;
     [ total_force, location/total_force];
   end:
```

USING LOCAL VARIABLES Here we test the third procedure with the previous data set.

```
> `3rd_try`([-2, 0.5],[-5.6, .9], [-1, 1],
   [-2, 0]);
```

$$[-10.6, .6641509434]$$

If a variable defined within a procedure is not explicitly declared local, the Maple parser issues a warning and, by default, treats it as if it were defined local.

IS IT LOCAL? In this example, a procedure is declared without declaring the variable *x* as local.

```
> test_local:= proc(a) x:=a^2 end:
Warning, `x` is implicitly declared local
```

FOR — IN The *for-in* construct provides a flexible and intuitive way of operating on every element in a list or set.

```
for count in expr do body od
```

The loop body is evaluated once for each element in `expr`, the loop count taking the value of the current element. Example:

```
for thing in [a, b, c] do thing^2 od
```

Although we should try to keep variables used within a procedure local, there are certain instances when it is necessary to be able to access variables globally. Global variables are declared in a similar manner to local variables using the `global` keyword. A global variable must be declared global in every procedure in which we wish to access it globally.

GLOBAL VARIABLES Our next procedure appends elements to a sequence stored in the global variable *answer*.

```
> add_2_answer:=proc(a)
   global answer;
   answer:=answer, [a, evalf(a^(3/2), 4)];
   end:
```

The variable answer is initialized to NULL, and a for loop is used to call the test procedure repeatedly.

```
> answer:=NULL:
  for n to 4 do
   add_2_answer(n)
  od:
```

Here we can see that the global variable has been updated as expected.

```
> answer;
```

$$[1, 1.], [2, 2.828], [3, 5.196], [4, 8.000]$$

FOR — DO Repetitive or looping operations can be performed with the *for-do* construct.

[? 5]
```
for count to stop do body od
for count to stop by inc do body od
```
> The loop body is evaluated once and the loop counter, initially 1, is incremented by 1 each time through the loop until the termination condition set by stop becomes valid. If the loop count is to be incremented by anything other than unity, the incrementor needs to be set using `inc`. The loop body can be any Maple expression sequence.
> Examples:
> ```
> for x to 5 do x! od;
> for x to -3.5 by -0.3 od;
> ```

```
for count from start to stop do body od
for count from start to stop by inc do body od
```
> In this form, the initial value of the loop count is explicitly set with start. Again the loop body is evaluated and the count incremented by either 1 or inc until the termination condition becomes valid.
> Examples:
> ```
> for y from -10 to -5 by 2 do y^3 od
> for cnt from 0 to 2 by .3 do
>   [ cnt, sin(cnt)]
> od
> ```

Other Procedure Options

Maple procedures can be defined with options that add special functionality. The most commonly used options are `remember` and `Copyright`.

Remember

Procedures can cache previously calculated answers used in remember tables and so avoid unnecessary recalculation. A remember table must be explicitly attached to a procedure by setting the option remember in the procedure definition. A remember table is a standard Maple table the indices of which are the procedure's calling argument patterns and the entries of which are the corresponding results returned by the procedure. A new entry is added to the table every time the procedure is invoked with a previously unused argument pattern. If the argument pattern exists, the previously calculated result is returned without the body of the procedure being evaluated.

REMEMBER By using a recursive definition, *n!!* is defined. By using the option `remember`, a remember table is attached to the procedure. As a test, each time the procedure body is evaluated, a message is printed.

```
> factorial2:=proc(n)
    option remember;
    print(`body evaluated`);
    factorial2(n-2)*n;
  end:
```

By making assignments to the procedure with specified arguments, entries are explicitly made in the remember table.

```
> factorial2(0):=1:
> factorial2(-1):=1:
> factorial2(-2):=1:
```

This calculates 2!! and shows that the procedure body is evaluated once.

```
> factorial2(2);
```

$$\textit{body evaluated}$$
$$2$$

Now try calculating 6!!. The procedure body is only evaluated twice because 2!! has already been cached.

```
> factorial2(6);
```

$$\textit{body evaluated}$$
$$\textit{body evaluated}$$
$$48$$

Finally, 4!! is calculated. The answer is already in the remember table, so the answer is returned without the procedure body being evaluated.

```
> factorial2(4);
```

$$8$$

By using nested `op` functions, the remember table can be viewed.

```
> op(op(4,eval(factorial2)));
```

$$[0 = 1, -1 = 1, -2 = 1, 2 = 2, 4 = 8, 6 = 48]$$

Using remember tables can result in substantial savings in computation time. The drawback of using remember tables is the increased system resource usage.

USING REMEMBER Now we redefine the `factorial2` procedure without the print statement.

```
> factorial2:=proc(n)
    option remember;
    factorial2(n-2)*n;
  end:
```

Here we initialize the remember table explicitly as before.

```
> factorial2(0):=1:factorial2(-1):=1:
  factorial2(-2):=1:
```

USING REMEMBER

As a test, we measure the CPU time taken to calculate 100!!. The test is repeated twice. The time of the second run is only 14% of the first, because the procedure is using the results "remembered" during the first run.

```
> 'time(factorial2(100))'$2;
```
$$.116, .016$$

The procedure, for comparison, is redefined without the remember option.

```
> factorial2:=proc(n)
    factorial2(n-2)*n;
  end:
```

Again, enter the initially known values, which are remembered. There is however, no remember table.

```
> factorial2(0):=1:
> factorial2(-1):=1:
> factorial2(-2):=1:
```

Repeating the test, the times are now the same as no caching has taken place and every calculations must be performed starting from scratch each time.

```
> 'time(factorial2(100))'$2;
```
$$.116, .116$$

MORE HELP

forget   Allows either complete or partial clearing of a function's remember table. This function is loaded using `readlib`.

`subsop(4=NULL, eval(function_name))`

Clearing the entire remember table can be done by setting it to NULL with `subsop`.

Copyright

By using the `Copyright` option, we can include information, that can be printed, at the top of a procedure. It is also possible to use this option as a way of obtaining only an abridged form of a procedure when it is printed. Any string beginning with `Copyright ... ` is considered a copyright option and will be printed along with the procedure.

COPYRIGHT   The following procedure contains a copyright notice.

```
> copy_right:= proc()
    option `Copyright Coded by Steve
    Adams`;
  end:
```

COPYRIGHT

?₇

With the interface variable verboseproc set to 1, the default, an
abridged form of the procedure is
printed using eval.

```
> eval(copy_right);

proc() ... end
```

Setting verboseproc equal to 2
allows us to view the body of the
procedure as we shall see.

```
> interface(verboseproc=2):
    eval(copy_right);

proc() options `Copyright Coded by Steve
Adams`;  end
```

MORE HELP

system	The system option identifies procedures as "system" functions. When used with remember, garbage collection is allowed to remove these functions' remember tables.
operator, arrow	The option operator indicates that special printing and manipulation rules apply because the procedure is an operator.
trace	When this option is present and the procedure is called, the entry and exit calls and the outcome of the internal assignments can be seen. See "Debugging" below.
interface(verboseproc=3)	Enables procedures to be viewed in their entirety, including the remember table, if present.

Parameter-Type Checking

Maple allows us to check the type of any parameter passed into a procedure at two distinct points during the calling process: prior to the procedure being called and in the procedure. Maple performs type checking through an algebra of types. This is a very powerful technique that allows complex types to be defined and tested quickly. The basic types introduced in Chapter 2 can be combined to form additional compound types.

COMPOUND TYPES

In this test, we are looking for a
list with specific element types:
name, name, and integer.

```
> type([ a, b, 1], [ name, name, integer]);
```
true

This test fails because the last element, which should be an integer,
is a range.

```
> type([ a, b, 1..4], [ name, name,
    integer]);
```
false

COMPOUND TYPES Type parameters can include sets to indicate valid alternate types. In this test, the last element can be either an integer or a range.

```
> type([ a, b, 1..4],
    [ name, name, { integer, range} ]);
```

$$true$$

Care should be exercised because types can quickly become extremely complex as a result of subtypes. In this example, a function with arguments *procedure, equation(name, range(integer, integer))), equation(name, string)* is expected.

```
> type(
    g(plot, x=1..2, title=`Title line`),
    anyfunc(procedure, name=integer..integer,
    name=string)
    );
```

$$true$$

MORE HELP

| `?type[ definition]` | This returns the help page describing how a type is defined in Maple. |
| `?type[ structured]` | This returns the help page for Maple's structured types, types that cannot be represented as strings. |

At the Top Level

If we choose to check the argument types at the top level, that is, prior to the procedure being evaluated, the procedure will only be called if all of the arguments match the expected types. This approach is the easiest to implement but does not allow us to recover gracefully from an error condition.

TOP-LEVEL TYPE CHECKING

```
procedure_name :=
proc(arg₁::type₁,arg₂::{ type₁,type₂, .., typeₙ} ,.., argₙ::..) body end;
```
The procedure will only be called if the types of the parameters match the expected types.

TYPE TESTS This will cause an error message to be returned because `sum` is called with an invalid argument.

```
> sum(x, sin(k));

Error, (in sum) second argument must be a
    name or name=a..b or name=RootOf
```

Type checking is easily included in a procedure definition. Here a list, a set or matrix, and an *equation(name, range(anything, positive integer)* are expected.

```
> type_test:=proc(a::list, b::{ set,
    matrix} , c::name=anything..posint)
    print( `Correct type sequence entered`)
    end:
```

TYPE TESTS First, the procedure is called with the correct argument sequence.

```
> type_test([ 1, 2], {}, test=g(x)..4);
```

Correct type sequence entered

This time invalid arguments are used and an error results.

```
> type_test([ 1, 2], {}, test=g(x)..1⁄2);
```

```
Error, type_test expects its 3rd argument,
c, to be of type name = anything ..
posint, but received test = g(x) .. 1⁄2
```

In order to incorporate some argument-type checking, we must modify our *force-location* procedure once again.

```
> `4th_try`:=proc(a::list)
    local total_force, location, n;
    total_force:=0:
    location:=0: #initialize
    for n in a do
      total_force:=total_force + n[ 1] ;
      location:=location + n[ 1]*n[ 2] ;
    od;
    [ total_force, location⁄total_force] ;
  end:
```

Within the Procedure

An alternative approach is to check the types of a procedure's arguments within the body of the procedure. This enables us, amongst other things, to define polymorphic functions and user-defined error-handling procedures.

CHECKING IN THE PROCEDURE The procedure defined on the right uses `type` in conjunction with a conditional statement to test for a symbolic argument. The difference between this and the previous example is that the test occurs after the procedure has been invoked.

```
> type_test_body:= proc(x)
    local ans;
    if type(x, name) then
      print(`A symbolic quantity has been
      entered`);
      ans:=x;
    else
      ans:=evalf(Bi(x))
    fi;
    ans;
  end:
```

Here the procedure is called with a valid numeric argument.

```
> type_test_body(3.6);
```

$$39.59271507$$

CHECKING IN THE PROCEDURE Now we call the same procedure again but with a symbolic argument. Instead of an error condition halting evaluation, as in the previous section, we are warned and the evaluation continues.

```
> type_test_body(lambda);
```

A symbolic quantity has been entered
λ

By using this method of type checking, the test procedure can be rewritten to include full type checking. The first parameter must be a list of lists with each sublist being a pair of numbers. The error message is printed using lprint.

```
> `5th_try`:=proc()
    local total_force, location, n;
    if not has(map(type, [args[1]],
     [numeric, numeric]), false) and
     type(args[1], list) then
     total_force:=0:
     location:=0:
     for n in args[1] do
         total_force:=total_force+n[1];
         location:= location + n[1]*n[2];
     od;
     [total_force, location/total_force];
    else
     lprint(`A list of lists expected.
     Each sublist must be a pair of
     numbers`);
    fi;
  end:
```

Here the current iteration of our test procedure is called with invalid parameters.

```
> `5th_try`(1, 2, 3);
```

A list of lists expected.   Each sublist
must be a pair of numbers

Now valid arguments are used and the expected result is

```
> `5th_try`([[-1, .2], [-10, .9]]);
```

[-11, .8363636364]

MORE HELP   match   Match tests for a pattern match between an expression and a test expression containing unknowns. If a match is found, a substitution list is returned that will turn the test expression into the given one.
Example:
```
match(x^2=x^F, x, 'subs_list')
```

(The variable subs_list contains { F=2} .)

MORE HELP   typematch   Typematch is similar to match. However, the type of the
                                                constituent parts can be specified.
                                                Example:
                                                ```
                                                typematch(x^2, C::name^F::integer,
                                                'subs_list')(
                                                ```

                                                (The variable subs_list contains [C=x, F=2].)

User Options

It is good to make procedures as flexible as possible. We can achieve this flexibility by including optional arguments that override default values. Many of the Maple built-in functions and
procedures support optional arguments. For example, numpoints is an option to plot that is
used to set the minimum number of plot points to something other than the default value of 49.
Options take one of two forms: an optional parameter or an optional equation of the form
option_name = new_value.

USER OPTIONS The option orthogonal forces
the dot product of the two lists to
be evaluated without the complex
conjugate of the second list being
taken.

```
> linalg[ dotprod] ([ 1, 2, 3], [ 1, -2, 3],
  orthogonal);
```

$$6$$

By overriding the defaults locally,
we plot the function $\sin 1/x$ using a
minimum of 100 points.

```
> plot(sin(1/x), x=0..1, numpoints=100);
```

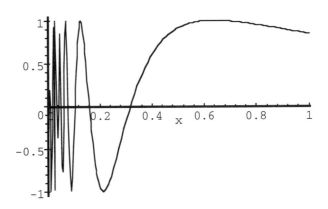

It is very easy to incorporate optional arguments into our functions that conform to either syntax. In the following example, we develop a procedure with a single optional argument. In this case, the equation format is used.

USER OPTIONS In defining the procedure, we will use three local variables, `opt`, `optd`, and `optf`. These are used to store the user option value, the default value, and the final option value, respectively. The default is used only if no valid option is supplied by the user. The user option, when supplied, is trapped using `select`. Then the variable `optf` is assigned using `subs`. The substitution equations are applied sequentially so that the user option is applied first, followed by the default. The first match sets the value of `optf`. By using the if-elif statement in conjunction with `optf`, the required operation is selected. The option name is `to_do`.

```
> `what_to_do?`:=proc()
    local opt, optd, optf;
  #set default value
    optd:= square_it;
  # trap all equations in the parameter
  # list
    opt:=select(type, [args], `=`);
  # set the option value
    optf:=subs(opt, to_do=optd, to_do);
  # test option value
    if optf=square_it then
      args[1]^2
    elif optf=root_it then
      sqrt(args[1])
    else
      RETURN(`Invalid option`);
    fi;
  end:
```

This uses the default value.

```
> `what_to_do?`(3*y + h);
```

$$(3\,y + h)^2$$

In this example, the default value is overridden.

```
> `what_to_do?`(3*y + h, to_do=root_it);
```

$$(3\,y + h)^{1/2}$$

RETURN   `RETURN( expr₁, expr₂, .., exprₙ )`
`RETURN()`

Using RETURN forces the current procedure to terminate, with control passing to the next level up. The value returned is determined by the arguments $expr_i$ passed to RETURN. A RETURN statement does not have to be present at the end of a procedure. The result of the last evaluation is returned by default.

MORE HELP	`` `plot/options` ``	Global variable holding the default plot options
	`` `plot/options3d` ``	Global variable holding the default plot3d options
	`?plot[ options]`	Returns the help page for the plot options
	`?plot3d[ options]`	Returns the help page for the plot3d options
	`?plot[ structure]`	Returns the help page for the plot structure

Error Handling

The two error-handling techniques standard to Maple are abort on error and trap error. Abort on error is easy to implement but trap error provides for more elegant error handling.

ERROR and ASSERT

The functions ERROR and ASSERT are used to force an abort on error from a procedure. Control passes to the point where the offending procedure was called and an error message is displayed.

ERROR This procedure simulates an error condition. The error message is formed from the arguments passed to ERROR.

```
> error_test := proc(x)
    ERROR(`Called with `, x)
  end:
```

So calling will result in an error condition.

```
> error_test(big_num);

Error, (in error_test) Called with ,
big_num
```

The ASSERT function differs from ERROR in that it is active and hence we can use it to detect offending conditions. When using ERROR, we have to call it explicitly following the discovered error condition. Additionally, an error condition generated with ASSERT cannot be trapped (see below). Hence, we use ASSERT to guarantee the condition of a variable either prior to or following an operation. The ASSERT function is enabled via kernelopts.

ASSERT Using ASSERT, we define a test function. The argument expected must be a nonzero number.

```
> f:= proc(x)
    ASSERT(type(x,numeric) and x<>0,
    cat(`Input must be numeric and nonzero
    - received `, x)):
  end:
```

ASSERT The ASSERT facility is enabled using kernelopts.

```
> kernelopts(ASSERT=true):
```

Calling the function *f* with a positive integer, we find nothing happens, as expected.

```
> f(2);
```

If we now use an invalid argument, an error condition is flagged.

```
> f(e);
```

```
Error, (in f) assertion failed,
Input must be numeric and nonzero -
received e
```

Traperror and Lasterror

By using the function traperror, we can inhibit the normal Maple error-handling process of abort on error (not applicable to ASSERT). This means that procedures can be written that include code that allows evaluation to continue even though an error has occurred. By using traperror(expr), a trap is set prior to the evaluation and simplification of expr. If an error occurs at any time during this process, the error message returned is trapped, enabling computation to continue. The error message returned is stored in the global variable lasterror where we can use it if necessary. If the operation is error-free, the result of expr is returned and computation continues as normal.

TRAPERROR AND LASTERROR

```
if traperror(expression) = lasterror then …
```
The standard syntax to allow error trapping using traperror and lasterror.

TRAPPING ERRORS This procedure uses traperror and lasterror to deal with possible error conditions. Using traperror allows the operation to be evaluated without risk of an abort-on-error condition terminating the procedure. The result is then used with lasterror as shown.

```
> trap_test:=proc(x)
    local err;
    err:=traperror(1/x);
    if err<>lasterror then
      print(err)
    else
      print(`zero entered - invalid,
      default returned`);
      1;
    fi;
  end:
```

TRAPPING ERRORS This invocation of the test procedure will not cause an error.

```
> trap_test(23);
```

$$\frac{1}{23}$$

This, on the other hand, will.

```
> trap_test(0);
```

zero entered - invalid, default returned
1

MORE HELP   procname   When using nested procedures, it is useful to know at what level an error occurs. Maple provides the system variable procname for use in such an event. In a chain of evaluations the 'last name evaluated' is held in procname. If there is no name, then the name unknown is substituted. Example:

```
RETURN(`Error in `, procname)
```

Rule-Based Programming

Rule-based programming is a relatively new way of problem solving with a computer. The two concepts on which rule-based programming is based are polymorphic function definitions and pattern matching. A polymorphic function is one that has a single name but supports multiple definitions. Each definition is uniquely identified by the pattern of its input arguments. The power of rule-based programming lies in the fact that it mimics closely human thought processes. We are provided with a choice of solutions to a given problem; the particular solution chosen is dependent on the parameters of the question. In other words, if we are given an input sequence α, we use method 1; an input sequence β, we use method 2; and so on.

RULE DEFINITIONS

```
function name:=(input pattern₁)->body₁

function name:=(input pattern₂)->body₂

function name:=(input pattern₃)->body₃

            ...

function name:=(input patternₙ)->bodyₙ
```

The problem to be tackled is defined in terms of a set of rules of the form input pattern $\Rightarrow$ output. Rules are defined until the problem is completely specified.

It is easy to grasp the technique by working through a simple example, say, performing a derivative. First, the rules describing all of the valid mappings need to be defined.

DERIVATIVE RULES

```
power_diff:=x^n->x^(n-1);
```
Differentiating a power

```
uv_diff:=u*v->u*std_diff(v) + v*std_diff(u);
```
Differentiating a product

```
u_over_v_diff:=u/v->(v*std_diff(u) - u*std_diff(v))/v^2;
```
Differentiating a quotient

```
symbolic_diff:=g(x)->g'(x);
```
Differentiating a symbolic function

Next we apply the rules to our test case: $d(x^2 f(x)/g(x))/dx$. Table 3.1 shows how the rules are applied and their outcomes.

u_over_v_diff	APPLIED TO	$x^2 f(x)/g(x)$	GIVES	$(g(x) \text{ diff}(x^2 f(x)) - x^2 f(x) \text{ diff}(g(x)))/g(x)^2$
uv_diff	APPLIED TO	$diff(x^2 f(x))$	GIVES	$x^2 \text{ diff}(f(x)) + f(x) \text{ diff}(x^2)$
symbolic_diff	APPLIED TO	$g(x)$	GIVES	$g'(x)$
symbolic_diff	APPLIED TO	$f(x)$	GIVES	$f'(x)$
power_diff	APPLIED TO	x^2	GIVES	$2x$

COMPLETE DERIVATIVE IS: $2x\, f(x)/g(x) + x^2\, f'(x)/g(x) - x^2\, f(x)/g(x)^2$

Table 3.1 Differentiation Through Rule Application

It should be noted however, that despite the power associated with rule-based programming, in practice no problem can be efficiently solved using only one basic style of programming. The best results are invariably obtained when all three styles are successfully combined.

Rule Definition: forall

The keyword `forall` is used to define a rule. Each rule is a single relationship linking an input pattern to an action. Hence, a specific input argument sequence causes the required action to be invoked. For each argument sequence, a separate `forall` statement must be defined.

If we now apply Maple to the previous example, we will need to develop four `forall` definitions as follows.

FORALL

First, we define the power rule for differentiation for the new function `new_diff`. The formal parameters are u and v.

```
> power_diff:=forall([ v, u],
    ''new_diff(v^u) = u*v^(u-1)''):
```

Then the product rule is defined. The input pattern is specified on the left-hand side of the transformation equation.

```
> uv_diff:=forall([ u, v], ''new_diff(u*v)
    = new_diff(v) + v*new_diff(u)''):
```

Next we define the quotient rule. Note the ' 's placed around each equation to delay its evaluation.

```
> u_over_v_diff:=forall([ u, v],
    ''new_diff(u/v) = (v*new_diff(u) -
    u*new_diff(v))/v^2''):
```

Finally, the rule to allow the manipulation of symbolic expressions is defined.

```
> symbolic_diff:=forall([ v, u],
    ''new_diff(v(u)) = cat(v, `'(`,
    u,`)`)''):
```

Rule Definition: define

The `define` mechanism is Maple's way of bringing together the function name and its associated rules in order that the new function can be built.

DEFINE

By using `define`, the rules are combined to form the new function.

```
> define(new_diff, power_diff, uv_diff,
    u_over_v_diff, symbolic_diff);
```

Here the new function is used to find the first derivative of $x^2g(x)$.

```
> new_diff(x^2*g(x));
```

$$x^2g'(x) + 2g(x)x$$

Type Checking within Rules

When we define a rule it is possible to include type checking. We can see just how type checking is incorporated into the rule definition process through three examples: the factorial and *Fibonacci* functions and the *Collatz* mappings. These are only defined for a specific range of arguments.

TYPE CHECKING IN RULES Here the transformation rule for the calculation of x! is defined. By using type checking, the scope of this rule is limited to positive integers.

```
> factorial_rule:=forall(posint(x),
    fac(x= x*fac(x-1)):
```

Here the *Fibonacci* numbers are defined over the integers using a recursive rule.

```
> fibonacci_rule:=forall(integer(x),
    fib(x)=fib(x-1) + fib(x-2)):
```

By using two rules, the *Collatz* mapping is fully defined. There is one rule for even numbers and one for odd.

```
> collatz_rule1:=
    forall(even(x), collatz(x)=x/2):
  collatz_rule2:=
    forall(odd(x), collatz(x)=(3*x + 1)):
```

We can check for any valid Maple type and can quickly extend this list by defining and using custom types.

Initial Conditions

Many functions have initially known states, such as 0!, which is defined as being equal to 1. Similarly, the first two entries in the *Fibonacci* sequence are 1 and 2, and the entries -17, -5, -1, and 1 in the *Collatz* mapping have the values, -17, -5, -1, and 1, respectively. These known values are incorporated into the rule base as follows.

INITIAL CONDITIONS Here the known values in the *Collatz* mapping are entered.

```
> ics_collatz:=collatz(1)=1,
    collatz(-1)=-1, collatz(-5)=-5,
    collatz(-17)=-17;
```

This sets the known value for 0!.

```
> ics_fac:=fac(0)=1;
```

Here the initially known values are included in the function definition for the new factorial function.

```
> define(fac, factorial_rule, ics_fac);
```

Here the initially known values are included in the function definition for the *Collatz* map.

```
> define(collatz, collatz_rule1,
    collatz_rule2, ics_collatz);
```

INITIAL CONDITIONS   Using `eval`, we can see how Maple has generated a procedural model of the rule base.

```
> eval(collatz);

proc()
local _AA,i,j,Sign;
options remember;
    _AA := [args];
    if _AA = [-17] then RETURN(-17) fi;
    if _AA = [-5] then RETURN(-5) fi;
    if _AA = [-1] then RETURN(-1) fi;
    if _AA = [1] then RETURN(1) fi;
    if type(_AA,[even]) then
      RETURN(1/2*_AA[1]) fi;
    if type(_AA,[odd]) then
      RETURN(3*_AA[1]+1) fi;
    'procname'(op(_AA))
end
```

User Types: type /...

In certain cases where we need to perform comprehensive argument checking, it is beneficial to define our own custom type or types. Custom types are equally applicable to procedural and rule-based programming styles. We can define a custom type by making a Boolean-valued procedure, one that returns either true or false, known to the Maple type checker `type`. This procedure will perform our test and will be of the form `type/custom_type_name`:= proc() ... end:. Once this procedure has been defined, our new type is known to the Maple system and we can test for it in the usual way, for example: `type(a, custom_type_name)`. Such a call actually generates the function call `type/custom_type_name`(a).

Returning to the *force-location* procedure defined previously, we are now in a position to extend it once again to include parameter type checking. For our function to behave correctly, its argument must be a list of lists with each sublist containing a pair of numbers. This enhancement is included in the following procedure definition.

A NEW TYPE   Type testing procedures are Boolean in nature, returning either true or false. The procedure `type/my_test` checks for a list of lists of numeric pairs.

```
> `type/my_test`:=proc(a)
    if type(a, listlist) and not
  has(map(type, a, [numeric,numeric]),
  false) then
      true
    else
      false
    fi
  end:
```

A NEW TYPE   This is a test list.

```
> a_list:=[[1, 2], [2, 3], [3, 4]]:
```

It is a valid list.

```
> type(a_list, my_test);
```

$$true$$

This list is invalid.

```
> type([[1], [1, 2]], my_test);
```

$$false$$

Here our example procedure is rewritten to incorporate type checking.

```
> `6th_try`:=proc()
    local total_force, location, n;
    if type(args[1], my_test) then
      total_force:=0: location:=0:
#initialize
      for n in args[1] do
         total_force:=total_force + n[1];
         location:= location+n[1]*n[2];
      od;
      [total_force, location/total_force];
    else
      print(`A list of lists expected. Each
sublist must be a pair of  numbers`);
    fi;
end:
```

SELECT AND PURE PROCEDURES   Pure procedures are particularly well-suited to be used in custom type checking routines (they are equally applicable in functions like `zip` and `map`). Like anonymous functions, anonymous or pure procedures are defined without including a tag or head.

By using a pure procedure and the select function, the procedure `type/my_test` can be rewritten as shown.

```
> `type/my_test`:=proc(a)
    if type(a, listlist) and select(
proc(x) not type(x, [numeric, numeric])
end, a)=[] then
      true
    else
      false
    fi
end:
```

Operators

Custom or neutral operators can also be defined and used in Maple. They can be either prefix or infix operators. Custom operators allow us limited formatting control of the input expressions. An operator name can be up to 495 characters long but must start with an ampersand (&) and end with a white space character. The name can contain alphanumeric characters, including underscores, but the second character cannot be numeric. Finally, an operator name cannot contain any of the following: &, |, (,), [,], {, }, ;, :, ', `, #, or a newline.

OPERATORS

This is how to define an operator using a function.

```
> `&add2`:=(a, b)->a + b:

> 12 &add2 (3*t);
```
$$12 + 3t$$

Here we use it as an infix operator.

We can also define operators using procedures

```
> `&add_many`:=
     proc() convert([args], `+`) end:
```

Here the infix form is used again with six arguments.

```
(a, b, c) &add_many (1, 2, 3);
```
$$6 + a + b + c$$

MORE HELP

`` `simplify/...` ``
`` `expand/...` ``
`` `series/...` ``
	Special rules for simplify, expand, and so on, can be defined using the same technique as applied to type checking. The only difference is an expression is returned and not either true or false.

`hastype`	Tests to see if an object contains a given type.

`` `type/PROC_NAMEargs` ``	Defines a global variable containing the valid argument types for the procedure PROC_NAME.
	Example:
	`` `type/TESTargs`:={set, list, matrix} ``
	`TEST:=proc() type([args], TESTargs) end`

`?operators`	Returns the help page on operators.
`?neutral`	Returns the help page on neutral operators.
`?procedures`	Returns the help page on procedures.
`?define[Linear]`	Returns the help page on defining linear operators.

MORE HELP

`?define[ Group]`	Returns the help page on defining the characteristics of a Group operator.
`?define[ operator]`	Returns the help page on defining operators.

Debugging

tracelast and trace

Once we have completed our program, there is a good possibility that it will contain a bug or two. The function `tracelast` allows us to pinpoint quickly the cause of the last error. Normally on an error condition, all we see is the standard error message giving the procedure name and very little else. We can now get additional information by immediately invoking `tracelast`. This gives us the original error message, the statement being executed, when the error occurred, and the arguments with which the function was called.

TRACELAST Here we call our test function again with an invalid argument and we receive the standard error message.

```
> f(A);

Error, (in f) assertion failed,
Input must be numeric and nonzero -
   received A
```

By immediately invoking `tracelast`, we can get additional information.

```
> tracelast;

Error, (in f) assertion failed,
Input must be numeric and nonzero -
   received A
executing statement: ASSERT(type(x,numeric)
   and x <> 0, cat(`Input must be numeric
   and nonzero - received `, x))
f called with arguments: A
```

We can also perform high-level debugging operations by using the functions `trace` and its synonym `debug`. These can be equally applied to both standard Maple and user-defined functions and procedures. When a function is traced, the calling and exit conditions can be viewed along with any internal functional calls and assignment.

USING TRACE This enables the debugging function for the random-number generator `rand`.

```
> trace(rand);
```
rand

USING TRACE Calling `rand` will cause the following debug information to be displayed.

```
> rand();

{--> enter rand, args =
```

$$p := 999999999989$$
$$a := 427419669081$$
$$s := 1000000000000$$
$$\_seed := 343633073697$$

```
<-- exit rand (now at top level) =
  343633073697}
```

$$343633073697$$

By looking at the code for `rand`, we can quickly see a correlation between the debug information the internals of the function.

```
> interface(verboseproc=2):
> eval(rand);

proc(r)
local a, p, s;
global _seed;
options `Copyright 1993 by Waterloo Maple
  Software`;
p := 999999999989;
a := 427419669081;
s := 1000000000000;
if not assigned(_seed) then _seed := 1 fi;
if nargs = 0 then _seed := irem(a*_seed,p)
else subs(
{_SHIFT = s,`rand/generator`(r,p),_MODULUS
  = p,_MULTIPLIER = a},
proc()
local t;
global _seed;
_seed := irem(_MULTIPLIER*_seed,_MODULUS);
t := _seed;
to _CONCATS do
_seed := irem(_MULTIPLIER*_seed,_MODULUS);
t := _SHIFT*t+_seed
od;
irem(t,_DIVISOR)+_OFFSET
end )
fi
end
```

USING
TRACE

Here the debugging is turned off.

```
> untrace(rand);
```

rand

MORE HELP	infolevel	Procedures can contain information messages. To turn on their printing, infolevel has to be set appropriately. Examples: `infolevel[ all] :=3;` `infolevel[ int] :=5;`
	userinfo	Information messages are defined using userinfo. Example: `userinfo(3, my_func, `this is a message for my_func`);`
	printlevel	Sets the echo level. To "see" assignments, and so on, made inside a procedure, set printlevel to at least 5. For every loop, add 1 or 2. Example: `printlevel:=15;`
	mint	*Mint* is the Maple syntax checker and is similar to *lint*, the UNIX syntax-checking utility. *Mint* is a stand-alone utility that is used to analyze files separately from Maple.
	undebug	This is a synonym for untrace.
	interface(verboseproc=3)	This causes a function's remember table and body to be printed when `print(proc_name)` and `eval(proc_name)` are used.
	?debugger	Returns the help page for the Maple line debugging facility.
!3	?profile	Return the help page for Maple's procedure profiling utility. This utility, unlike *Mint*, is used from within Maple and returns information about function and memory usage.

NEW FUNCTIONS AT A GLANCE	`$ range` `expr $ times`	The sequence operator. The first form will generate a sequence over `range`. The sequence is of the form $x, x+1,$ .., y, where `range` is `x..y`. The second form will produce `times` copies of `expr`.
	`` `expr` ``	By using the hold evaluation quotes, the evaluation of `expr` is delayed one level.
	`<>`	The inequality operator.
	`@`	The function composition operator.
	`@@`	The repeated function composition operator.
	`::`	Type tag operator.
	`anyfunc`	The Maple type specifying any function.
	`anything`	The Maple type specifying any type.
	`apply[ func ] ( data )`	Found in the `stats` subpackage `describe`, `apply` applies `func` to each element in `data`.
	`args`	The global variable containing the argument sequence passed to the current procedure.
	`arrow`	The built-in procedure option denoting the standard function syntax.
	`ASSERT( t, message )`	If `t` evaluates to false, an untrappable error condition is generated and `message` is printed. A NULL is returned otherwise.
	`Bi( expr )`	This calculates the Airy wave function Bi(*expr*).
	`cat( expr`$_1$`, expr`$_2$`, .., expr`$_n$` )`	This concatenates the expressions `expr`$_i$.
	`` `Copyright string` ``	The built-in procedure option denoting a copyright notice comprising `string`.

NEW **FUNCTIONS** **AT A GLANCE**	`dotprod( list`$_1$`, list`$_2$`, opt )`	Found in the `linalg` package, this calculates the dot product of the lists. If `opt` is present and set to `orthogonal`, the product is calculated without taking the complex conjugate of the elements in `list`$_2$.
	`ERROR( expr`$_1$`, expr`$_2$`, .., expr`$_n$` )`	
		Abort on error, returning `expr`$_i$ as an error message.
	`even`	The Maple type specifying an even integer.
	`false`	A Boolean constant.
	`forget( func, entry )` `forget( func )`	The `readlib`-defined function for the clearing entries of `func`'s remember table.
	`Heaviside( expr )`	The Heaviside step function, zero for `expr` < 0 and one for `expr` ≥ 0
	`if ... fi` `if ... elif ... fi`	The conditional if construct.
	`infinity`	Either a real or complex infinity.
	`infolevel[ func ]:=level`	Causes the information of level `level` associated with `func` to be displayed when `func` is invoked.
	`integer`	The Maple type specifying an integer.
	`invfunc`	The inverse function table.
	`lasterror`	The global variable containing the last error message generated.
	`lhs( expr )`	This returns the left-hand side of `expr`.
	`list`	The Maple type specifying a list.
	`local var`$_1$`, var`$_2$`, .., var`$_n$	
		The keyword identifying local variables `var`$_i$.
	`lprint(expr`$_1$`, expr`$_2$`, .., expr`$_n$` );`	
		This line prints `expr`$_i$ separated by three blanks.

NEW FUNCTIONS AT A GLANCE `map2(func , var, expr );`	This maps `func` onto each element of `expr`, taking `var` as the first parameter and the element of `expr` as the second.
`matrix`	The Maple type specifying a matrix.
`multiapply[ func ]( [ data₁, data₂ ] )`	The `stats[ describe]` function `multiapply` applies `func` to $data_1$. The arguments of `func` coming from $data_1$ and $data_2$.
`name`	The Maple type specifying a name.
`nargs`	The global variable containing a value equal to the number of parameters passed to the current procedure.
`numeric`	The Maple type specifying a number.
`odd`	The Maple type specifying an odd integer.
`operator`	The built-in procedure option denoting that the procedure is to be printed in function notation.
`option opt₁, opt₂, .., optₙ` `options opt₁, opt₂, .., optₙ`	The keyword identifying the options opt_i.
`orientation = [ alpha, beta ]`	A `plot3d` option setting the view orientation.
`orthogonal`	Option to `linalg[ dotprod]` .
`posint`	The Maple type specifying a positive integer.
`printlevel := level`	Set the print level to `level`.
`procedure`	The Maple type specifying a procedure.
`procname`	The global variable containing the name of the last procedure in the current evaluation chain.
`rand( )`	A random-number generator.
`range`	The Maple type specifying a range.

`Re( expr )`	Return the real part of `expr`.
`remember`	The built-in procedure option attaching a remember table to the procedure.
`RETURN( expr`$_1$`, expr`$_2$`, .., expr`$_n$` )`	Force an explicit return from a procedure with `expr`$_i$`.
`set`	The Maple type specifying a set.
`string`	The Maple type specifying a string.
`style = expr`	A `plot` option setting the point style.
`surd( expr, n )`	Calculate the nth real root of `expr`.
`system`	The built-in procedure option identifying it as a system procedure.
`time( expr )`	Return the CPU time taken to perform `expr`.
`title = string`	A `plot` and `plot3d` option setting the plot title to `string`.
`trace( func`$_1$`, func`$_2$`, .., func`$_n$` )`	Enable debugging of functions `func`$_i$`.
`tracelast`	Trace the last error condition. Must be invoked immediately after the error has been flagged.
`traperror( expr`$_1$`, expr`$_2$`, .., expr`$_n$` )`	Trap any errors occurring when `expr`$_i$ are evaluated.
`true`	A Boolean constant.
`unapply( expr, vars )`	Form a function from `expr` with parameter `vars`.
`undebug( func`$_1$`, func`$_2$`, .., func`$_n$`)`	A synonym for `untrace`.
`untrace( func`$_1$`, func`$_2$`, .., func`$_n$` )`	Inhibit debugging of functions `func`$_i$`.

FAQs 1: Can a function be coerced into containing a sequence of operations?

Yes, by wrapping the expressions in an if .. fi construct. The condition must always evaluate to true for this to work, i.e.,

```
f:=x->if true then expr₁; expr₂;
    ... exprₙ fi:
```

Maple will automatically cast this into a procedure.

2: When I asked for the real and imaginary parts of the expression $a + ib$, I was expecting $[a, b]$ to be returned. Why has Maple not done this?

Maple does not know anything about a or b, therefore complex variables are assumed.

3: Whenever a function or procedure containing an if — fi statement is operated on the message, 'cannot evaluate boolean' is returned. Why?

This is a result of Maple's order of evaluation. Consider plotting the function $g(x)$.

```
> g:= proc(x) if x<=0 then
    cos(x) else sin(x) fi; end:
```

If we try to plot this using `plot`, an error results because $g(x)$ is evaluated before a value for x is substituted. Maple cannot successfully compare the unknown x with the numeric quantity zero. The simplest solution is to delay the evaluation $g(x)$ using delayed evaluation quotes `' '`.

```
> plot('g'(x), x=-1..1);
```

This will not work in all instances as is confirmed if a numerical integral is calculated using `evalf(int( ... ))`. To deal with this situation, the conditional statement needs to be altered to test first if x is a symbol. If it is, the function is returned; if not, the numeric value.

```
> g:=proc(x)
    if type(x, name) then 'g'(x)
    elif x<=0 then cos(x)
    else sin(x)
```

FAQs 3: Continued.

```
    fi;
end:
```

The function returned must be quoted to avoid an infinite loop.

4: Can local variables be given built-in function names?

Yes. Variable names corresponding to built-in function names such as `sum`, when defined as local, will not clash with the function names in the global context, and therefore, can be used in the same way as any other local variable.

5: What happens if the stop value is omitted from the for statement?

In this case, the end condition is taken as infinity. Therefore, an endless loop will result.

6: How fast is the remember table?

The time taken to access a remember table is independent of the table size. The index is used to access a hash table, the output of which points to the table entry. If a hash table collision occurs when a new entry is being added, the entire hash table is rebuilt.

7: How can I see the code for Maple library procedures?

First, set the interface variable `verbose-proc` equal to 2 and then either `eval` or `print` the function name.

8: Why are the bodies of the rule definitions delayed twice?

The extra level of delay is needed because the expression will be evaluated once when the rule is assigned and again when the rules are combined using `define`.

9: Does the right-hand side of a transformation rule have to call another rule?

No, the right-hand side of the rule can be any valid Maple expression. Complex operations are more easily implemented through a procedure.

10: Is rule order important?

Yes. Maple first checks for the initially known states and then works sequentially through the rules from left to right. Hence, care always should be the taken.

FAQs 11: Why can an error condition occur when a rule is modified and the function redefined?

If only a subset of the rules are modified, the remainder will still be in a partially evaluated state. When the function is redefined, these are evaluated fully and will cause the error. Either restart or clear and reenter the rules and the definition.

BEWARE 1: In releases Vr3 and older, there is an alternate function definition syntax. The angle bracket syntax was useful because it supported local variables.

```
function_name:=< body | arg₁, arg₂, .., argₙ>
function_name:=
<body | arg₁, arg₂, .., argₙ | local₁, local₂, .., localₙ>
```
Function definition using the angle bracket operator.

Here the convolution integral is defined using the angle bracket notation. The ability of this form to include local variables is used to advantage.

```
> convolve:=<int(f1(tau)*f2(t - tau),
  tau=-infinity..infinity) | f1, f2 |t,
  tau>:
```

This defines two functions, f and g.

```
> f:=< exp(-t)*Heaviside(t) | t>:
> g:=< exp(-0.5*t)*Heaviside(t) | t>:
```

Here the convolution of the two functions is computed.

```
> ans:=convolve(f, g);
```

$$ans := -\frac{2}{e^t} + \frac{2}{e^{t/2}}$$

2: In previous releases, the operator associating argument names to types was the colon (:), for example, `arg:type`. Although this will still work, a warning will be issued and the correct syntax should be used.

3: The profile utilities have been reintroduced for Vr4 after having been removed in Vr3.

Working with External Data

With Maple we are not restricted solely to using data sets that have been previously generated by Maple. Generally, an external data set is taken to mean a data file. This can be either a file created by Maple or a file created by an external application such as a word processor, spreadsheet, or another analysis package. Maple has 24 input/output (I/O) functions with which to read, write, and manipulate data from sources other than Maple. In many instances, these functions are not used on their own but are used as an integral part of a user-defined or custom function that has been developed to address a specific need. In this chapter, we will take a look at many of the Maple I/O functions and investigate how they can be used in our own functions and procedures. All of the data files used in the following discussions are available on the program disk that accompanies this text; they are also listed, for convenience in Appendix A.

Reading Maple Files

Maple can read two basic file formats: human-readable and machine-readable. A human-readable file is flat ASCII, whereas the machine-readable format is proprietary and can only be produced by Maple during a Maple session. Files saved using the proprietary format have the extension *m*, whereas human-readable ones can have any name and any extension other than *m*. As a rule, the extension *mws* is used to identify human-readable Maple Worksheet files.

read

Both data and predefined user functions can be easily read into a Maple session using `read`. As `read` is used for both file types, the file's extension is used as a switch to distinguish between the two. If we use `read` to access a file with an extension other than *m*, a flat ASCII file is assumed. The file is read one statement at a time, with Maple treating the input as if we had used the keyboard. Therefore, the data in the file must be syntactically correct if we are to avoid an error condition aborting the read.

READING ASCII FILES

The file *data1.txt*, containing two commands: a list definition and a conversion, is read into the current Maple session.

```
> read(`data1.txt`);
```

$$a\_list := [\, [1, 2, 3], [a, b, c], [A, B, C] \,]$$

$$\begin{bmatrix} 1 & 2 & 3 \\ a & b & c \\ A & B & C \end{bmatrix}$$

READING ASCII FILES When we read the file *data2.txt*, a syntax error is detected and the read operation is aborted

```
> read(`data2.txt`);
```

$$b\_list := [[1a, 2a, 3a], [aa, ba, ca], [Aa, Ba, Ca]]$$

```
on line 2, syntax error:
op(op(1 2, b_list));
```

If the extension of the file we want to read is *m*, Maple assumes that it is machine-readable, in which case the file is read into the current Maple session immediately. In the following example, we read a previously defined procedure into our current Maple session.

READING .M FILES Is the function `my_listplot` known to Maple? No!

```
> eval(my_listplot);
```

$$my\_listplot$$

This reads the file *mylistpt.m*, containing the function definition, into the current session. The file is in machine-readable format.

```
> read(`mylistpt.m`);
```

This generates a list plot from 15 random numbers. The function `my_listplot` was loaded with the previous command. As the function is now part of the session, it is possible to view its code, as we shall see next.

```
> my_listplot([ 'rand()'/10^12$15] );
```

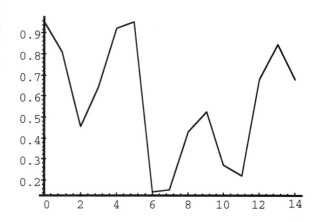

READING .M FILES After setting `interface(verboseproc=2)`, we can view the function's code using `eval`.

```
> interface(verboseproc=2):
  eval(my_listplot);

proc()
local pts,x,n;
options `Copyright coded by Dr. Steve
  Adams 1995`;
  if nargs = 0 then
     RETURN(`listplot(list, opts)`)
  elif 0 < nargs and not type(args[1],
  list) then
     ERROR(`badargs, a list expected`)
  else
  x:=[ seq(n,n =0 .. nops(args[1])-1)];
  pts:=zip((x, y)->[x, y], x, args[1]);
  plot(pts, args[2 .. nargs])
  fi
end
```

Reading Other Files

More often than not we will want to use Maple to investigate a data set obtained from somewhere else. It is extremely unlikely that such a data file will be in a "Maple-friendly" format. By using either `readdata` or `readline`, such files can be read and the data extracted and used.

readdata

We can use `readdata` if we are reading a data file containing only integers and floats formatted in columns that are delimited with white spaces. It is important to emphasize that the data should be either integers or floating-point numbers because all nonnumeric entries are ignored. To read entries from a file of floats contained in a single column, we only have to use `readdata`, giving the file name as the only function argument. This is because by default a file containing a single column of floating-point numbers is assumed. If this is not the case, we will have to supply the number of columns and the data type as necessary.

In the following examples, the data file *data3.dat*, containing four rows of five columns, is used. The file contains both integers and floats.

READING DATA FILES The data file is read using the default settings: a single column of floating-point numbers.

```
> readdata(`data3.dat`);
```

$$[1., 1., 1., 1.200000000000000]$$

READING
DATA FILES
By setting the column count to 5, we can read all of the data.

```
> readdata(`data3.dat`, 5);
```

$$[[1., 2., 3., 4., 5.], [1., 4., 9., 16., 25.],$$
$$[1., .5000000000000000, .3000000000000000,$$
$$.2500000000000000, .2000000000000000],$$
$$[1.200000000000000, 34., 5.600000000000000, 789.,$$
$$100.]]$$

If we set the options so that only two columns are read and integers are expected, the list on the right is returned.

```
> readdata(`data3.dat`, integer, 2);
```

$$[[1, 2], [1, 4], [1], [1]]$$

readline

In the event that we either do not know a file's structure and contents, or it contains nonnumeric entries, we can use the general file-reading function `readline` to extract the data. Every call to `readline` will cause a read from the current input stream to be attempted. If the read is successful, a string minus any carriage returns and/or line feed characters is returned. This string can have a maximum length of 499 characters, so if a data entry exceeds this upper limit, it must be read in pieces using multiple calls to `readline`.

When the first call to `readline` is made, the source file is automatically opened for reading; the first line of the file is returned as a string. If for any reason a read is unsuccessful, the numeric zero is returned instead of a string; for example, a zero will be returned when the end of file is reached. When the end of a file is reached, `readline` automatically closes the file. The number of files that we can have open simultaneously is platform-specific, but in general will be at least 5.

READING
TEXT FILES
The file *eigentes.t*, produced by *Mathematica*, another CAS, is a flat ASCII text file. Using `readline` in a loop, we read the first four lines.

```
> to 4 do readline(`eigentes.t`) od;
```

$$(*^$$

$$::[\ frontEndVersion = \text{"Macintosh Mathematica Notebook}$$
$$\textit{Front End Version 2.1"};$$
$$macintoshStandardFontEncoding;$$

Now using a while loop, we read the rest of the file until the end of file is reached. The data are discarded after each read operation.

```
> while 0 <> readline(`eigentes.t`) do od;
```

WHILE — DO The *while-do* construct is yet another incarnation of the for loop.

```
for count while test do body od
      while test do body od
```
The loop body is evaluated while test is true.
Examples:
```
x:=3:
while x! < ithprime(x) do x:=x + 1: od
for z while ithprime(z) < z^3 do
   z; z:=z + 1;
od
while a^2 + b^2=c^2 do
   c:=c + 2; a:=a - 1; b:=b/2;
od
```

sscanf

Once we have retrieved a line from a file using `readline`, it is usual to parse it into its constituent parts. The function `sscanf`, which is based on the C *stdio* library function of the same name, is ideally suited to this task. Using `sscanf`, we can split up a string according to a format statement. The format statement is a concatenation of format objects, one for each part of the string being parsed. Each format object has the same form: `%[ *][ width][ type]`. It should be noted that for `sscanf` to return predicable results, we must know the structure of the string being parsed beforehand.

FORMAT OBJECT		
	%	Marks the beginning of a format object.
	*	Object if found is to be discarded. This parameter is optional.
	width	Number of characters of the object to be returned. This can be used to split objects into smaller chunks and is optional.
	type	Type of object being scanned for.

USING SSCANF First, we will fake a read by entering a string by hand.

```
> read_string:=`string X 3.14159 12345
  1/sqrt(5) `:
```

!₂ Next we define the format string: a string (`%s`), a character (`%c`), a float (`%f`), an integer (`%d`), and an algebraic expression (`%a`). All elements are space-delimited.

```
> objects:=`%s %c %f %d %a`:
```

USING SSCANF Now we can split up the test string as specified by the format string using `sscanf`.

```
> sscanf(read_string, objects);
```

$$\left[string,\ X,\ 3.141590000000000,\ 12345,\ \frac{1}{sqrt(5)} \right]$$

By specifying that the delimiter is a decimal point, the mantissa and the fractional part of a floating-point number can be isolated.

```
> sscanf(`123.456`, `%d.%d`);
```

$$[\ 123,\ 456\ ]$$

The delimiter can be any expression. Here the floating-point number following `asExp=` is returned. The `%e` format object is used.

```
> sscanf(`asExp=123456E-3`,`asExp=%e`);
```

$$[123.4560000000000]$$

Semicolon delimited numbers can be parsed and returned as floats.

```
> sscanf(`1; 2.90; -33`,`%f;%f;%f`);
```

$$[1.,\ 2.900000000000000,\ -33.]$$

Parsed objects can be discarded. Here only the exponent is returned

```
> sscanf(`123.456`, `%*d.%d`);
```

$$[456]$$

Strings can be parsed and only specified characters returned. In this example M is discarded and only lowercase characters in the range a to s and y to z are returned (`%[ ^t-x]`).

```
> sscanf(`Maple system`, `%*[ A-Z]%[ ^t-x] `);
```

$$[aple\ sys]$$

Example 1: Reading a Flat Data File

In our first major example, we will use a home-grown procedure to tackle a common problem encountered when using Maple: wanting to read data from an external file. Our procedure accepts a data file that can have up to 20 columns of floating-point data separated with a delimiter. If no delimiter is specified, it is assumed to be a comma. Finally, the actual number of columns in the file is determined automatically.

The procedure is called *flat_file_read* whose code follows. The code or this and all subsequent author-defined procedures can be found on Prentice Hall's ftp and world wide web sites. By now you should be able to read the Maple code without too much trouble, but because everybody's coding style is different, the gray boxes throughout the code contain hints as to what is going on.

Procedure name, no formal parameters are defined.

```
> flat_file_read:=proc()
```

Local variable definitions.

```
local opts, src, line, fmt, temp, delim, old, c;
```

Initialize local variables: `temp` is a temporary variable and `c` is a counter used in the production of the format object definition.

```
temp:=NULL;
c:=1;
```

If the procedure is called with no arguments, use ERROR to display a message and exit.

```
if nargs=0 then
    ERROR(`expected source file, delimiter = expr - default
        delimiter is ,`)
fi;
```

Get the file name and any optional arguments.

```
src:=args[1];
opts:=select(type, [args], `=`);
```

Set the delimiter, using the default if none is specified in the calling sequence.

```
delim:=subs(opts, delimiter=`,`, delimiter);
```

Read the first line from the source file, construct the basic format object, and scan the input looking for a single floating-point entry. The entry is assigned to the temporary variable.

```
line:= readline(src);
fmt:=cat(`%f`,delim);
temp:=sscanf(line, cat(fmt$c));
```

The number of columns in the file is automatically determined as follows. By using the while loop, the first line from the source file is repeatedly scanned looking for one additional floating-point entry each time. When the number of entries returned no longer changes, the loop is terminated with `c` containing the number of columns plus one.

```
while old<>temp do
    old:=temp;
    c:=c + 1:
    if c=21 then ERROR(`Only 20 columns supported`); fi;
    temp:=sscanf(line, cat(fmt$c));
od;
```

The format object is now constructed, one entry for each column found.

```
fmt:=cat(fmt$(c - 1));
```

By using a while loop the file is read and parsed a line at a time. The parsed objects are appended to the temporary variable.

```
temp:=NULL;
while line<>0 do
    temp:=temp, sscanf(line, fmt);
    line:=readline(src);
od;
```

The contents of the temporary variable are returned.

```
[temp];
end:
```

By using this utility, two data files are read, one is comma-delimited and the other uses semi-colons.

```
> flat_file_read(`ff1.dat`);
```

$$[[1., 2., 3., 4., 5.], [11., 22., 33., 44., 55.],$$
$$[1.200000000000000, 3.400000000000000, 5.600000000000000,$$
$$7.800000000000000, 9.]]$$

```
> flat_file_read(`ff2.dat`, delimiter=`;`);
```

$$[[1200., .008999999999999999, 45.],$$
$$[3.141500000000000, 2.718281828000000, 0],$$
$$[1.414000000000000, .7070000000000000, .1234567 \ 10^7]]$$

MORE HELP	related(iolib)	Get a list of all of the I/O functions.
	feof	Test for end-of-file stream.
	filepos	Set the offset into a file.
	fprintf	Write formatted data to a file stream.
	fscanf	Read and parse data directly from a file or stream.
	readbytes	Read data from a file or stream.
	Menu item FILE:IMPORT	Import text into the current Worksheet (Macintosh only).

Writing to Files

It is not only important to read data from files, we must also be able to store data in files as well. In most cases we would default to the Worksheet as our preferred method of saving data, text, and mathematical content in a form that can be reused again and again. There are, however, a few notable exceptions when the Worksheet paradigm is inappropriate; for example, saving user-developed functions and packages and saving data sets for use in other analysis tools. It is these exceptions that we will be addressing here.

save

The save function is the complement of the read function. When it is necessary to write data to a file, this is the function that we will use. In this case, data are taken to mean a set of assigned names. Like read, save can be used to save data in either human-readable form or in the Maple internal format, the destination file's extension acting as the switch. If it is *m,* the data will be saved using the internal format; otherwise, it will be saved as ASCII. You should always exercise care when writing to a file because if it already exists, it will be overwritten without warning.

SAVING DATA

? 4

Here all the assigned names (functions and variables) in the current session are saved in *file1*.

```
> save(`file1`):
```

Whereas the previous command results in an ASCII file, this saves the session using the Maple internal format.

```
> save(`file1.m`):
```

By using this form only, the definitions of the specified objects are saved in *file2*.

```
> save(data1, func1, proc1, `file2`):
```

Again, this form saves the specified objects using the Maple internal format.

```
> save(data1, func1, proc1, `file2.m`):
```

writeto and appendto

We can also save data by redirecting Maple output, from, say, the Worksheet to a file using writeto and appendto. When using this method of saving data, we first open the destination file using either writeto or appendto. Once the destination file is open, all subsequently generated output is redirected to it. Finally, we complete the process by redirecting the output back to the Worksheet. This automatically closes the open data file. Both functions save data as flat ASCII.

REDIRECTING TO A FILE We can mimic data by printing procedure definitions.	```> interface(verboseproc=2):```
The first step is to open the destination file to accept the redirected output.	```> writeto(`proc_body`):```
Instead of the Maple code for `tan` being echoed to the Worksheet, it is redirected to the file *proc_body*.	```> eval(tan);```
By redirecting the output back to the Worksheet, we terminate the process and close the open data file.	```> writeto(terminal);```
A file can be reopened so that data can be appended to it using `appendto`.	```> appendto(proc_body):```
This time the code for the `cot` is saved.	```> eval(cot);```
Resetting the redirection closes the file once again.	```> appendto(terminal);```

Both `writeto` and `appendto` take a file name as their argument; if the file does not exist, a new file is automatically created. If we use `writeto` with an already existing destination file, its contents will be overwritten without a warning. If, on the other hand, we use `appendto`, the new output is appended to the end of the file's contents.

writebytes and writeline

The previous functions all write data to a file but they do so in such a way that it is either difficult or impossible to control the process on a character-to-character basis. This level of control is needed if, for example, we wanted to write to a file data, generated with Maple, in another tool's data format. The functions `writebytes` and `writeline` give us the level of fine control required because they both lineprint expressions to a file. In fact `writebytes` is capable of lineprinting data as either strings or raw bytes. Both functions lineprint expressions to a file but only `writeline` terminates each write with a carriage return. Therefore, expressions that will appear on a single line can be written to a file using `writebytes`, whereas each expression will appear on a separate line if `writeline` is used. Both functions maintain a buffer to reduce the amount of I/O activity, so a write operation is only performed when the buffer is full, the destination file is closed or a `writeline` is performed. Both functions return the number of bytes written to the respective file if the write operation is successful, and in both cases, the destination file must have been opened prior to the write operation being performed.

WRITEBYTES AND WRITELINE

This opens *file3* for writing using the low-level I/O command `open`.

```
> open(`file3`, WRITE);
```

The first line of data is written to the destination file. Because `writebytes` is used, no carriage return is added.

```
> writebytes(`file3`, `this is the first
  line`);
```
$$20$$

Next some more text is appended to the file and this time a carriage return is added.

```
> writeline(`file3`, `this completes the
  first line`)
```
$$29$$

Using `writebytes`, we write to the test file a space followed by the characters *A*, *B*, and *c* as a list of bytes.

```
> writebytes(`file3`, [ 32, 65, 66, 99]):
```

Having completed our task, we close file 3.

```
> close(`file3`);
```

MORE HELP	`readline(terminal)`	Reads input from the top level — normally, the keyboard. Can be used to redirect a file so that Maple can be run in batch mode.
	`parse`	Parses a string and evaluates the result in the same way as if the string had either been typed or read in from a file.
	`readstat`	Prompts for input from the user.
	`searchtext` `SearchText`	Returns the position of a pattern in a string. The first form is not case-sensitive but the second is.
	`importdata`	Found in the `stats` package, `importdata` is used to import statistical data from a file.

MORE HELP	`convert/bytes`	Convert an expression to bytes.
	writestat	Write comma-separated expressions terminated with a newline to a file. Similar to lprint.
	Menu item FILE:SAVE AS	Export the current Worksheet as text.

Example 2: Saving Maple Objects in a MATLAB Data File

In this example, we consider a second commonly encountered problem: saving Maple objects in a form that can be used by another software tool, here taken to be MATLAB. In this example, we will develop a main procedure, a type checker, and a conversion utility.

The conversion utility fabricates the MATLAB matrix structure and is called whenever a list of lists, a set of sets, or an array is detected, and the type checker tests for sets of sets. The main routine is save_as_matlab, the type checker is `type/setset`, and the converter is `convert/tospecial`.

Main Procedure

Procedure name, no formal parameters defined.

```
> save_as_matlab:=proc()
```

Options and local variable definitions.

```
local tosave, temp, n, nn;
```

Open the destination file for writing. The name of the destination file is taken as the last parameter in the input sequence.

```
open(args[ nargs] , WRITE);
```

By using a for loop, every Maple object is tested to see if it is unassigned, a list of lists, a set of sets, an array, a set, a vector, a list, a table, or something else. The object type determines the amount of conversion necessary. Tables are not supported and a NULL is written to the file if one is encountered.

```
for n in args[ 1..nargs-1] do
  if n=eval(n) then tosave:=n;
  elif type(eval(n), { listlist, setset, array} ) then
    tosave:=n=convert(eval(n), tospecial);
  elif type(eval(n),{ set, vector, list} ) then
    tosave:=n=convert(eval(n), list);
  elif type(eval(n), table) then tosave:=NULL;
  else tosave:=n=[ eval(n)] ;
  fi;
```

> Write the converted object to the destination file.

```
    writeline(tosave);
  od;
```

> Tidy up and end.

```
    close(dst);
  end:
```

Custom Converter

> Procedure name, one formal parameter is defined.

```
>  `convert/tospecial`:=proc(x)
```

> Options and local variable definitions.

```
  local temp, result, n, nn;
  result:=`[ `;
```

> Check for a list of lists, a set of sets, and an array. The type of conversion required is determined by the object type discovered. A matrix results in each case.

```
  if type(x, listlist) then temp:=convert(x,matrix);
  elif type(x, setset) then temp:=[ op(map(convert, x, list))];
    temp:=convert(temp, matrix);
  else temp:=convert(x, matrix);
  fi;
```

> By using nested for loops, the Maple matrix structure is transformed into the corresponding MATLAB structure. The last column and row are manipulated separately.

```
  for n to linalg[ rowdim] (temp) do
    for nn to linalg[ coldim] (temp) - 1 do
      result:=cat(result, convert(temp[ n, nn] , string), ` `);
    od;
```

> Add the last column element with the semicolon delimiter.

```
    result:=cat(result, convert(temp[ n, nn] , string), `;`);
  od;
  cat(substring(result, 1..length(result) - 1), `] `);
```

> Remove the last semicolon and replace it with a close square bracket to complete the structure. The complete structure is returned.

```
  end:
```

Custom Type Checker

Procedure name, one formal parameter is defined.

```
> `type/setset`:=proc(x)
```

The new type is defined. The new type is a set of sets.

```
   type(x,set) and not has(map(type, x, set),false) and nops(x)>0
end:
```

Trying out our new utility on the data set shown, we get the expected results.

```
> a:=3:n:b:=[ 1,2,3] :c:={ 4,5,6,7} :d:=array(1..2,1..2,[[ 1,2] ,[ 6,7]] ):
> save_as_matlab('a','n','b','c','d', `to_mlab`);
```

$?_5$

```
a = [3]
n
b = [1, 2, 3]
c = [4, 5, 6, 7]
d = [1 2;6 7]
```

writedata

With the inclusion of the function `writedata` in Maple's I/O suite, it is now very easy to save one- and two-dimensional Maple data structures such as lists, matrices, and vectors to a file as tab-delimited data as floats, integers, or strings . The actual format used is user-selectable, through an optional format argument at the time of writing, but this facility is ignored; the default is to save the data in a floating-point format. When using `writedata`, it is important to be aware of the format used by Maple to store the data in the file: vectors and one-dimensional lists are saved one element per line, whereas matrices and lists of lists (or two-dimensional lists) are saved one row or sublist per line.

WRITEDATA This stores a list of numbers as floats in the file *wdata1.dat*. If the file is not already open, it will be opened and closed automatically.

```
> writedata(`wdata1.dat`, [1, 1.2, 4]):
```

First, define a numeric matrix.

```
> num_mat:=
    matrix([[1, 2.3], [4, 100.09]], list):
```

Now save it as integers in a file. This operation forces floating-point numbers to be cast into integers.

```
> writedata(`wdata2.dat`, num_mat,
    integer):
```

WRITEDATA If we want to save more than one data structure in a single file, we must first explicitly open the file, write the data, and then explicitly close the file. Here we open the destination file.

```
> fopen(`big_file.dat`, WRITE):
```

Next we save a vector, a list of lists, and a matrix in the same file.

```
> writedata(`big_file.dat`,
    vector([ a, b, c] ), string):
> writedata( `big_file.dat`,
    [[ 1] , [ 2]] , integer):
> writedata(`big_file.dat`,
    num_mat, float):
```

Finally, we close the file.

```
> fclose(`big_file.dat`):
```

Example 3: Parsing a *Mathematica* NoteBook

In this final example, we combine elements of the previous two examples by developing the Maple code to read a file, manipulate the acquired data, and then save the result in a second file. The resulting utility is a combination of three procedures: one to isolate valid input regions in the source file and perform some housekeeping, one to perform syntax conversion, and one to write the modified data to the destination file . The procedures are `get_ip_regions`, `change_syntax`, and `write_it`, respectively.

Main Procedure

Procedure name and formal parameter definition.

```
> get_ip_regions:=proc(src::string, dst::string)
```

Options and local variable definitions.

```
local line;
```

Read first line from source file. Use `searchtext` to see if (*^ are the first three characters of the file; if not, `error`, tidy up, and leave.

```
line:=readline(src);
if searchtext(`(*^`, line)<>1 then
```

To tidy up, we use an empty while loop to read every line in a file to the end of file. Use ERROR to exit.

```
    while readline(src) <> 0 do od;
    ERROR(`Not a NoteBook file, (*^ expected line 1 char 1`)
else
```

Write header information to the destination file. The file is opened automatically.

```
writeline(dst, `# This file contains the input regions`);
writeline(dst, `# from the Mathematica NoteBook`, src);
writeline(dst):
```

Read the next line before entering the while loop.

```
line:=readline(src);
```

Use the while loop to read lines from the file until the end of file. Again searchtext is used to isolate the lines beginning with the pattern :[font = input;. If found, the source file name and control are passed to write_it.

```
while line<>0 do
        if searchtext(`:[ font = input;`, line) = 1 then
                line:=write_it(src, dst);
        else line:=readline(src);
        fi:
    od:
```

The end of file detected. Close the source and destination files and exit.

```
        close(dst, src);
    fi;
end:
```

Disk Write Routine

Procedure name and formal parameter definition.

```
> write_it:=proc(src, dst)
```

Options and local variable definitions.

```
local line, n, nn, string, end;
```

Read the next line in the file. If it is not the end of file, continue; else return zero.

```
line:=readline(src):
if line=0 then RETURN(0) fi:
```

Again we use searchtext to find the end of the input region. However, while in an input region, each line is saved, following a syntax adjustment, to the destination file. The second call to searchtext checks to see if we are still in the NoteBook text. A NoteBook ends with the text pattern ^*).

```
while searchtext(`:[ font`, line)<>1 and
        searchtext(`^*)`, line)<>1 do
```

The string read from the source file is altered using `change_syntax`.

```
string:= change_syntax(string);
```

Once the syntax has been adjusted, the string is written to the destination file and the next line is read from the source file.

```
writeline(dst, substring);
line:=readline(src);
```

If the end of file is detected, zero is returned to the calling procedure. This way the end of file is propagated upward.

```
    if line=0 then RETURN(0) fi:
od;
```

When the end of the current input region is encountered, a test for the end of file is made. If the test returns false, the next line is returned and the search for the next input region begins.

```
    RETURN(line);
end:
```

Syntax Converter

Procedure name and formal parameter definition.

```
> change_syntax:=proc(l::string)
```

Options and local variable definitions.

```
local new, nn, t, r, L;
```

Initialize local variables: `L` is the length of the string, `t` is the number of 20 character chunks in the string, and `r` is the remainder.

```
L:=length(l):
new:=NULL:
t:=iquo(L, 20):
r:=L mod 20;
```

So that the syntax can be adjusted, the input string is split into a list of characters. Then a substitution can be performed prior to the characters being concatenated to reform the new string. The string is split into 20 character chunks using `substring`; each chunk is split into characters with `sscanf`, which is stored in n.

```
for nn from 0 to t+1 do
    new:=new, op(sscanf(substring(l, 1 + 20*nn..(1 + nn)*20),
        cat(`%c`$20)));
od;
new:=new, op(sscanf(substring(l, 1 + 20*nn..(1 + nn)*20),
cat(`%c`$r));
```

By using `subs`, tabs are changed to single white spaces, curly braces are changed to square brackets and equalities are changed to assignments.

```
new:=subs(`      `=` `,`{ `=`[ `, `} `=`] `, `=` = `:=`, [ new] );
```

Finally, all of the characters are reformed into a single string, which is returned.

```
  cat(op(new));
end:
```

Testing the new utility with the *Mathematica* NoteBook *eigentst,* we get

```
> get_ip_regions(`eigentst`, `test.txt`);
```

```
# This file contains the input regions
# from the Mathematica NoteBook, eigentst

mat:= .1*[[19., -50., 88.], [ -53.,85.,49.], [78.,17.,72.]]
MatrixForm[%%]
Eigensystem[mat]
 [-6.519805426, 1., [[ 1.782474996, 1., -1.137283254 ]]]
%[[2,1]]
%/%[[2]]
```

Visualizing External Data

We can use Maple to visualize external data in either two or three dimensions with a minimum of fuss. If the data are in the form of coordinate pairs, `plot` can be used directly; if the data are stored as *(x, y, z)* triplets, `surfdata` (see `?plots`) is used, and if the data are an array of height values, then `matrixplot` (see `?plots`) is applicable.

VIEWING DATA First, we read the data from *usa.dat* into our Maple session. The data format is a list of *x–y* coordinates like so: $USA:=[[[x_1, y_1], [x_2, y_2], ..., [x_n, y_n]], [...], ...]]$. A list of lists is used to accommodate any islands.

```
> read(`usa.dat`):
```

VIEWING DATA By first converting the topmost list to a set, we can plot the groups of data points easily using `plot`. By using the color option, we force the outline to be black.

```
> plot(convert(USA, set),color=BLACK,
    axes=NONE);
```

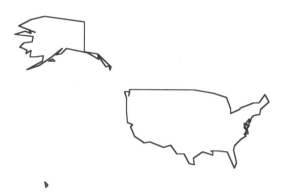

The data in *sdata.dat* are in the form of a list of lists of amplitudes: $data:=[[z_{11}, z_{12}, .., z_{1n}],$
$[z_{21}, z_{22}, .., z_{2n}], [...],$
$[z_{m1}, z_{m2}, .., z_{mn}]]$. These data are read into our session using `read`.

```
> read(`sdata.dat`);
```

Using `matrixplot`, we plot the data as a three-dimensional surface. The grid is generated automatically from the number of array entries and the amplitude is given by the data.

```
> plots[ matrixplot](data, shading=ZHUE,
    orientation=[ -180, 2],
    style=PATCHCONTOUR, title=`Visualization
    of data sdata.dat`);
```

Visualization of data sdata.dat

VIEWING DATA The data for our third example are in *pole.dat*. This file contains data triplets of the form:

$[[[x_{11}, y_{11}, z_{11}], [x_{12}, y_{12}, z_{12}], ..,$
$[x_{1n}, y_{1n}, z_{1n}]], [[x_{21}, y_{21}, z_{21}], [$
$x_{22}, y_{22}, z_{22}], .., [x_{2n}, y_{2n}, z_{2n}]], ..,$
$[[x_{m1}, y_{m1}, z_{m1}], [x_{m2}, y_{m2}, z_{m2}], ..,$
$[x_{mn}, y_{mn}, z_{mn}]]].$

```
> read(`pole.dat`);
```

After reading in the data, we assign the tag *data1* to it.

```
> data1:=" :
```

Using `surfdata`, we generate the three-dimensional surface shown on the right.

```
> plots[ surfdata] (data1),
    style=PATCHCONTOUR, shading=ZHUE,
    title=`Visualization of pole.dat`);
```

Visualization of pole.dat

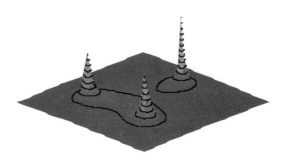

Here we use the Maple I/O function `readdata` to read a column of floating-point numbers from the data file *vect.dat*. The data are assigned to the variable *y*.

```
> y:=readdata(`vect.dat`);
```

$y := [0, .9453559925000000, .9381374240000000,$
$.8786893259000000, .6884614320000000,$
$.9666666666000000, .5884614320000000,$
$.5453559926000000, .9381374240000000,$
$.9453559925000000, -.06666666671000000,$
$-.6786893260000000, -1.004804091000000,$
$-.6120226594000000, -.5884614321000000,$
$-.7666666668000000, -.6551280988000000,$
$-.5453559927000000, -1.071470757000000,$
$-.7120226593000000, 0]$

VIEWING DATA Because the data are in vector form, they must be transformed into pairs before they can be plotted. The corresponding x coordinates are quickly generated with the `seq` command as shown and the point pairs are formed by the application of `zip`.

```
> x:=[ seq(n, n=0..nops(y) - 1)];
```

$$x := [0, 1, 2, 3, 4, 5, 6, 7, 8, 9, 10, 11, 12, 13, 14, 15, 16, 17, 18, 19, 20]$$

```
> data_pairs:=zip((x, y)->[ x, y] , x, y];
```

$$
\begin{aligned}
\textit{data\_pairs} := &[[0, 0], [1, .9453559925000000], \\
&[2, .9381374240000000], [3, .8786893259000000], \\
&[4, .6884614320000000], [5, .9666666666000000], \\
&[6, .5884614320000000], [7, .5453559926000000], \\
&[8, .9381374240000000], [9, .9453559925000000], \\
&[10, -.06666666671000000], [11, -.6786893260000000], \\
&[12, -1.004804091000000], [13, -.6120226594000000], \\
&[14, -.5884614321000000], [15, -.7666666668000000], \\
&[16, -.6551280988000000], [17, -.5453559927000000], \\
&[18, -1.071470757000000], [19, -.7120226593000000], \\
&[20, 0]]
\end{aligned}
$$

The list of points is now plotted using `plot`.

```
> plot(data_pairs, style=POINT, title=`Vec-
```

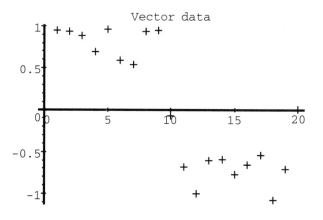

Vector data

MORE HELP   MESH   Create a surface from a mesh. The points on the mesh are of the form $[x, y, z]$.
Example:
```
PLOT3D(MESH([[[ 1,  1,  1] , [ 2,  2,  2]] ,
    [[ 3,  3,  3] , [ 4,  4,  4]]]))
```

MORE HELP	ISOSURFACE	Create an isosurface from a list of points. The points on the isosurface are of the form *[x, y, z, amp]*, where *amp* is the value of the isosurface at the point *[x, y, z]*. Example: `PLOT3D(ISOSURFACE([[[1, 1, 1, 1], [2, 2, 2, 2]], [[3, 3, 3, 3], [4, 4, 4, 4]]]))`
	listplot	Found in the `plots` package, `listplot` can be used to plot lists and vectors of data points in two dimensions.
	listplot3d	Found in the `plots` package, `listplot3d` can be used to plot lists of data points in three dimensions.
	listcontplot	Found in the `plots` package, `listcontplot` can be used to plot a two-dimensional contourplot from a rectangular grid of values.
	listcontplot3d	Found in the `plots` package, `listcontplot3d` can be used to plot a three-dimensional contourplot from a rectangular grid of values.
	?stats[statplots]	Return the help page for the statistical plotting routines.

NEW FUNCTIONS AT A GLANCE	`appendto( file )`	Redirect output to `file`, appending new data to existing data.
	`close( file )`	Close an unbuffered file.
	`coldim( array )`	Return the column dimensions of `array`.

`fclose( file_1, file_2, .., file_n )`
> Closes the buffered files `file_i`.

`fopen( file, oper )`
> Open a buffered `file` for either reading or writing. The type is set with `oper`.

`matrixplot( array, opts )`
> Found in the `plots` package, this displays a three-dimensional image of height values stored in `array`. The options are the same as for `plot3d`.

`open( file, oper )`
> Open an unbuffered `file` for either reading or writing. The type is set with `oper`.

`read( file )`
> Read the contents of `file` into the current Maple session.

`readdata( file, type, cols )`
`readdata( file )`
> Read white-space-delimited numerical data from `file`. The argument `type` can be either integer or float, which is the default. If the file contains more than a single column of data, the number of columns read is set by `cols`.

`readline( file )`
> Read a line from `file`.

`save( expr_1, expr_2, .., expr_n, file )`
`save( file )`
> Save `expr_i` to `file`. The second form will save all assigned names to `file`.

`searchtext( patt, string, range )`
`SearchText( patt, string, range )`
`searchtext( patt, string )`
`SearchText( patt, string )`
> Return the position of `patt` in `string`. If `range` is present, only that portion of `string` is searched. The second form performs a case-sensitive search.

`sscanf( string, fmt )`
> Scan `string` for objects given in the format statement `fmt`.

NEW FUNCTIONS AT A GLANCE		
	`substring( string, range )`	Take the portion of `string` indicated by `range`.
	`surfdata( pts, opts )`	Found in the `plots` package, this displays a three-dimensional image of the data points `pts`. The data points have the form: $[[[x_{11}, y_{11}, z_{11}], [x_{12}, y_{12}, z_{12}], .., [x_{1n}, y_{1n}, z_{1n}]], [[x_{21}, y_{21}, z_{21}], [x_{22}, y_{22}, z_{22}], .., [x_{2n}, y_{2n}, z_{2n}]], .., [[x_{m1}, y_{m1}, z_{m1}], [x_{m2}, y_{m2}, z_{m2}], .., [x_{mn}, y_{mn}, z_{mn}]]]$. The options are the same as for `plot3d`.
	`to n do body od`	A degenerate form of the for loop, equivalent to `for x to n do body od`.
	`while test do body od`	The body is evaluated while `test` is true.
	`writebytes( file, expr`$_1$`, expr`$_2$`, .., expr`$_n$` )`	Lineprint `expr`$_i$ to `file`.
	`writedata( file, data, type )`	Write tab-delimited data to `file` of type `type`. The data can be a vector, a list a list of lists, or a matrix, and `type` can be `float`, `integer`, or `string`.
	`writeline( file, expr`$_1$`, expr`$_2$`, .., expr`$_n$` )`	Lineprint `expr`$_i$ to `file` followed by a carriage-return linefeed.
	`writeto( file )`	Redirect output to `file`. Existing data will be overwritten.

FAQs

1: How do I stop the input statements from being echoed when reading from a file?

Maple is parsing each statement as it is read from the file. To suppress the output, each statement must be terminated with a colon.

2: What happens when a file entry is encountered that cannot be cast in to the specified type?

The read operation is aborted for that line.

3: When using `readline` to retrieve data from a file, what happens if I miss the end of file?

When the end of file is encountered, Maple will close the file. This means that the next call to `readline` will start reading data from the beginning of the file again.

4: Are the parentheses necessary when using `save` and `read`?

No, they can be omitted provided that the basic syntax is adhered to.

5: Why are the names quoted with delayed evaluation quotes?

If the quotes are omitted, Maple would evaluate the names prior to the routine being called. Therefore, the data associated with each of the names would be passed to the procedure and not the names.

BEWARE

1: The file extension *mws* is new to Vr4; in older releases, *ms* was used.

2: The format type `%i` is only recognized in versions Vr3 and older. Use `%d` instead.

3: The file-writing functions `writebytes` and `writeline` are only recognized in versions following Vr3. They replace `write` and `writeln`.

4: The function `close` now takes a file name as an argument so that specified files can now be closed. This differs from Vr3 in which all open files would be closed following the use of `close`.

Using Maple

In this chapter, we take a look at how Maple can be easily applied to problems from as diverse areas as finance and engineering. In many instances, we can use Maple to analyse a problem without resorting to programming; in fact, quite often we only have to find and apply the appropriate Maple function or functions in order to gain some insight into the problem. In some cases, however, we will have to undertake some simple programming to tackle our problem effectively. Although it is not their intent, the tutorials can be used as solution templates that you can quickly adapt and apply to your own problems. As already mentioned, do not be discouraged if you do not immediately recognize or feel comfortable with all of the problem areas. If your knowledge of a topic is sketchy, just concentrate on the way in which Maple is applied and on the functions that are used to get a result.

Finance

Although the finance industry seems at first glance to be preoccupied with only numerical (mainly floating-point approximations) quantities and operations, a second look shows otherwise. We have already considered the money to be made if we could only adjust the number of significant digits used by our calculators. Moreover, the *Black-Scholes* model, a closed-form analytic option pricing model, is available in Maple. Additionally, we only have to look at the financial pages of any newspaper to see that many financial quantities are quoted exactly; for example, a bond yield might be 10-3/16% over 15 years. Finally, the ability to manipulate unknowns means that sensitivity analysis is possible.

Maple comes with a set of common financial functions. These functions are found in the finance package, the contents of which follow.

THE FINANCE PACKAGE		
	annuity	Calculate the present value of annuities with fixed cash flows.
	cashflows	Calculate the present value of a list of cash flows, one per period.
	growingannuity	Calculate the present value of annuities where the cash flows increase.
	growingperpetuity	Calculate the present value of perpetuities where the cash flows increase.
	levelcoupon	Calculate the present value of a level coupon bond of face value and coupon rate in maturity periods.

THE FINANCE PACKAGE	`perpetuity`	Calculate the present value of an instrument that pays a fixed cash flow forever.
	`amortization`	Compute an amortization table.
	`blackscholes`	Calculate the option price using the Black-Scholes formula.
	`effectiverate`	Compute the effective rate from a compound interest rate.
	`futurevalue`	Calculate the future value of a quantity.
	`presentvalue`	Calculate the present value of a quantity.
	`yieldtomaturity`	Calculate the yield to maturity of a bond.

Example F1: Options

In this example, we develop models for both a *put* and a *call* option based on the built-in Black-Scholes option pricing model. A *put* option is used by the investor to bet that the price of a stock will decline (put down), whereas for a *call* option, the reverse is true (call up). By plotting these two financial instruments as functions of the strike price and the volatility, it is possible to see how the compound straddle option is affected. Finally, we define the gamma (the second derivative of the option premium with respect to the underlying investment) for the option and show graphically how it is linked to the performance of the straddle.

OPTION PRICING

This "loads" the finance package.

```
> with(finance):
```

!1 The *call* function is defined using the built-in *Black-Scholes* model and takes the strike price, volatility, and the time to maturity, as a fraction of a year, as arguments. We assume that the option price is unity and that the risk-free interest rate is 0%.

```
> call:= (sp, t, v) -> blackscholes(1, t,
  sp, v, 0);
```

$$call:=(sp, t, v) \rightarrow blackscholes(1, t, sp, v, 0)$$

Using `call`, we define the put function easily.

```
> put:= (sp, t, v) -> call(sp, t, v) -
  (sp-1);
```

$$put:=(sp, t, v) \rightarrow call(sp, t, v) - sp + 1$$

OPTION PRICING We visualize the straddle by plotting both functions together using plot3d. The time to maturity is 100 days.

```
> plot3d({ call(sp, 100/365, v), put(sp,
  100/365, v)}, sp=0..2, v=0..1,
  axes=BOXED, title=`A straddle using a
  call and a put`, labels=[ `Strike Price`,
  `Volatility`, ``], style=PATCHNOGRID,
  shading=ZHUE);
```

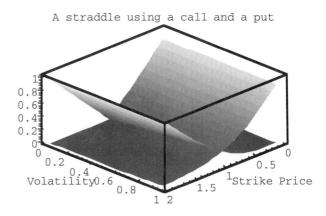

This plot will be used later on, so we store it by assigning it (the plot structure) to a variable. Note that the output is suppressed. If we did not do this, the plot structure itself would be printed to the screen.

```
> p1:=" :
```

Next we define γ for the preceding option. We start by defining the cumulative normal density function.

```
> Int(exp(-1/2* s^2)/sqrt(2* Pi),
  s=-infinity..x);
```

$$\int_{-\infty}^{x} \frac{\exp(-1/2\ s^2)\sqrt{2}}{2\sqrt{\pi}}\, ds$$

This definition is transformed into a function using unapply.

```
> N:=unapply(", x);
```

$$N := x \rightarrow \int_{\infty}^{x} \frac{\exp(-1/2\ s^2)\sqrt{2}}{2\sqrt{\pi}}\, ds$$

OPTION PRICING Using this functional representation, we can take the first derivative of the cumulative normal density function with respect to its upper limit x.

```
> diff(N(x), x);
```

$$\frac{\exp(-1/2\ x^2)\sqrt{2}}{2\sqrt{\pi}}$$

The quantity d_1 is dependent on the strike price, the volatility, and the time to maturity, and is defined here.

```
> d[1]:=ln(sp)/(v*sqrt(t)) + t*v/2:
```

A function describing the g surface for the option is formed by substituting d_1 in the first derivative calculated before and using `unapply` as shown.

```
> gamma_surface:=unapply(subs(x=d[1],
  "")/(sp*v*sqrt(t)), sp, v, t):
```

Now we can plot the surface using `plot3d`. Note the scaling applied. This makes for better viewing of the final plot.

```
> p2:=plot3d(gamma_surface(sp, v,
  100/365)/6, sp=0.1..2, v=0.1..1,
  axes=BOXED, style=PATCHNOGRID,
  shading=ZHUE):
```

By combining plots `p1` and `p2`, the complete picture is generated.

```
> plots[display3d]({p1, p2},
  title=`Straddle with Gamma`);
```

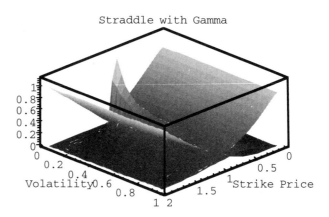

Example F2: Markets

In the second example, we develop a stock exchange using nested tables. A list of stock exchanges is stored using a table and each exchange is a table holding the stocks traded on that exchange. As we develop this example, we perform operations commonly encountered when working with real data, namely, read the data in, manipulate the data, and store it for future use as well as develop tools to access the data and display the data graphically.

The Maple program that follows is a utility function that reads a data file, the format of which is *company name price price price price price*. Each line contains the stock price for the five days, Monday through Friday. The price data are placed in a table, the indices of which are the days of the week. The table name is set by the company name.

Read A Data File

Procedure name, one formal parameter defined: the name of the data file.

```
> make_data:=proc(src)
```

Options and local variable definitions.

```
local days, company, data, prices, companies;
companies:=NULL;
days:=[ Monday, Tuesday, Wednesday, Thursday, Friday] ;
```

Load the assign function, which is readlib-defined.

```
readlib(assign);
```

Start to read the file.

```
data:=readline(src);
```

While not the end of file, manipulate the data. The line is parsed using `sscanf` and the variables `company` and `prices` are set accordingly.

```
while data<>0 do
  data:=sscanf(data, `%s %f %f %f %f %f`);
  company:=op(data[ 1] );
  prices:=[ data[ 2..6]] ;
```

The prices and days are zipped together to form a list of equalities. These are then converted to a table that is then assigned to the company name.

```
  assign(company, convert(zip((x, y)->x=y, days, prices), table));
  companies:= companies, company;
```

Read the next line and continue.

```
  data:=readline(src);
od;
fclose(src);
[ companies] ;
end:
```

MAKING A MARKET Using the new utility, we read a file containing dummy data placing the data in the current Maple session. The list returned by the utility shows the company names for which data have been supplied.

```
> make_data(`prices.dat`);
```

$$[IBM, ITT, NEC, DEC]$$

Here we explicitly create a table whose entries are the stock exchanges we are interested in.

```
> stock_exchange[ FT100] :=FT100:
  stock_exchange[ NYSE] :=NYSE:
  stock_exchange[ NASDQ] :=NASDQ:
```

Next we populate one of the test exchanges with the price data read in before.

```
> FT100[ IBM] :=IBM:
  FT100[ ITT] :=ITT:
  FT100[ NEC] :=NEC:
  FT100[ DEC] :=DEC:
```

By using Maple's ability to alias names, we define two tools used to access the database. In this case, `lookat` behaves like `indices` and `lookatstock` behaves like `eval`.

```
> alias(lookat=indices,
  lookatstock=eval):
```

Here we use the tools to access the stock date. First, we see what stock exchanges are available, next we return the companies traded on the *FT100* stock exchange, and, finally, the week's prices for a single company are obtained.

```
> lookat(stock_exchange);
```

$$[NYSE], [FT100], [NASDQ]$$

```
> lookat(stock_exchange[ FT100] );
```

$$[IBM], [ITT], [NEC], [DEC]$$

```
> lookatstock(stock_exchange[ FT100][ DEC] );
```

> *table([*
> *Tuesday = 28.12307709000000*
> *Friday = 26.04848045000000*
> *Wednesday = 24.51231043000000*
> *Thursday = 26.56714806000000*
> *Monday = 27.*
> *])*

MAKING A MARKET Here we manipulate the stock exchange database directly to return a list of the companies quoted.

```
> the_stocks:=map(op, [ lookat(
  stock_exchange[ FT100] )] );
```

$$the\_stocks := [\mathit{ITT}, \mathit{IBM}, \mathit{DEC}, \mathit{NEC}\,]$$

Using a for-in loop, we easily obtain the stock price data for each stock on a particular day, in this case, Thursday.

```
> for n in the_stocks do
    n=lookatstock(stock_exchange[ FT100]
    [ n][ Thursday] )
  od;
```

$$\mathit{ITT} = 15.02296338000000$$
$$\mathit{IBM} = 55.41123357000000$$
$$\mathit{DEC} = 26.56714806000000$$
$$\mathit{NEC} = 4.735726282000000$$

!₂ Using one of Maple's statistical plotting routines, we display the price data for IBM and DEC. The function `display` is used to alter the look and feel of the resulting plot.

```
> plots[ display] ({
  stats[ statplots, scatter2d] (
  convert(IBM, list ),
  convert(DEC, list))},
  title=`IBM vs DEC`, symbol=BOX);
```

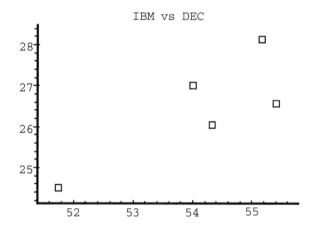

MAKING A
MARKET

Three sets of data are displayed simultaneously with a space-curve plot. Using nested `zip` functions, we form triplets from our data sets prior to plotting them.

```
> data:= zip((x, y)->[ op(x), y],
    zip((x, y)->[ x, y] convert(NEC, list),
    convert(ITT,list)), convert(DEC, list));
```

$$data := [5., 14.50000000000000, 27.],$$
$$[4.735726282000000, 15.02296338000000,$$
$$26.56714806000000], [5.184423884000000,$$
$$13.49671852000000, 28.12307709000000],$$
$$[4.987859313000000, 15.18700463000000,$$
$$26.04848045000000], [5.815843191000000,$$
$$14.64595034000000, 24.51231043000000]$$

Here we plot the points formed before in three space.

```
> plots[ spacecurve] ({ data}, style=POINT,
    symbol=DIAMOND, tickmarks=[ 2, 2, 2],
    labels=[ `NEC`, `ITT`, `DEC`],
    color=BLACK, title=`NEC vs ITT vs DEC`
    orientation=[ 47, 66], axes=FRAME,);
```

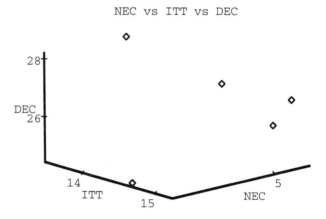

Example F3: Counting the Days

In our final financial example, we develop four utility functions for determining elapsed time. Being able to calculate accurately the time to maturity of a financial instrument is very important in the business world. Although this seems like a reasonably straightforward problem to solve, there are some pitfalls that we should be aware of; for example, financiers use a number of bases when calculating time—actual time and 30-day time are the two most common. Actual time is where the actual number of days between two dates is used in calculation, so the number of days between January 1, 1992 and January 1, 1993, is 366. Thirty-day time, on the other hand, artificially splits the year into 12 months of 30 days (that is by 360 days in a single year). Therefore, using this second method, the number of days between the January 1, 1992 and the January 1, 1993 is 360.

In the following code, the functionality to test for a leap year and to count in either actual or 30-day time is developed. The day-counting function uses two day counters, one counter calculates the number of days from January 1, 1900, to a specified date and the other calculates the days between two specified dates. A date is specified as a list of the form [*day, month, year*].

Custom Type Test

Procedure name, one formal parameter defined: the object to be tested.

```
>  `type/leapyear`:=proc(x)
     if x mod 400 = 0 then true
     elif x mod 100=0 or x mod 4<>0 then false
     else true
     fi;
   end:
```

Year and day data held in global variables.

```
>  _datedataactual:=[[ 31,28, 31, 30, 31, 30, 31, 31, 30, 31, 30, 31],
   [ 365, 365, 365, 366]]:
>  _datedata360:=[[ 30,30, 30, 30, 30, 30, 30, 30, 30, 30, 30, 30],
   [ 360, 360, 360, 360]]:
```

Counting the Days from January 1, 1900

Procedure name, two formal parameters defined: the date and the counting basis.

```
> daysfrom:=proc(date, style)
```

Define and initialize the local and global variables. The number of leap days is held in lds, the number of leap centuries is held in cds the appropriate global data is copied to the local variable data. Finally, year contains the number of days in a year.

```
   local lds, cds, data, year;
   global _datedataactual, _datedata360;
   if style=`actual` then
     data:=_datedataactual; year:=365;
     lds:=max(0, iquo((date[ 3] - 1900 - 1), 4) -
     iquo((date[ 3] - 1900 - 1), 100));
     cds:=max(0, iquo(floor((date[ 3] - 1900)/100 + 3 - 0.01), 4));
   else
```

```
      data:=_datedata360; year:=360;
      cds:=0;
    fi;
    convert([ year*(date[ 3]  - 1900), lds, cds, op(data[ 1][ 1..date[ 2]  -
1] ), date[ 1]  - 1] , `+`);
  end:
```

Counting the Days Between Two Dates

> Procedure name, no formal parameters defined: valid argument sequences are date$_1$, date$_2$ and date$_1$, date$_2$, option (year = actual or 360).

```
> daysbetween:=proc()
```

> Local variable definitions. The variable theopts contains a sequence: any optional arguments followed by the default. This is used to set opt.

```
  local opt, n, theopts;
  theopts:=op(select(type, [ args] ,`=`)), year=actual;
  opt:=subs(theopts, year);
```

> Call daysfrom to compute the day count.

```
  daysfrom(args[ 2] , opt) - daysfrom(args[ 1] , opt);
  end:
```

Counting Time as a Fraction of a Year

> Procedure name, no formal parameters defined: valid argument sequences are date$_1$, date$_2$ and date$_1$, date$_2$, option (year = actual or 360).

```
> get_time:=proc()
```

> Local variable definitions. If two parameters are present, then two dates are assumed; if three, two dates and an option. Anything else is an error.

```
  local t, t1, opt;
  if nargs=2 then
    t:=args[ 1] ;
    t1:=args[ 2] :
```

> Two arguments, therefore, set the default counting basis.

```
    opt:=year=actual:
  elif nargs=3 then
    t:=args[ 1] ;
    t1:=args[ 2] :
    opt:=args[ 3] :
  else ERROR(cat(procname, `(`, args, `) `, `called with bad args`));
  fi;
```

> Call `daysbetween` to count the days and divide by the year length.

```
    if rhs(opt)=360 then daysbetween(t, t1, year=360)/360;
    else daysbetween(t, t1, year=actual)/365;
    fi
end:
```

COUNTING DAYS Here we calculate the time, as a fraction of a year, between January 1, 1992, and January 2, 1993 using actual time.

```
> get_time([ 1, 1, 1992], [ 2, 1, 1993]);
```

$$\frac{367}{365}$$

Here we calculate the time as a fraction of a year between July 4, 1995 and January 1, 1990, using 30-day time.

```
> get_time([ 4, 7, 1995], [ 1, 1, 1990],
    year=360);
```

$$\frac{217}{60}$$

Using actual time, we count the number of days in February 1992.

```
> daysbetween([ 31, 1, 1992], [ 1, 3, 1992],
    year=actual);
```

$$29$$

Now we repeat the exercise using 30-day time.

```
> daysbetween([ 31, 1, 1992], [ 1, 3, 1992],
    year=360);
```

$$30$$

This counts the number of days, in actual time, between April 25, 1959, and July 4, 1995.

```
> daysbetween([ 25, 4, 1959],
    [ 4, 7, 1995]);
```

$$13219$$

Finally, we calculate the days between July 4, 1995, and January 1, 1990 using 30-day time.

```
> daysbetween([ 4, 7, 1995], [ 1, 1, 1900],
    year=360);
```

$$-34383$$

Control Engineering

Intuitively, control engineering, like any other discipline, can take advantage of Maple's power in a number of ways. We can determine, for instance, if a closed-form solution to a particular problem can be found, we can use Maple as a powerful differential equation solver, and we can look at our results quickly. Possibly Maple's most useful feature from a control engineer's view point is its well-established linear algebra package. The ability to manipulate symbolic and numeric matrices and vectors easily and without error, either interactively or by using a program, makes Maple immediately useful.

Example CE1: Control Plots

In the first example, we use Maple's graphing abilities to plot the Root-Locus, Bode, Nichols and Nyquist diagrams of different dynamical systems.

CONTROL PLOTS

First, define the test system, in terms of *s*.

```
> sys:=K*(s^2 + 2*s + 4)/
    (s*(s + 4)*(s + 6)*(s^2 + 1.4*s + 1)):
```

The Root-Locus plot is the locus of the poles of the closed-loop system as the forward path gain K is varied for zero to infinity. Here we obtain the closed-loop system response when unity-negative feedback is applied.

```
> cl_sys:=simplify(sys/(1 + sys));
```

$$cl\_sys := $$
$$\frac{5\,K\,(s^2 + 2s + 4)}{5s^5 + 57s^4 + 195s^3 + 218s^2 + 120s + 5\,Ks^2 + 10\,Ks + 20\,K}$$

Using the Root-Locus plotting function we plot the locus of the closed-loop system as the gain is swept from 0 to 200.

```
> plots[ rootlocus] (sys/K, s, 0..200);
```

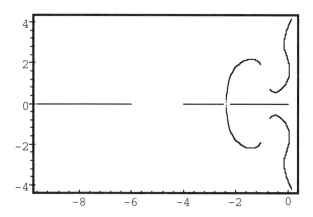

CONTROL PLOTS

Another common method of representing a control system graphically is the Bode plot. A Bode plot has two components: a gain plot and a phase plot. The system that we are investigating is defined opposite.

```
> sys:=K*(s + 3/10)*(s^2 + s/10 +
  401/400)/((s^2 + 7/5*s + 949/100)*(s^2 +
  6*s + 45/4));
```

$$sys := \frac{K\left(s + \frac{3}{10}\right)\left(s^2 + \frac{1}{10}s + \frac{401}{400}\right)}{\left(s^2 + \frac{7}{5}s + \frac{949}{100}\right)\left(s^2 + 6s + \frac{45}{4}\right)}$$

The Bode plot provides information in the frequency domain, so we need to replace the *s* in the Laplace transform with *jw*. The gain is also set to *-100*.

```
> alias(j=sqrt(-1));
```

$$I, j$$

```
> Sys:=subs(K=-100, s=I*w, sys):
```

The gain portion of the Bode plot plots *20 log₁₀(gain)* against *log₁₀(frequency)*. Here we use Maple's `semilog` function, which is found in the `plots` package.

```
> plots[ semilog] (20*log10(abs(Func)),
  w=0.1..100, axes=FRAME, title=`The Gain
  Response`, labels=[ `Log(w)`, `dBs`] );
```

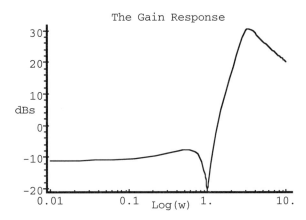

CONTROL PLOTS The next plot is the other half of the Bode plot, the system phase response. Both plots have logarithmic ordinate axes and linear abscissi. The abscissa of gain plot is graduated in decibels (dB) and the abscissa of phase plot is graduated in degrees.

```
> plots[ semilog] (evalf(180*
   (argument(Func))/Pi), w=0.1..100,
   axes=FRAME, title=`The Phase Response`,
   labels=[ `Log(w)`, `Degrees`]);
```

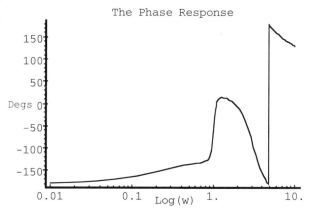

Another common plot used to represent a dynamic system's behavior is the Nyquist plot. We use Maple's two-dimensional plotting function `plot` but alias it to the function name `nyquistplot`.

```
> alias(nyquistplot=plot);
```

I, j, nicholsplot, nyquistplot

Here we create two functions, one to return the *x* and one to return the *y* coordinate from the system transfer function and frequency.

```
> X:=(sys, w)->abs(sys)*cos(evalf(
   argument(sys))):
   Y:=(sys, w)->abs(sys)*sin(evalf(
   argument(sys))):
```

CONTROL PLOTS A Nyquist plot is the trajectory of the system response, as a function of frequency, plotted on the complex plane. The trajectory is graduated in frequency.

```
> nyquistplot([ X(Sys, w), Y(Sys, w),
    w=0.01..10], labels=[ `Re`, `Im`],
    scaling=CONSTRAINED,
    title=`G(jw) Trajectory`);
```

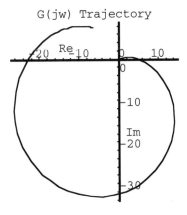

The final plot that we will consider here is the Nichols Chart. The Maple plotting routine `logplot`, which is part of the `plots` package, can be used. Using `alias`, we give it a more meaningful name.

```
> alias(nicholsplot=plots[ logplot]);
```

I, j, nicholsplot

The Nichols chart displays both the system's gain and phase response on the same plot. The trajectory is graduated in frequency. We display the trajectory and the graduations by generating two separate plots, a line plot and a point plot, which are then displayed together to get the required effect.

```
> p:=nicholsplot([ evalf(180*(argument(Sys)
    )/Pi), abs(Sys), w=0.01..10]):
> p1:=plots[ display] (p, style=POINT,
    symbol=CIRCLE):
```

CONTROL
PLOTS
Here we display the complete plot. The discontinuity is caused by the actual phase becoming less than -180 degrees and the plot "wrapping" around to the positive value.

```
> plots[ display] ({ p, p1}, title=`Nichols
    Plot`, labels=[ `Degrees`, `|G|`]);
```

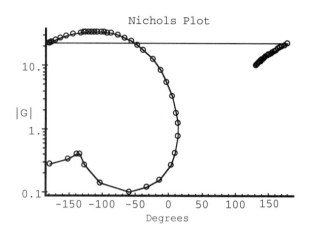

Example CE2: Nonlinear Control

In our second example, we investigate how Maple can be applied to a nonlinear control problem. In this example, we use a describing function to represent the nonlinear element. The nonlinear component in question is a gain element for which the forward path gain is a function of the input amplitude. We model this in Maple using the `piecewise` function. Using the Maple code solver, we obtain the error response for a nonlinear closed-loop control system. The control system is shown in the Figure 5.1, and the input/output characteristic for the nonlinear gain element is shown in Figure 5.2. By way of comparison, this particular example was considered numerically by Katsuhiko Ogata (*Modern Control Engineering*, 2nd ed. Englewood Cliffs, NJ: Prentice Hall, pp. 593–596).

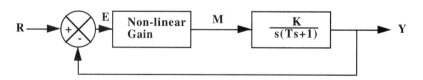

Figure 5.1 Nonlinear Control System

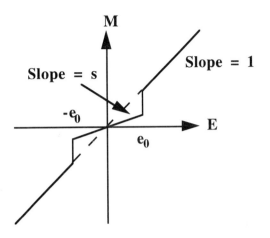

Figure 5.2 Response of the Nonlinear Gain Element

NONLINEAR ELEMENTS By using the `piecewise` function, it is easy to define the behavior of the nonlinear gain element. We set the value of s equal to 1/2. It should be noted that the error function $err(t)$ has been defined as a function of time as we will need to differentiate with respect to time later.

We can plot the gain response of the nonlinear element, even though it contains the `piecewise` function, in the same way as any other function using `plot`.

```
> s:=1/2:
> gain:=piecewise( err(t)>=-1 and
  err(t)<=1, s, err(t)<-1 or err(t)>1, 1);
```

$$gain := \begin{cases} 1/2 & -1 - err(t) \le 0 \text{ and } err(t) - 1 \le 0 \\ 1 & err(t) + 1 < 0 \text{ or } 1 - err(t) < 0 \end{cases}$$

```
> plot(e*subs(err(t)=e, gain), e=-2..2);
```

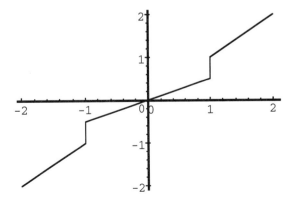

NONLINEAR ELEMENTS

Next we define the system dynamics. Here we describe them using a second-order differential equation, where $y(t)$ is the system output.

```
> System:=T*diff(y(t), t, t) +
  diff(y(t), t) = K*m;
```

$$System := T\frac{\partial^2}{\partial t^2}\, y(t) + \frac{\partial}{\partial t}\, y(t) = K\, m$$

Using `isolate`, we make the output signal $y(t)$ the subject of the system error equation (see Figure 5.1). The function `isolate` is readlib-defined.

```
> readlib(isolate)(err(t)=r(t) - y(t),
  y(t));
```

$$y(t) = -err(t) + r(t)$$

As we are interested in the error response of the system, the next stage is to eliminate $y(t)$ from the original code.

```
> new_System:=subs(", System);
```

$$new\_System := T\frac{\partial^2}{\partial t^2}(-err(t) + r(t)) + \frac{\partial}{\partial t}(-err(t) + r(t)) = Km$$

At this point, we have to cajole Maple into solving our problem. First, we expand the new code.

```
> new_System:=expand(new_System):
```

Next we convert the piecewise definition into a list of constraints.

```
> M:=convert(gain, list);
```

$$M := [-1 - err(t) \leq 0 \text{ and } err(t) - 1 \leq 0, 1/2,$$
$$err(t) + 1 < 0 \text{ or } 1 - err(t) < 0, 1]$$

Here we solve the differential equation `new_System` obtained earlier for each of the constraints. We do this interactively using a for loop as shown to apply the constraints one at a time and solve the resulting differential equation. The input $r(t)$ is a unit step, the forward path gain K is 3 and the initial conditions are $err(0) = 2$ and $err(0) = 0$. The results are stored in the variable `ans`.

```
> ans:=NULL:
> for n from 2 to nops(M) by 2 do
    ans:=ans, M[n-1], rhs(dsolve(
    {simplify(subs(r(t)=1, K=3, T=1,
    m=M[n]*err(t), new_System)),
    D(err)(0)=0 ,err(0)=2}, err(t)));
  od:
```

NONLINEAR ELEMENTS This converts the answer back into a piecewise function for future use.

```
>  piecewise(ans);
```

$$\begin{cases} 2\dfrac{\sqrt{5}}{5}\, e^{-t/2} \sin\!\left(\dfrac{\sqrt{5}}{2}\, t\right) + 2\, e^{-t/2} \cos\!\left(\dfrac{\sqrt{5}}{2}\, t\right) \\ \qquad -1 - \mathrm{err}(t) \le 0 \text{ and } \mathrm{err}(t) - 1 \le 0 \\[2mm] 2 e^{-t/2} \cos\!\left(\dfrac{\sqrt{11}}{11}\, t\right) + 2\, e^{-t/2} \sin\!\left(\dfrac{\sqrt{11}}{2}\, t\right) \\ \qquad \mathrm{err}(t) + 1 < 0 \text{ or } 1 - \mathrm{err}(t) < 0 \end{cases}$$

By using `unapply`, we convert the piecewise expression into a function that will return a value.

```
>  f:=unapply(subs(err(t)=err, "), t, err):
```

Plotting this particular piecewise function is a little more involved than normal, due to the nature of the gain element. The value of the next output is related to the previous one; hence, we must always remember the previous answer in order that we can compute the next. This is easy to do iteratively using a for loop.

```
>  pts:=NULL:
>  pt:=2: for n from 0 to 12 by 0.1 do
     pt:=evalf(f(n, pt));
     pts:=pts, [n, pt];
   od:
```

Here we plot the time response calculated before.

```
>  plot([pts], title=`Response for
   err(0)=2`);
```

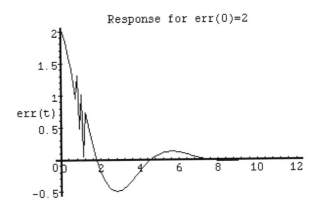

NONLINEAR ELEMENTS Functions containing piecewise elements can be manipulated in the same way as continuous functions. In this particular instance, we are interested in the first derivative, with respect to *t*, of the error function.

```
> f_dot:=unapply(diff(f(t, err), t), t,
  err):
```

By adapting the body of the previous for loop, we can generate the phase portrait of *err* versus *erṙ*.

```
> pts:=NULL:
> pt:=2:
> for n from 0 to 12 by .1 do
    pt:=evalf(f(n, pt));
    pts:=pts, [evalf(f_dot(n, pt)), pt];
  od:
```

This plots the phase portrait for the system with an initial value of error dot of 2.

```
> plot([pts], title=`err vs err dot`);
```

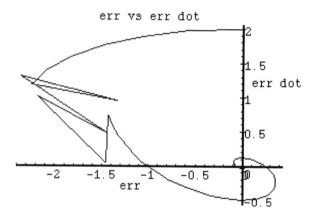

Example CE3: Full State-Feedback Control of a Cart and an Inverted Pendulum

In this control engineering example, we take a look at how Maple can help us in the design a full state-feedback controller. The system that we have to control has an inverted pendulum mounted on a cart, as shown in Figure 5.3. The object of the exercise is to keep the pendulum upright while the system is being subjected to disturbances. This is a popular control example that has been covered numerically by many authors. In our case, we are using, for comparison, the parameters used by Katsuhiko Ogata (*Modern Control Engineering,* 2nd ed. Englewood Cliffs, NJ: Prentice Hall, pp. 787–795).

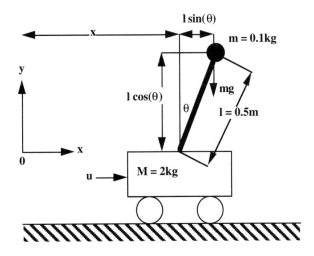

Figure 5.3 Cart and Inverted Pendulum

STATE FEEDBACK This "loads" the linear algebra package.

```
> with(linalg):
```

Warning, new definition for norm
Warning, new definition for trace

By using the functions `seq` and `cat` as shown, it is easy to generate variable names of the form *xi(t)* for *i*=1..4. In this case, we use the variables to define the state vector **X**.

```
> X:=matrix([ seq(cat(x, n)(t), n=1..4)]);
```

$$X := \begin{bmatrix} x1(t) \\ x2(t) \\ x3(t) \\ x4(t) \end{bmatrix}$$

STATE **Next we define the A, B, C, Y,**
FEEDBACK **and Ẋ matrices for the system. In**
creating the matrices, we have linearized the system by making the
following assumptions: θ is small
so that $\sin\theta \approx \theta$ and $\cos\theta \approx 1$ and $\dot\theta$
is small so $\theta\dot\theta^2 \to 0$.

```
> A:=matrix([[ 0, 1, 0, 0], [ (M+m)*g/(M*l),
  0, 0, 0], [ 0, 0, 0, 1], [ -m*g/M, 0, 0,
  0]]):
```

```
> B:=matrix([ 0, -1/(M*l), 0, 1/M]):
```

```
> C:=matrix([[ 1, 0, 0, 0], [ 0, 0, 1, 0]]):
```

```
> Y:=matrix([ seq(cat(y, n)(t), n=1..2)]):
```

```
> X_dot:=matrix([ seq('diff'(cat(x, n)(t),
  t), n=1..4)]):
```

The next task is to find the rank of
the augmented matrix. The rank
is 4 indicating that the system is
completely state-controllable.

```
> Mat:=
  augment(B, A &* B, A^2 &* B, A^3 &* B):
  rank(Mat);
```

$$4$$

Using `charpoly`, we generate
the characteristic equation of the
system. We then use it to determine positions of the desired
closed-loop poles.

```
> cpoly:=charpoly(A, lambda);
```

$$cpoly := \frac{\lambda^2 (-\lambda^2 Ml + gM + mg)}{Ml}$$

First, we tidy up the previous
polynomial by expanding and
then collecting terms.

```
> ecpoly:=collect(expand(cpoly), lambda);
```

$$ecpoly := \lambda^4 + \left[\frac{g}{l} - \frac{m}{Ml}\right]\lambda^2$$

Here we pick out the polynomial
coefficients and save them for
future use.

```
> alpha:=[ seq(alpha.n=coeff(ecpoly, lambda,
  n), n = 0..3)];
```

$$\alpha := \left[\alpha 0 = 0, \alpha 1 = 0, \alpha 2 = -\frac{g}{l} - \frac{m\,g}{M\,l}, \alpha 3 = 0 \right]$$

Intuitively, we want our system to
have a damping factor of 0.5 and
a settling time of 2 seconds. The
corresponding closed-loop poles
are shown opposite.

```
> cl_poles := [ mu1=-2 + I*3.5,
  mu2=-2 - I*3.5, mu3=-10, mu4=-10]:
```

STATE FEEDBACK Using the new closed-loop poles, we generate a new characteristic equation.

```
> new_cpoly:=subs(cl_poles, mul((lambda-
  mu.n), n=1..4));
```

$$new\_cpoly := (\lambda + 2. - 3.5I)(\lambda + 2. + 3.5I)\ (\lambda + 10)^2$$

Before continuing, we expand and collect the coefficients of the new equation as before.

```
> new_alpha:=[ seq(alpha.n=
  coeff(expand(new_cpoly), lambda, n),
  n=0..3)] :
```

!5 The difference between the new and the old α's can now be calculated.

```
> k:=matrix([ map(rhs, new_alpha-alpha)] );
```

$$k := \left[\ 1625.00\ \ 725.00\ \ 196.25 + \frac{g}{l} + \frac{mg}{Ml} - 24.\ \right]$$

Now we need to define two additional matrices, **w** and **T,** so that we can calculate the elements of the state-feedback gain matrix **K**.

```
> w:=matrix([[ alpha1, alpha2, alpha3, 1],
  [ alpha2, alpha3, 1, 0],
  [ alpha3, 1, 0, 0], [ 1, 0, 0, 0]]):
```

```
> T:=Mat &* subs(alpha, evalm(w)):
```

The state-feedback gain matrix **K** is defined as **kT⁻¹** and is used to shift the poles of the original system to their new locations. By shifting the system's poles, we alter the system's behavior.

```
> K:=evalm(k &* inverse(T));
```

$$K :=$$

$$\left[\frac{-1625.00\ Ml^2 - 196.25\ Ml\ g - g^2M - mg^2}{g}\ ,\right.$$

$$-\frac{Ml\ (725.00l + 24.g)}{g}\ ,$$

$$\left.-\frac{1625.00\ Ml}{g}\ ,\ -\frac{725.00\ M\ l}{g}\right]$$

We can now describe the new system using a matrix equation. The equation describes the new system in terms of the old system's parameters, its states, and their rates of change.

```
> mat_eqn:=X_dot=(A - B &* K) &* X;
```

$$mat\_eqn := X\_dot = (A - (B\ \&*\ K))\ \&*\ X$$

STATE FEEDBACK Up to this point, we have represented system parameters as symbolic quantities. Here we define their numeric values.

```
> params:=[ M=2, l=0.5, g=9.81, m=0.1];
```

$$params := [M = 2, l = .5, g = 9.81, m = .1]$$

The symbolic quantities, in the matrix equation defined before, are replaced with their numerical values using `subs`.

```
> odes:=subs(params, map(evalm, mat_eqn)):
```

Using `zip`, we transform the numerical matrix equation into a list of linear first-order coupled differential equations.

```
> eqns:=convert(zip((x, y)->x=y,
  convert(lhs(odes), vector),
  convert(rhs(odes), vector)), list):
```

The cart is initially at rest and the pendulum is 0.1 radians from the vertical.

```
> ics:=x1(0)=.1, x2(0)=0, x3(0)=0,
  x4(0)=0;
```

$$ics := x1(0) = .1, x2(0) = 0, x3(0) = 0, x4(0) = 0$$

Using Maple's numerical differential equation solver, we solve the system of equations using the default solver, a *Fehlberg* fourth-fifth-order *Runge-Kutta* algorithm. Maple returns a procedure. The `dsolve` procedure expects list or set arguments, hence the conversion performed on *eqns*.

```
> eqns:=convert(eqns, list):

> response:=dsolve({ op(eqns)}, ics},
  (convert(X,set), type=numeric);
```

```
response:=proc(rkf45_x) ... end
```

The time response of the system is obtained by sampling the system states at 20 Hz for the period 0 to 4 seconds using `seq`.

```
> curves:=seq(response(t/20), t=0..80):
```

This results in a list of lists with each sublist containing entries for the time step, *x1(t)*, *x2(t)*, *x3(t)*, and *x4(t)*.

```
> curves[ 2];
```

$$[1 = 1/20, x1(1) = .07459155597145141,$$
$$x2(1) = -.8090875136028038,$$
$$x3(1) = -.01342268413055248,$$
$$x4(1) = .4492089443064456]$$

STATE FEEDBACK By using nested maps, the right-hand side of each equation is isolated and stored in a matrix. The data are stored as follows: column 1—time, columns 2 through 5—the state values.

```
> T:=convert(map(x->map(rhs, x), [curves]),
    matrix):
```

The next Maple statement does two operations at once: The coordinate pairs are generated using `zip` and a list of plot structures is built using `seq`.

```
> pl:=[ seq(plot(zip((x, y)->[ x, y],
    col(T, 1), col(T, n)), title=cat(`x`,
    (n-1), `(t)`)), n=2..5)] :
```

This plots as a graphics array the time responses of system states x1(t) through x4(t).

```
> plots[ display] (matrix([ pl[ 1..2],
    pl[ 3..4]] ));
```

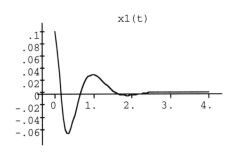

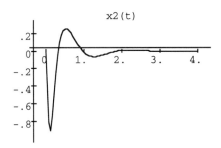

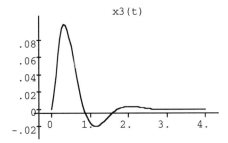

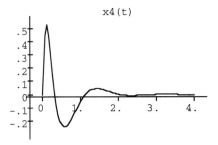

Example CE4: Analytical or Graphical Analysis?

The graphical tools shown in Example CE2 were developed as a way of avoiding the complex mathematics associated with analyzing complex control systems. Although the various graphical techniques are still useful and provide a great deal of insight into many control problems, the control engineer now has access to analytical tools that are capable of dealing with much of the complex mathematics.

As we have already seen, Maple is an ideal tool with which to generate the various graphical representations commonly used by control engineers. In this final set of control engineering examples, we see how Maple can replace the graphical techniques used to obtain system parameters, like gain and phase margins, maximum allowable forward gain for stable operation, and so on, with analytical ones.

REPLACING THE GRAPH With reference to the Root-Locus plot generated in Example CE2, we see that the system is conditionally stable when the locus has sections in the right-hand half plane. Using Maple, we can determine the values of gain that will result in unstable operation. First, we redefine the system.

```
> sys:=K*(s^2 + 2*s + 4)/
    (s*(s + 4)*(s + 6)*(s^2 + 1.4*s + 1)):
```

```
> cl_sys:=simplify(sys/(1 + sys));
```

$$cl\_sys := \frac{5K\,(s^2 + 2s + 4)}{5s^5 + 57s^4 + 195s^3 + 218s^2 + 120s + 5Ks^2 + 10Ks + 20K}$$

Using Maple's assume facility, we make some assumptions about w and K.

```
> assume(w, real);
> assume(K, real);
```

We can also find out what assumptions, if any, have been made about a variable.

```
> about(w);
```

```
Originally w, renamed w~: is assumed to
    be: real
```

In this and the next example, we will use j to represent the complex constant.

```
> alias(j=sqrt(-1));
```

$$I, j$$

By using `subs`, we replace s in the Laplace transform with the frequency variable jw. Note how the variables with assumptions have been renamed. This does not effect how we interact with them.

```
> cl_w:=subs(s=j*w, cl_sys);
```

$$cl\_w := (5K\!\sim (-jw\!\sim^2 + 2.jw\!\sim + 4.))/$$
$$(5jw\!\sim^5 + 57w\!\sim^4 - 195.jw\!\sim^3 - 218.w\!\sim^2 + 120.jw\!\sim$$
$$- 5.K\!\sim w\!\sim^2 + 10.K\!\sim jw\!\sim + 20.K\!\sim)$$

REPLACING THE GRAPH The system poles are given by the roots of the transfer function's denominator.

```
> denom(cl_w);
```

$$5jw\sim^5 + 57w\sim^4 - 195.\,jw\sim^3 - 218.w\sim^2 + 120.jw\sim$$
$$- 5.K\sim w\sim^2 + 10.K\sim jw\sim + 20.K\sim$$

By equating the real and imaginary components of the denominator to zero, we generate two simultaneous equations in w and K.

```
> Im(")=0;
```

$$5.w\sim^5 - 195.w\sim^3 + 120.w\sim + 10.K\sim w\sim = 0$$

```
> Re("")=0;
```

$$57.w\sim^4 - 218.w\sim^2 - 5.K\sim w\sim^2 + 20.K\sim = 0$$

If we solve for w and K, we will find the points at which the locus crosses the frequency axis and the corresponding values of the forward path gain.

```
> solve({", ""}, {w, K});
```

$$\{w\sim = 0, K\sim = 0\},$$
$$\{K\sim = 15.61062138, w\sim = -1.213031763\},$$
$$\{K\sim = 67.51260052, w\sim = -2.150900362\},$$
$$\{K\sim = 163.5567781, w\sim = -3.755287150\},$$
$$\{w\sim = 3.755287150, K\sim = 163.5567781\},$$
$$\{K\sim = 67.51260052, w\sim = 2.150900362\},$$
$$\{K\sim = 15.61062138, w\sim = 1.213031763\}$$

In the next example, we find the phase and gain margins for the system for which the Bode, Nichols, and Nyquist plots were constructed in Example CE2. As before, we redefine the system.

```
> new_sys:=K*(s + 3/10)*(s^2 + s/10 +
  401/400)/((s^2 + 7/5*s + 949/100)*(s^2 +
  6*s + 45/4)):
> Sys:=subs(K=-100, s=j*w, new_sys):
```

$$Sys := \frac{K\left(s + \dfrac{3}{10}\right)\left(s^2 + \dfrac{1}{10}s + \dfrac{401}{400}\right)}{\left(s^2 + \dfrac{7}{5}s + \dfrac{949}{100}\right)\left(s^2 + 6s + \dfrac{45}{4}\right)}$$

To calculate the phase margin, we have to find the frequency at which the system's gain is unity.

```
> solve(Sys=1, {w});
```

$$\{w\sim = RootOf(-42960\,j\,\_Z^3 - 27656\,\_Z + 70376\,j\,\_Z^2$$
$$+ 54735 + 400\,\_Z^4)\}$$

The first attempt is not very successful so we try again. This time we help Maple by making some additional assumptions about the variables w and k. As before we check w before continuing.

```
> assume(w, positive);
> additionally(w, real); about(w);

Originally w, renamed w~:
  is assumed to be:
  RealRange(Open(0),infinity)
```

REPLACING THE GRAPH Next we perform some pre-processing before we invoke the `solve` function.

```
> abs(Sys);
```

$$\frac{10\sqrt{(9 + 100w\sim^2)}\sqrt{(160000w\sim^4 - 319200w\sim^2 + 160801)}}{\left(\sqrt{(10000w\sim^4 - 170200w\sim^2 + 900601)}\sqrt{(16w\sim^4 + 216w\sim^2 + 2025)}\right)}$$

This solves the previous expression equal to unity for *w* using `solve`. By using `evalf`, we force floating-point solutions to be returned.

```
> evalf(solve("=1, {w}));
```

$$\{w\sim = .6596519896 - .5874866049\,j\},$$
$$\{w\sim = .6596519896 + .5874866049\,j\}$$

Again this is not what we would expect from the Bode plot. This time we find the solution using purely numerical techniques by using `fsolve`.

```
> fsolve(abs(Sys)=1,{w});
```

$$\{w\sim = 1.312739569\}$$

By substituting the preceding value for *w* back into the system's transfer function, we get the value for the phase, as a complex number, of the system at this frequency. By using `argument`, we convert this to radians.

```
> argument(subs(", Sys));
```

$$.2427627068$$

The difference between this and -180° is the phase margin.

```
> `Phase Margin`=
  evalf(convert(-Pi-",degrees),4);
```

$$Phase\ Margin = -193.9\ degrees$$

Next we find the system's gain margin. To do this, we first need to find the phase cross-over frequency (the frequency at which the phase is equal to -180°). First, we tidy up the transfer function.

```
> normal(Sys, expanded);
```

$$\frac{-40000\,j\,w\sim^3 - 16000\,w\sim^2 + 41300\,j\,w\sim + 12030}{-400\,w\sim^4 + 2960\,j\,w\sim^3 + 11656\,w\sim^2 - 29076\,j\,w\sim - 42705}$$

REPLACING THE GRAPH The phase of the system is given by $\tan^{-1}[\Im(Sys)/\Re(Sys)]$; hence, we need to get both the real and the imaginary parts of *Sys*.

```
> evalc(Re("));
```

$$\frac{(-16000w{\sim}^2 + 12030)\,(-400w{\sim}^4 + 11656w{\sim}^2 - 42705)}{(-400w{\sim}^4 + 11656w{\sim}^2 - 42705) + (2960w{\sim}^2 - 29076w{\sim}^3)^2}$$
$$+\frac{(-40000w{\sim}^3 + 41300w{\sim})\,(2960w{\sim}^3 - 29076w{\sim})}{(-400w{\sim}^4 + 11656w{\sim}^2 - 42705) + (2960w{\sim}^2 - 29076w{\sim}^3)^2}$$

Once the real and imaginary components are found, the phase as a function of frequency can be calculated. We are interested in the frequency at which the phase is equal to -180°.

```
> evalc(Im("")):
> phase:=arctan(", ""):
> evalf(solve(phase=-Pi, {w}), 4);
```

$$\{w{\sim} = 0\},\ \{w{\sim} = 4.769 + .00001456\,j\},$$
$$\{w{\sim} = -4.769 - .00001456\,j\},$$
$$\{w{\sim} = 1.088 + .0007184\,j\},\ \{w{\sim} = -1.088 - .0007184\,j\},$$
$$\{w{\sim} = 1.814 - .0005263\,j\},\ \{w{\sim} = -1.814 + .0005263\,j\}$$

As with the gain margin calculation, the results are unexpected and we are forced to use numerical techniques once again.

```
> fsolve(phase=-Pi, {w});
```

$$\{w{\sim} = 4.768890885\}$$

By substituting the frequency value back into the system transfer function, the gain at that frequency is calculated.

```
> subs(", normal(Sys, expanded));
```

$$-22.70826403 + .9051378576* 10^{-8}\,j$$

The returned value is a complex number that is converted to Decibels, as shown.

```
> evalf(20*log10(abs(")))*dB;
```

$$27.12367870\ dB$$

MORE HELP

`?plots[ structure]`		Returns the help page on the Maple plot structure.
`?DEtools`		Returns the help page for the DEtools (differential equations tools) package.
`?dsolve[ numeric]`		Returns the help page for Maple's default numeric ode solver.

Statistical Tools

Statistical analysis is a mature branch of mathematics. In general, statisticians will apply algebraically derived formulas to real data sets. Therefore, they need a tool that is capable of both manipulating symbolic expressions and performing computationally intensive tasks. Additionally, the ability to visualize the data in a number of different ways is an advantage. Maple, being capable of all of these tasks, is therefore ideally suited to the job.

Maple has a well-rounded statistics package containing functions for importing and exporting statistical data, data manipulation, regression analysis, and statistical plotting, amongst others. This package, unlike the others in Maple, contains six subpackages that are listed in what follows. In addition to the statistics package, curve-fitting routines and a basic random-number generator can be found in the standard Maple library.

THE STATS PACKAGE		
	`describe`	Contains the data analysis functions.
	`fit`	Contains the linear regression functions.
	`transform`	Contains the data manipulation functions.
	`random`	Contains the random-number generators. They support both built-in and custom specified distributions.
	`statevalf`	Contains the functions for the numerical evaluation of distributions.
	`statplots`	Contains the plotting functions.

Example S1: Random Numbers

This first example is not strictly an example. We will take a brief look at Maple's random-number generators, starting with the basic generator and moving onto the more sophisticated ones found in the statistics package. Along the way, we will take a look at the kinds of distributions supported and some of the basic statistical tests available to us.

RANDOM NUMBERS

Using Maple's standard random-number generator, we obtain five random integers between plus and minus 10.

```
> 'rand'(-10..10)()$5;
```

$$-4, 9, 3, -10, 1$$

RANDOM NUMBERS This particular random-number generator produces 12-digit integers and can be called as a function.

```
> random_num:='rand'():
```

Using the function defined before, we generate five 12-digit random numbers.

```
> 'random_num'()$5;
```

772367257706, 329341722897, 750579080033, 355209441783, 6653134116

We can generate floating-point random numbers with a specific distribution using functions in the statistics subpackage random. This is "loaded" using with, as shown.

```
> with(stats);
```

[*describe, fit, importdata, random, statevalf, statplots, transform*]

This generates five random numbers with a β distribution.

```
> random[ beta[ 1,2]] (5);
```

.0009987317914, .4104476824, .4242845645, .02026636957, .4147548131

Here we generate five random numbers with an *f-ratio* distribution.

```
> random[ fratio[ 1,2]] (5);
```

.4084130079, 19.36212304, 3.401074763, 1.959374711, 2.681616286

We can plot the distributions supported by Maple using plot. In this particular case, we plot the continuous probability function of a γ distribution. Note how a point on the probability distribution function is returned as a floating-point value using statevalf.

```
> plot(statevalf[ pdf,gamma[ 1, 2]] (x),
  x=0..5, title=`The gamma distribution`);
```

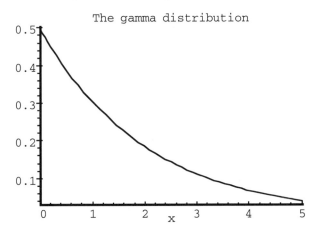

RANDOM NUMBERS This time we plot the cumulative density function for the χ^2 distribution.

```
> plot(statevalf[ cdf, chisquare[ 1]] (x),
  x=0..5, title=`The chi-squared
  distribution`);
```

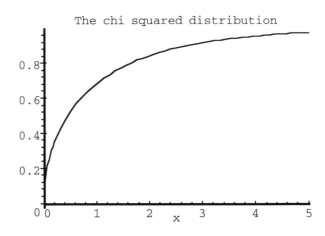

Here we generate some test data.

```
> data:=[ stats[ random, studentst[ 3]] (100)] :
```

This computes the mean of the data created before.

```
> describe[ mean] (data);
```

$$.06196491775$$

Now we obtain the standard deviation of the data.

```
> describe[ standarddeviation] (data);
```

$$1.731855571$$

Next the skewness of the data is calculated.

```
> describe[ skewness] (data);
```

$$.7814724328$$

Finally, we get the data's variance.

```
> describe[ variance] (data);
```

$$2.999323719$$

Example S2: Curve Fitting

In this example, we investigate curve fitting with Maple. In the first problem, we perform a linear fit to some data, and in the second, we demonstrate how Maple can be used to perform nonlinear data fits. In both problems, we use Maple's `fit` function.

LINEAR FIT As we will be using functions from the statistics package, we will first "load" it.

```
> with(stats):
```

This operation creates some data for us to use in this example.

```
> digits:=convert(numer(convert(evalf(Pi,
  21 ), rational, exact)), base, 10):
```

Using $, we generate a list of numbers from 0 to 20.

```
> ord:=[ $0..20] :
```

The two lists created are the *y* and *x* values, respectively, of our test data. Here we compute the linear least-squares fit to our test data.

```
> the_fit:=fit[ leastsquare[[ x,y]] ] ([ ord,
  digits] );
```

$$the\_fit := y = \frac{1297}{231} - \frac{29}{770} x$$

This generates a function of *x* from the equation returned by the least-squares fit procedure. This is necessary in order that we can test the goodness of fit to the original data.

```
> f:=unapply(rhs(the_fit), x):
```

Here we form the test data into coordinate pairs and plot them.

```
> plot(zip((x, y)->[ x, y] , ord, digits),
  style=point, symbol=cross):
```

This plots a curve corresponding to the fit function.

```
> plot(f(x), x=0..20):
```

LINEAR FIT Finally, we display the fit and the original data together for the sake of comparison. In this particular example, a linear least-squares fit does not return very good results.

```
> plots[ display] ({", "", title=`Raw data
  and fit`});
```

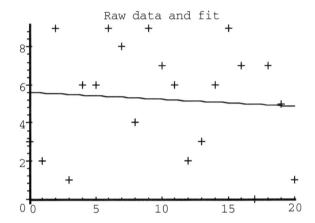

Raw data and fit

Although Maple does not currently come with any nonlinear curve-fitting algorithms, such as the *Levenburgh-Marquet* algorithm, it does give us the tools to linearize nonlinear data prior to attempting a standard fit. For example, if the data is exponential, then it can be linearized by taking the natural logarithm. Then the coefficients returned by the linear fitting routine will be equal to natural logarithms of the real coefficients. Such a case is explored in the next problem.

NONLINEAR FIT Again we will be using functions from the statistics package, so we will "load".

```
> with(stats):
```

In this example, we use test data gathered previously and stored on file. Here we read the data into the current Maple session. The data are stored as a two-column matrix.

```
> pts1:=readdata(`stats.dat`, 2):
```

The first column contains the *x* values and the second, the *y* values. Here we split the matrix in two and convert the data into lists. The fit procedure requires that the data be in this form.

```
> x:=convert(linalg[ col] (pts1, 1), list):
> y:=convert(linalg[ col] (pts1, 2), list):
```

NONLINEAR FIT This plots the raw data. With reference to the plot, it appears that the data has an exponential bias.

```
> plot(zip((x, y)->[ x, y] , x, y),
    title=`Raw data`);
```

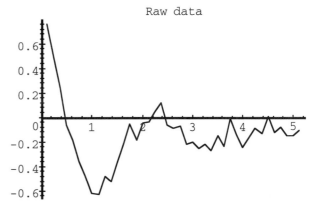

Here we linearize the data by taking the natural logarithm of the y values.

```
> y:=map(x->Re(log(x)), y):
```

This plots the linearized data and saves the plot structure for later use.

```
> plot(zip((x, y)->[ x, y] , x, y),
    title=`Transformed data`);
    aplot:=" :
```

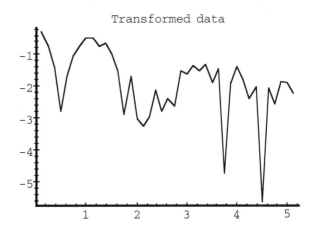

NONLINEAR FIT Now that we have a linearized data set, we can use Maple's `leastsquare` function to calculate the linear least-squares fit to the data.

```
> fit[ leastsquare[[ X, Y]]] ([ x, y]);
```

$$Y = -1.099459029 - .3095949099 \, X$$

As before, we transform the equation returned by the least-squares fit into a function so that we can plot it.

```
> f:=unapply(rhs("),X);
```

$$f := X \rightarrow -1.099459029 - .3095949099 \, X$$

This generates a plot of the fit function.

```
> plot('f'(t), t=.125..5.125):
```

Once again, we display the linearized data and the computed fit function on the same graph for easy comparison. The spikes in the linearized data correspond to data points approaching zero. These spikes may result in a poor fit being calculated.

```
> plots[ display] ({ p2, aplot},
    title=`Transformed data and fit`);
```

Transformed data and fit

This operation generates a list of data values at the same sample points as the original data using the calculated best fit.

```
> t_data:=[ seq(f(t/8), t=1..41)]:
```

Here we compute the linear correlation of the raw data and the fit data. It appears that we have an average fit.

```
> describe[ linearcorrelation] (y, t_data);
```

$$.4311019858$$

MORE HELP	?interp	Returns the help page for the polynomial interpolation function.
	?sinterp	Returns the help page for the sparse multivariate modular polynomial interpolation function.
	?spline	Returns the help page for the spline segment function
	?thiele	Returns the help page for Thiele's continued fraction interpolation formula.
	?dinterp	Returns the help page for the probabilistic degree interpolation function.
	?simplex	Returns the help page for the linear optimization package.

Example S3: Life and Death Processes

Our final statistical example is how to model a *life-death* statistical process. We are actually modeling the arrivals and departures of vehicles at a bridge tollbooth. The point of modeling this process is to help us decide how many tollbooths need to be open during the day given a certain probability of cars arriving and the maximum acceptable queue time. Our model assumes that the vehicles arrive with a normal distribution centered on 08:00 with a standard deviation of 1, and the time to pass through an open booth is 30 seconds. The wait is given by the following expression: $wait = wait_{ave}/(1 - (wait_{ave}\ arrivals))$, where $wait_{ave}$ is the average time it takes for a car to pass through a tollbooth and *arrivals* is the number of vehicles arriving per unit time. In this example, the output from the model is a graphic showing the relative queue time against the number of tollbooths operating throughout the day.

LIFE-DEATH PROCESSES

This "loads" the statistics package.

```
> with(stats):
```

Here we define the wait model that we are using.

```
> cars:=x->
    statevalf[ pdf, normald[ 3, 1]] (x)*2:
```

This is a function returning the number of arrivals at a specific time.

```
> wait:=(n, l)->
    (.5/floor(n))/(1 - (.5/floor(n))*l):
```

LIFE-DEATH PROCESSES Here we plot the expected distribution of arrivals against the time of day. The peak corresponds to the 08:00 rushhour.

```
> plot(statevalf[ pdf, normald[ 3, 1]] (x),
  x=0..8);
```

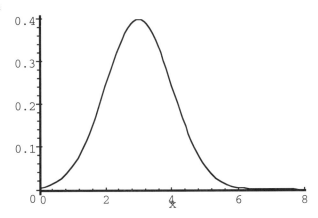

This three-dimensional surface shows how the wait changes as a function of tollbooths open throughout the morning rush hours.

```
> plot3d([ floor(n), t + 6, wait(n,
  cars(t))], t=0..6, n=1..10,
  orientation=[ -50, 60], axes=FRAME,
  labels=[ `Booths`, `Hour`, `t`]);
```

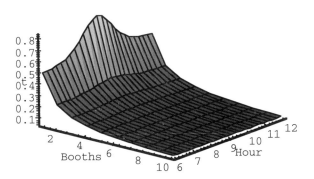

MORE HELP		
	`?data`	Returns the help page on Maple's representation of statistical data.
	`?updates`	Returns the help page on how to update from Maple V Release 2 or earlier to the current release.
	`?distributions`	Returns the help page on the statistical distributions supported by `stats`.

Digital Signal Processing

At first glance, a computer algebra system like Maple does not seem particularly well suited to the field of digital signal processing (DSP) applications. On the contrary, Maple is a very useful and powerful tool and its application in this area is often beneficial; at the very least, Maple can be used to render images quickly and simply.

Maple comes with an integral transform package that makes it easy to transform and manipulate continuous and discrete functions. The `inttrans` package contains many of the most commonly used transformations such as the *Laplace* and the continuous *Fourier* transform pairs. Along with the continuous *Fourier* transform, the forward and inverse *Fast Fourier* transforms (FFTs) are available as readlib-defined functions. These, however, are only one-dimensional at present.

Filter designers can use Maple in a number of ways, such as its ability to represent numbers to an arbitrary level of precision to determine the effects of finite word length and roundoff error on a filter's response and the way that it can be used to handle and manipulate large matrices easily. Once an image has been digitized, it can be thought of as a matrix of intensity values. If we are dealing with a monochrome image, we have only a single matrix to manipulate; if, however, we are manipulating a color image we have to deal with multiple matrices, one for each color plane.

In the following examples, we will investigate how Maple can be used as a DSP engine capable of manipulating both two- and three-dimensional images.

Example DSP1: FFTs

In the first example, we show how frequency analysis of complex time-varying signals can be done using Maple's FFT routine. The one-dimensional routine is extended, only in terms of the amplitude, to demonstrate how this type of analysis can be easily performed in two dimensions.

THE FFT Here we create a three-dimensional plot of the data points that we will use as our test data.

```
> plot3d(sin(x*y), x=-3..3, y=-3..3,
  numpoints=15^2):
```

By using nested ops, we can strip out the amplitude information from the plot structure We than convert the data points to an array.

```
> pts:=convert(op([ 3, 1], [ op(")])),
  array):
```

Here we form a zero matrix with the same dimensions as the amplitude array `pts`.

```
> imag:=map(0, pts):
```

THE FFT By looking at the first row of the matrix **pts**, we quickly check that the data are as we expect following their conversion from the plot structure format.

```
> x:=linalg[ row] (pts, 1);
```

$$x := [.4121184852417566, .9985433453746050,$$
$$.3115413635133787, -.7727644875559871,$$
$$-.8715757724135885, .1411200080598659,$$
$$.9738476308781949, .5646424733950364,$$
$$-.5646424733950344, -.9738476308781955,$$
$$-.1411200080598681, .8715757724135877,$$
$$7727644875559877, -.3115413635133779,$$
$$-.9985433453746049, -.4121184852417582]$$

This does the same for the zero matrix.

```
> y:=linalg[ row] (imag, 1);
```

$$y := [0, 0, 0, 0, 0, 0, 0, 0, 0, 0, 0, 0, 0, 0, 0, 0]$$

We are now ready to perform the FFT on the first row of data. Note that FFT is readlib-defined.

```
> readlib(FFT)(4, x, y);
```

$$16$$

The FFT routine overwrites the data structures with which it is called with the transformed data. As x is an array, we use eval to look at its contents.

```
> eval(x);
```

$$[0, .0152, .1222, 4.369, -.3970, -.266,$$
$$-.2296, -.2168, -.2112, -.2148, -.2296,$$
$$-.265, -.3970, 4.374, .1222, .0172]$$

The data returned are in the form of a real and a complex array. Therefore, to plot the amplitude and phase response, we need the modulus and argument of each complex number.

```
> freqdata:=convert(zip((a, b)->
  convert(a+I*b,polar),x,y),list):
```

Here we form the data into triplets: [*modulus, argument, ordinate*].

```
> freqpts:=zip((a, b)->[ op(a), b],
  freqdata, [ $0..15] ):
```

THE FFT This plots the amplitude and the phase response on a single graph. The amplitude response has two distinct spikes, one at the frequency that we are interested in, say, f_0, and one at the sampling frequency minus f_0. There is a similar wrapping present in the phase response.

```
>  plot({ map(x->[ x[ 3], x[ 1]], freqpts),
   map(x->[ x[ 3], x[ 2]], freqpts)},
   axes=NORMAL, title=`Amplitude and
   Phase`);
```

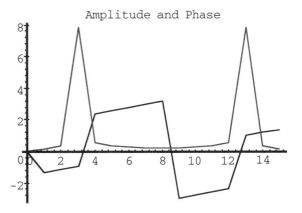

The one-dimensional case is easy to analyze with Maple as the functions already exist; sadly, this is not the case if we wish to analyze a two-dimensional image. We can overcome this shortfall in Maple' ability by combining the existing FFT routine and our Maple programming skills. The following code extends the one-dimensional FFT to two dimensions, at least for the amplitude case. We do this by developing two new routines: a main routine to manipulate the input data and call the existing FFT routines and an iterative routine that applies the built-in FFT routine to each row of the input matrices.

The Main Routine

Procedure name, three formal parameters defined: the size of the arrays as 2^m, the amplitude array, and the zero array.

```
>  `2dFFT`:= proc(m, x, y)
```

Local variable definitions.

```
   local a1, a2, n, nn, ans;
```

Create an empty array to be filled and returned.

```
   ans:=array(1..2^m, 1..2^m, [ ]);
```

Compute the FFT across the rows.

```
   a1:=do_FFT(m, x, y);
```

Compute the FFT across the columns.

```
a2:=do_FFT(m,linalg[ transpose] (x), linalg[ transpose] (y));
a2:=linalg[ transpose] (a2);
```

Calculate the resultant amplitude from the individual arrays.

```
for n to 2^m do
  for nn to 2^m do
      ans[ n, nn] :=sqrt(a1[ n, nn] ^2 + a2[ n, nn] ^2);
  od;
od;
```

Return the answer.

```
  ans;
end:
```

The Iterative Routine

Procedure name, three formal parameters defined: the size of the arrays as 2^m, the amplitude array, and the zero array.

```
> do_FFT:=proc(m, x ,y)
```

Local variable definitions.

```
local ans, n, X, Y:
X:=x: Y:=y: ans:=NULL:
```

Initialize the local variables and "load" FFT.

```
readlib(FFT):
```

Compute the FFT for each row.

```
for n to 2^m do
```

Store a row using local variables.

```
  X:=linalg[ row] (x, n):
  Y:=linalg[ row] (y, n):
  FFT(m, X, Y):
```

Calculate the amplitude only. Note the use of `eval` because `ans` is an array.

```
  ans:=eval(ans), zip((x, y)->sqrt(x^2 + y^2), eval(X), eval(Y)):
od:
```

Build the array to be passed out of the routine.

```
  linalg[ stack] (ans);
end:
```

2-D FFT For the data set `pts` defined earlier, we compute the two-dimensional FFT amplitude response using our new function `` `2dFFT` ``.

```
> `2dFFT`(4, pts, imag):
```

This procedure returns a matrix of amplitude points that we plot using `matrixplot`, which is found in the `plots` package.

```
> plots[ matrixplot] (", axes=FRAME,
    title=`Amplitude of FFT`);
```

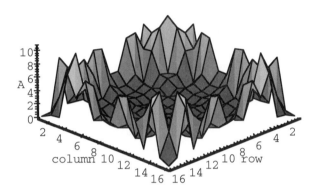

Amplitude of FFT

Example DSP2: Discrete Convolution

A common way of filtering continuous signals is through convolution. We can use a similar technique to filter digitized images: discrete convolution. The process of discrete convolution computes a new image from an original by sweeping a window or kernel over it and combining the kernel elements with the corresponding image elements mathematically; the result of this operation is a new image element. The basic technique is demonstrated in Figure 5.4.

Maple does not come with any discrete convolution functions as standard, so we are going to have to do some programming. The procedures that we will develop in this exercise enable us to accomplish the following operations: convolution, sum the elements of an array, and multiply the corresponding elements of two lists and sum the result.

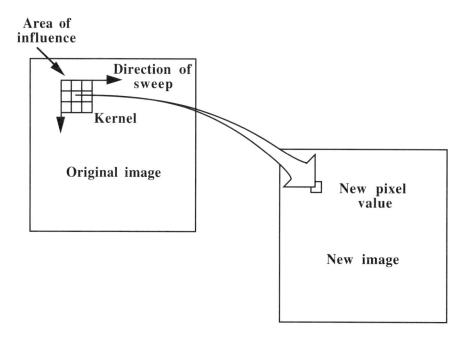

Figure 5.4 Forming a New Image Through Discrete Convolution

The Convolution Routine

Procedure name, two formal parameters defined: the image and the kernel.

```
> convolve:=proc(image::matrix, kern::matrix)
```

Local variable definitions.

```
local i, j, new, klim, d, rown, coln, sm;
```

Sum the elements in the kernel so that the new pixel can be normalized.

```
d:= sum_array(kern);
```

Get the image dimensions and form a new zero matrix.

```
rown:=rowdim(image);
coln:=coldim(image);
new:=matrix(rown, coln, 0);
```

Get the size of the kernel (assumed to be square).

```
klim := rowdim(kern);
```

Sweep kernel over old image to form new one.

```
for i to rown - ceil(klim/2.0) do
  for j to coln-ceil(klim/2.0) do
    sm:=submatrix(image, i..i + klim - floor(klim/2.0),
    j..j + klim - floor(klim/2.0));
    new[ i + 1, j + 1]:=(sm &** kern)/d;
  od;
od;
```

Return the new image.

```
  new;
end:
```

The Summing Function

Function definition with a single formal parameter.

```
> sum_array:=x->convert(map(convert, convert(x, listlist), `+`), `+`):
```

The Custom Operator

Procedure name, two formal parameters defined: list one and list two.

```
> `&**`:=proc(a, b)
```

Local variable definitions.

```
  local A, B, temp;
```

Multiply the corresponding list elements and sum the results.

```
  A:=convert(a, listlist):
  B:=convert(b, listlist):
  temp:=zip((x, y)->zip((X, Y)->X*Y, x, y), A, B);
  add(map(op, temp));
end:
```

IMAGE FILTERING As we will be using functions from the linear algebra and plots packages, we will "load" them into our session.

```
> map(with, [ linalg, plots]):

Warning, new definition for norm
Warning, new definition for trace
```

Using the new custom operator, we multiply the corresponding elements of two lists and sum the result.

```
> [[ 1, 2], [ 3, 4]] &** [[ a, b], [ c, d]];
```

$$a + 2b + 3c + 4d$$

IMAGE FILTERING

Here we test the new `sum_array` function.

```
> sum_array(linalg[matrix]([[a, b],
  [c, d]]));
```

$$a + b + c + d$$

Using the test image produced earlier, we convolve it with an arbitrary kernel.

```
> P:=convolve(pts, matrix(3, 3,
  [[1, 0, -1], [0, 1, 0], [-1, 0, 1]])):
```

By displaying both the original and the convolved images together in a graphics array, we can compare the pre- and post-filtered images easily. The original image is shown at the top.

```
> display3d(array(1..2, 1..1,
  [[matrixplot(pts)], [p]]));
```

Example DSP3: FIR Filters

In this DSP example, we consider how Maple's arbitrary precision arithmetic allows the digital filter designer to investigate the effects of word length on a filter's performance. All digital filters sample their input waveforms and produce a sampled output, *t,* which is commonly filtered to approximate a continuous signal. The amplitude of the output signal at any sampling instance is a weighted sum of previous input and output values; therefore, digital filters contain memory in order that previously sampled values may be used. Both the sampling and memory characteristics of a digital filter can be modeled using Maple.

In this section, we develop a model, in Maple, of a third-order elliptic filter designed by Oppenheim and Schafer (*Digital Signal Processing,* Englewood Cliffs, NJ: Prentice Hall, p.225. Initially we use exact arithmetic to implement the filter model. For comparison, we then use a floating-point arithmetic implementation and reduce the word length in order to determine the effects on the filter's step response.

ELLIPTIC FILTER First, define the general transfer function for a continuous third-order elliptic filter.

```
> TF:=
  a1*(s^2 + a2)/
  ((a3*s + a4)*(s^2 + a5*s + a6));
```

$$TF := \frac{a1(s^2 + a2)}{(a3\ s + a4)(s^2 + a5s + a6)}$$

Then set the parameter values for our particular design.

```
> a1:=623/500: a2:=163/125: a3:=3294/5000:
  a4:=153/625:
  a5:=2521/10000: a6:=4313/10000:
```

Using `unapply`, create a function of s from the transfer function.

```
> H[ a] :=unapply(TF, s):
```

The bilinear transform is defined as a function of z in Maple as follows:

```
> bilinear:=
  z->2*(1 - z^(-1))/(T*(1 + z^(-1)));
```

$$bilinear := z \rightarrow 2\frac{1 - 1/z}{T(1 + 1/z)}$$

Using the bilinear transform, we effectively transform the continuous filter into a discrete one.

```
> H[ z] :=unapply(normal(subs(s=bilinear(z),
  T=1/3, H[ a] (s))), z):
```

Next the filter's transfer function, as a function of the discrete variable z, is obtained.

```
> H[ z] (z);
```

$$H_z := z \rightarrow$$
$$\frac{124600}{9}\ \frac{(z + 1)(4663z^2 - 8674z + 4663)}{(379439z^2 - 711374z + 349187)(583z - 515)}$$

The next stage is to expand and normalize the preceding expression prior to isolating the numerator and denominator.

```
> normal(H[ z] (z), expanded):
> de:=denom("):
> nu:=numer(""):
```

This isolates the denominator and the numerator of the filter transfer function.

```
> de:=expand(de):
> nu:=expand(nu):
```

ELLIPTIC
FILTER

It is normal to represent the transfer function of a digital filter in terms of z, $1/z$, $1/z^2$, and so on. This adheres to the convention that z^0 is the current clock cycle, $1/z$ is the previous cycle, $1/z^2$ is the cycle prior to that, and so on. Using Maple, we transform the numerator and denominator polynomials into lists of terms, and order them so the term in z^0 is first, the term in $1/z$ is the next, and so on.

```
> lde:=convert(de, list);
```

$$lde := [1990916433z^3, -5491279143z^2,$$
$$5129402679z, -1618481745]$$

```
> lnu:=convert(nu, list);
```

$$lnu := [581009800z^3, -499770600z^2,$$
$$-499770600z, 581009800]$$

```
> lc:=op(1, lde);
```

$$lc := 1990916433z^3$$

```
> lde:=map(x->x/lc, lde);
```

$$lde := \left[1, \frac{-610142127}{221212937z}, \frac{569933631}{221212937z^2}, \frac{-179831305}{221212937z^3} \right]$$

To form a list of input and output weightings, we have to extract the coefficients from the lists of terms obtained before. These lists are r and yprime, respectively.

```
> lnu:=map(x->x/lc, lnu):

> r:=map(coeffs, lnu, z):

> yprime:=map(coeffs, lde[2..4], z);
```

$$yprime := \left[\frac{610142127}{221212937}, \frac{569933631}{221212937}, \frac{-179831305}{221212937} \right]$$

A digital filter works by sampling and remembering both its input and its output signals, applying the appropriate weights, and summing the result. The operator `&*+` is designed to do this. Note that if the third parameter is zero, exact arithmetic is used; a nonzero positive integer, on the other hand, will set the number of significant digits used in the computation.

```
> `&*+`:=proc(a, b, n)
    if n=0 then
      convert(zip((x, y)->x*y, a, b), `+`)
    else
      evalf(add(zip((x, y)->x*y, a, b)), n)
    fi;
  end:
```

ELLIPTIC FILTER The lists Y[z] and R[z] contain the filter's initial condition. The output is zero and the initial, $t = 0$, input is unity.

```
> Y[ z] :=[ 0, 0, 0] :
> R[ z] :=[ 1, 0, 0, 0] :
```

Using exact arithmetic, we compute the filter's next output, $t = 1$.

```
> output:=r &*+ (R[ z], 0) -
  yprime &*+ (Y[ z], 0);
```

$$output := \frac{581009800}{1990916433}$$

The output at $t = 1$ is calculated again, but this time using 10 significant figures.

```
> output:=r &*+ (R[ z], 10) -
  yprime &*+ (Y[ z], 10);
```

$$output := ..2918303302$$

The procedure opposite calculates the filter's unit step response. The previous inputs and outputs are stored in the variables oldi and oldo, respectively. The variable temp holds the current output and ans holds the cumulative response.

```
> calc_output:=proc(i, o, t, nn)
  local oldi, oldo, n, ans, temp:
  oldi:=i; oldo:=o;
  ans:=[ 0, 0], [ 1, 0];
  for n from 0 to t - 1 do
    temp:=r &*+ (oldo, nn) -
    yprime &*+ (oldi, nn):
    ans:=ans, [ n, temp], [ n + 1, temp];
    oldi:=[ 1, op(oldi[ 1..nops(oldi) - 1])];
    oldo:=[ temp, op(oldo[ 2..nops(oldo)])];
  od;
  [ ans];
  end:
```

This calculates the step response of the filter using exact arithmetic and plots it.

```
> plot(calc_output(R[ z], Y[ z], 10, 0),
  title=`Filter Step Response`);
```

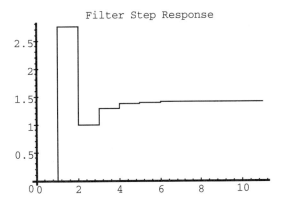

ELLIPTIC FILTER Here we create a table of plot titles. The table index corresponds to the number of significant digits used.

```
> t[ 0] :=`Exact`:
> t[ 1] :=`1 Significant digit`:
> t[ 2] :=`2 Significant digits`:
> t[ 4] :=`4 Significant digits`:
```

This next command generates a sequence of plots, one for each model specified before.

```
> pics:=seq(plot(calc_output(R[ z] , Y[ z] ,
    10, q), title=t[ q] ), q=[ 0, 1, 2, 4] ):
```

The resulting plots are displayed in a graphics array, allowing easy comparison of the calculated step responses.

```
> display(array([ [ pics[ 1..2]] ,
    [ pics[ 3..4]] ] );
```

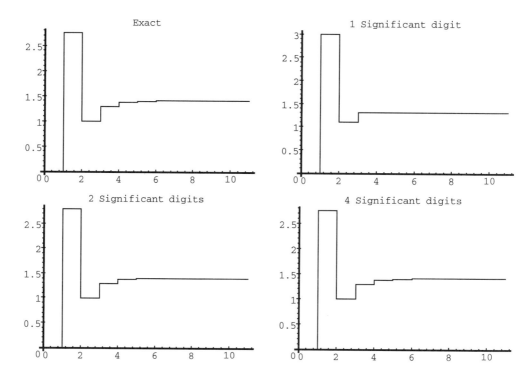

Example DSP4: The Wavelet Transform

In this example, we use Maple to develop a simple implementation of the discrete *Daubechies'* four-coefficient wavelet transform for the analysis of discontinuous waveforms in the same way that the *Laplace* and *Fourier* transforms are used to analyze continuous ones.

The discrete wavelet transform of a signal is a list of wavelet coefficients generated from 2^n samples of the original signal, where n is a positive integer. There will be 2^n wavelet coefficients produced, which can be considered as a list of approximation and detail coefficients. The first coefficient pair, sometimes called the mother wavelet, can be thought of as an excessively smooth version of the input data; the next two coefficients give the first detail information; the following four the next level of detail information; and so on. As we step through the coefficients, the scale at which the detail information applies successively decreases.

All of the transformation matrices used to calculate *Daubechies'* wavelet transform are built up using the same four basic coefficients: $\sqrt{2}(1 + \sqrt{3})/8$, $\sqrt{2}(3 + \sqrt{3})/8$, $\sqrt{2}(1 - \sqrt{3})/8$ and $\sqrt{2}(3 - \sqrt{3})/8$. The transformation matrices are developed in what follows.

THE BASIC ELEMENTS

As we make a great deal of use of Maple's linear algebra routines, we "load" the `linalg` package.

```
> with(linalg):
```

```
Warning, new definition for norm
Warning, new definition for trace
```

For clarity, we set the number of digits used and displayed to 4.

```
> Digits:=4:
```

With reference to the four basic coefficients given, we can see that there is a constant term common to all of them, namely, $\sqrt{2}/8$.

```
> const:=1/(4*sqrt(2));
```

$$const := \frac{\sqrt{2}}{8}$$

A matrix of the four *Daubechies* coefficients are defined in Maple as shown. The constant is applied to each term by using `scalarmul`.

```
> D_coeffs:=scalarmul(matrix([[ 1 + sqrt(3),
  3 + sqrt(3), 3 - sqrt(3),
  1 - sqrt(3)]]), const);
```

$$D\_coeffs :=$$
$$\left[\frac{\sqrt{2}\ (1 + \sqrt{3})}{8}, \frac{\sqrt{2}\ (3 + \sqrt{3})}{8}, \frac{\sqrt{2}\ (3 - \sqrt{3})}{8}, \frac{\sqrt{2}\ (1 - \sqrt{3})}{8} \right]$$

Using the basic coefficients, we construct a sequence of transformation matrices whose size increases as a power of 2, starting at 4, up to the size of the sample data set. For example, if we have 16 sample points, then we would generate transformation matrices of size 4 by 4, 8 by 8, and 16 by 16. The first two rows in the first transformation matrix, a 4 by 4 matrix, are defined manually. The next two are formed from the first by performing two shift-right-logical operations on the basic matrix. That is, the elements in the matrix are shifted to the right twice and the extreme rightmost elements being prepended to the left-hand side each time.

THE FIRST TRANSFORM MATRIX Manually, we define the first two rows of the first transformation matrix using the four basic coefficients.

```
> first:=matrix([[ df[ 1,  1], df[ 1,  2],
  df[ 1,  3], df[ 1,  4]],[ df[ 1,  4],
  -df[ 1,  3], df[ 1,  2], -df[ 1,  1]]]);
```

$$first := \begin{bmatrix} df_{1,1} & df_{1,2} & df_{1,3} & df_{1,4} \\ df_{1,4} & -df_{1,3} & df_{1,2} & -df_{1,1} \end{bmatrix}$$

Rows 3 and 4 are formed from the first two by shifting them using the `submatrix` and `augment` commands.

```
> second:=augment(submatrix(first, 1..2,
  coldim(first) - 1..coldim(first)),
  submatrix(first, 1..2, 1..coldim(first)
  - 2));
```

$$second := \begin{bmatrix} df_{1,3} & df_{1,4} & df_{1,1} & df_{1,2} \\ df_{1,2} & -df_{1,1} & df_{1,4} & -df_{1,3} \end{bmatrix}$$

The first transformation matrix is formed by stacking matrices **first** and **second** using the `stack` command.

```
> TM4:=stack(first, second);
```

$$TM4 := \begin{bmatrix} df_{1,1} & df_{1,2} & df_{1,3} & df_{1,4} \\ df_{1,4} & -df_{1,3} & df_{1,2} & -df_{1,1} \\ df_{1,3} & df_{1,4} & df_{1,1} & df_{1,2} \\ df_{1,2} & -df_{1,1} & df_{1,4} & -df_{1,3} \end{bmatrix}$$

The first transformation matrix, **TM4**, is fabricated by shifting the columns of matrix **first** left twice to form a second matrix; the two matrices are then stacked together. By repeating this pattern, the development of the larger transformation matrices is easy.

HIGHER-ORDER MATRICES As the matrix **first** only has four columns and the next transformation matrix is 8 by 8 it must be zero-padded.

```
> t0:=augment(first, matrix([[ 0$4],
  [ 0$4]])):
```

The shift operation must be a total of four times with the results of one shift operation being stored and used during the next shift operation. This is achieved with a for loop.

```
> for n to 3 do
    t.n:=augment(submatrix(t.(n - 1), 1..2,
    coldim(t0) - 1..coldim(t0)),
    submatrix(t.(n - 1), 1..2,
    1..coldim(t0) - 2));
  od:
```

HIGHER-ORDER MATRICES

The previous operation returns a sequence of shifted matrices assigned to the variables $t0$, $t1$, $t2$, and $t3$. These matrices are stacked together to form the transformation matrix **TM8**.

```
> TM8:=stack('t.nn'$nn=0..n - 1);
```

$$TM8 :=$$

$$
\begin{bmatrix}
df_{1,1} & df_{1,2} & df_{1,3} & df_{1,4} & 0 & 0 & 0 & 0 \\
df_{1,4} & -df_{1,3} & df_{1,2} & -df_{1,1} & 0 & 0 & 0 & 0 \\
0 & 0 & df_{1,1} & df_{1,2} & df_{1,3} & df_{1,4} & 0 & 0 \\
0 & 0 & df_{1,4} & -df_{1,3} & df_{1,2} & -df_{1,1} & 0 & 0 \\
0 & 0 & 0 & 0 & df_{1,1} & df_{1,2} & df_{1,3} & df_{1,4} \\
0 & 0 & 0 & 0 & df_{1,4} & -df_{1,3} & df_{1,2} & -df_{1,1} \\
df_{1,3} & df_{1,4} & 0 & 0 & 0 & 0 & df_{1,1} & df_{1,2} \\
df_{1,2} & -df_{1,1} & 0 & 0 & 0 & 0 & df_{1,4} & -df_{1,3}
\end{bmatrix}
$$

Using the procedure `make_TM`, developed from the previous code and shown in Appendix B, we construct the final transformation matrix for this particular example, **TM16** (assuming a data set containing 16 data points).

```
> TM16:=make_TM(first, 16):
```

The transformation matrices have an interesting characteristic: pre-multiplying by their transpose will produce an identity matrix.

```
> TMI:=evalm(transpose(TM4) &* TM4);
```

$$
TMI := \begin{bmatrix}
\%1 & 0 & \%2 & 0 \\
\%1 & 0 & \%2 & 0 \\
\%2 & 0 & \%1 & 0 \\
0 & \%2 & 0 & \%1
\end{bmatrix}
$$

$$\%1 := df_{1,1}^{2} + df_{1,4}^{2} + df_{1,3}^{2} + df_{1,2}^{2}$$
$$\%2 := 2\, df_{1,1}\, df_{1,3} + 2\, df_{1,4}\, df_{1,2}$$

The preceding matrix is symbolic in the variables $df_{11} .. df_{14}$, which represent the four *Daubechies* coefficients. By using `zip` as shown, a list of substitution equations are formed that can be used with the symbolic matrixes.

```
> coeff_eqn:=zip((x, y)->x=y, df[ 1, 1] ,
  df[ 1, 2] , df[ 1, 3] , df[ 1, 4] ],
  convert(convert(D_coeffs, vector),
  list)):
```

HIGHER-ORDER MATRICES   Substituting for the coefficients $df_{11} .. df_{14}$ in the symbolic matrix, we get the expected identity matrix.

```
> map((x, y)->simplify(subs(y, x)), TMI,
  coeff_eqn);
```

$$\begin{bmatrix} 1 & 0 & 0 & 0 \\ 0 & 1 & 0 & 0 \\ 0 & 0 & 1 & 0 \\ 0 & 0 & 0 & 1 \end{bmatrix}$$

Here we substitute for the symbolic variables in all of the transformation matrices, thus creating numeric transformation matrices.

```
> TM4n:=evalf(map((x, y)->subs(y, x), TM4,
  coeff_eqn));
```

$$TM4n := \begin{bmatrix} .4829 & .8364 & .2241 & -.1294 \\ -.1294 & -.2241 & .8364 & -.4829 \\ .2241 & -.1294 & .4829 & .8364 \\ .8364 & -.4829 & -.1294 & -.2241 \end{bmatrix}$$

```
> TM8n:=evalf(map((x, y)->subs(y, x), TM8,
  coeff_eqn), 4):
> TM16n:=evalf(map((x, y)->subs(y, x),
  TM16, coeff_eqn), 4):
```

A signal's discrete wavelet transform is generated by sampling the signal and then successively applying the transformation matrices to the sampled data points, as shown in what follows.

FORWARD TRANSFORM   First, we define a discontinuous signal using the piecewise function.

```
> f:=t->simplify(evalf(piecewise(t>=0.5 and
  t<=2*Pi-0.5,1/4*(1-cos(t))^2+0.2))):
```

The discontinuous signal is then sampled, in this case, 16 times, and the values are stored in a matrix. The sampled data are used to compute the discrete Wavelet Transform.

```
> sample:=
  matrix([[ seq(f(2*Pi*t/15), t=0..15)]]);
```

$sample := [0, 0, .2274, .3194, .5053, .7625, 1.018, 1.178,$
$1.178, 1.018, .7625, .5053, .3194, .2274, 0, 0]$

The wavelets coefficients and their corresponding smoothed data are computed starting at the finest level and finishing with the mother wavelet.

```
> T16:=evalm(TM16n &* transpose(sample)):
  transpose(");
```

$[.00963, .0360, .3914 , -.0466, .9576, .0463, 1.609,$
$.0980, 1.526, .0133, .8330, -.0546, .3444, -.09229, 0, 0]$

FORWARD TRANSFORM The odd entries of **T16** are a smoothed version of the original data. Weighted average smoothing has been used.

```
> sd16:=[ seq(T16[ (2*n - 1), 1], n=1..8)];
```

$$sd16 :=$$
$$[.00963, .3914, .9576, 1.609, 1.526, .8330, .3444, 0]$$

The even entries of **T16** are the wavelet coefficients at this level.

```
> w16:=[ seq(T16[ 2*n, 1], n=1..8)];
```

$$w16 :=$$
$$[.0360, -.0466, .0463, .0980, .0133, -.0546, -.09229, 0]$$

Using the smoothed data **sd16** and the next transformation matrix **T8,** we generate the next set of wavelet coefficients and smoothed data.

```
> T8:=
  evalm(TM8n &* transpose(matrix([ sd16]))):
  transpose(");
```

$$[.3385, -.0651, 2.042, .3892, 1.511, -.0961, .1178, -.2255]$$

As before, we separate the smoothed data and the coefficients for this level.

```
> sd8:=[ seq(T8[ (2*n - 1), 1], n=1..4)];
```

$$sd8 := [.3385, 2.042, 1.511, .1178]$$

```
> w8:=[ seq(T8[ 2*n, 1], n=1..4)];
```

$$w8 := [-.0651, .3892, -.0961, -.2255]$$

Once again we use the smoothed data, in this case, **sd8**, to calculate the coefficients and data at the next level.

```
> T4:=
  evalm(TM4n &* transpose(matrix([ sd8]))):
  transpose(");
```

$$[2.196, .7057, .6399, -.9249]$$

The penultimate step is to separate the wavelet coefficients and the data at this level resulting in the lists **w4** and **sd4,** respectively.

```
> sd4:=[ seq(T4[ (2*n - 1), 1], n=1..2)];
```

$$sd4 := [2.196, .6399]$$

```
> w4:=[ seq(T4[ 2*n, 1], n=1..2)];
```

$$w4 := [.7057, -.9249]$$

FORWARD TRANSFORM We have now used each of the transformation matrices once we have all of the data necessary to produce the Wavelet Transform. The Wavelet Transform is formed by stacking the approximation data, **sd4**, and the sets of coefficients, **w4**, **w8**, and **w16**, together.

```
> FT:=
    matrix([ map(op, [ sd4, w4, w8, w16])]);
```

$FT := [2.196, .6399, .7057, -.9249, -.0651, .3892, -.0961, -.2255, .0360, -.0466, .0463, .0980, .0133, -.0546, -.09229, 0]$

The inverse transform is computed by reversing the procedure leading to the forward transform, meaning that we work from the coarsest level of coefficients and smoothed data to the finest, premultiplying the data by the inverse, which in this case is the transpose, of the relevant transformation matrix. Before we compute the inverse transform from the forward data obtained before we reset two of the transform coefficients, which has the effect of filtering the original discontinuous test signal.

INVERSE TRANSFORM First, filter the original signal by resetting coefficients 6 and 7 of the forward transform.

```
> FT[ 1,6] :=0:FT[ 1, 7] :=0: eval(FT);
```

$FT := [2.196, .6399, .7057, -.9249, -.0651, 0, 0, -.2255, .0360, -.0466, .0463, .0980, .0133, -.0546, -.09229, 0]$

The first step in calculating the inverse transform is to isolate and reorder the first four coefficients in the forward transform and then premultiply by the inverse (the transpose) of the transform matrix **TM4n**.

```
> itf4:=transpose(evalm(transpose(TM4n) &*
    transpose(matrix([[ FT[ 1,1], FT[ 1,3],
    FT[ 1,2], FT[ 1,4]]]))));
```

$itf4 := [.3384\ 2.043\ 1.511\ .1175]$

This produces the level-2 smoothed data, which is combined with the level-2 coefficients using `submatrix` and `zip`, as shown. The resulting data are assigned to a temporary variable because it is used in the calculation of the next level of data.

```
> Coeffs4:=submatrix(FT, 1..1, 5..8);
```

$Coeffs4 := [-.0651\ 0\ 0\ -.2255]$

```
> temp:=map(op,zip((x, y)->[ x, y],
    convert(convert(itf4, vector), list),
    convert(convert(Coeffs4, vector),
    list)));
```

$temp := [.3384, -.0651, 2.043, 0, 1.511, 0, .1175, -.2255]$

INVERSE TRANSFORM The preceding process, resulting in level-2 data, is repeated using the level-2 data stored in `temp` and the inverse of the next transformation matrix **TM8n**.

```
> itf8:=transpose(evalm(transpose(TM8n) &*
  transpose(matrix([ convert(temp,
  list)])))));
```

$$itf8 := [.0095, .3913, 1.008, 1.697, 1.188, .9996, .4245, -.04669]$$

The data **itf8** is combined with the next level coefficients using `submatrix` and `zip`, as before. Again the result is stored for future use in the variable `temp`.

```
> Coeffs8:=submatrix(FT, 1..1, 9..16);
```

$$Coeffs8 := [.0360, -.0466, .0463, .0980, .0133, -.0546, -.09229, 0]$$

```
> temp:=map(op, zip((x, y)->[ x, y],
  convert(convert(itf8, vector),list),
  convert(convert(Coeffs8, vector),list)));
```

$$temp := [.0095, .0360, .3913, -.0466, 1.008, .0463, 1.697, .0980, 1.188, .0133, .9996, -.0546, .4245, -.09229, -.04669, 0]$$

The final step is to premultiply the data stored in `temp` by the inverse of the final transformation matrix **TM16n,** which results in a sampled version of the filtered signal.

```
> itf16:=transpose(evalm(transpose(TM16n)
  &* transpose(matrix([ temp])))));
```

$$itf16 := [-.01053, -.005920, .2272, .3191, .5295, .8046, 1.071, 1.244, 1.034, .7237, .7671, .6882, .3952, .2729, -.00461, -.04941]$$

INVERSE TRANSFORM This displays the original and the filtered signal on the same plot for comparison. The original signal is the heavier line.

```
> plots[ display] ({ plot([ seq([ (n - 1)*2*Pi/15,
  itf16[ 1, n]], n=1..16)]),
  plot([ seq([ (n - 1)*2*Pi/15,
  f(2*Pi*(n - 1)/15)], n=1..16)],
  thickness=2)}, color=BLACK,
  title=`Original and Filtered`,
  labels=[ `t`, ``]);
```

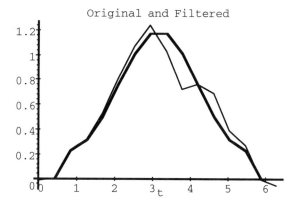

The three Maple processes, generating the transformation matrices, the forward transformation, and the inverse transformation, outlined in the previous section have been encapsulated and enhanced in the three procedures, Make_TM, WaveletTF, and InvWaveletTF, respectively. It should be noted that the procedure Make_TM is only called by the other two, so that the transformation matrices can be constructed automatically. These procedures are listed in Appendix B and also can be found on Prentice Hall's ftp and world wide web sites.

USING THE PROCEDURES In the first example, we obtain the discrete Wavelet Transform for the function $f(t) = \sin t$ for $0 \leq t \leq 2\pi$ and $f(t) = 0$ elsewhere. Here we sample the function.

```
> pts:=[ evalf(seq(sin(2*Pi*n/15), n=0..15),
  4)];
```

$pts := [0, .4067, .7433, .9510, .9945, .8660, .5878, .2080,$
$-.2080, -.5878, -.8660, -.9945, -.9510, -.7433, -.4067, 0]$

Here we form a matrix of the four basic coefficients arranged to give the first two rows of the first transformation matrix. The coefficients are defined in coeff_eqn and the order is set in **first**, both defined earlier.

```
> mat:=subs(coeff_eqn, eval(first));
```

$$mat := \begin{bmatrix} .4829 & .8364 & .2241 & -.1294 \\ -.1294 & -.2241 & .8364 & -.4829 \end{bmatrix}$$

USING THE PROCEDURES The procedure `WaveletTF` takes a matrix of the basic coefficients and matrix of the signal samples and returns a list of the transform coefficients.

```
> WaveletTF(mat, matrix([ pts] ));
```

$$[1.338, -1.338, -1.435, 1.126, .5275, -.1684, -.4687,$$
$$-.08250, .0714, .1043, .0684, -.0129, -.0855, -.1015,$$
$$-.0505, -.1438]$$

It is possible to view the individual wavelets. We do this by first creating a list of data with all its entries set to zero except the wavelet that we wish to see, whose entry is set to 1, in this case wavelet number 3.

```
> data:=[ 0, 0, 1, 0$61] :
```

The corresponding wavelet is produced by obtaining the inverse transform of this data. Here we use the procedure `InvWaveletTF` to do this. The procedure `InvWaveletTF` takes a matrix of the basic coefficients and matrix of the transform coefficients and returns a list of the signal samples. Here we plot the third-level wavelet.

```
> inv_data:=InvWaveletTF(mat,
  matrix([ data] )):
> plot(seq([ n, inv_data[ 1, n]], n=1..64,
  title=`Third-Level Wavelet`);
```

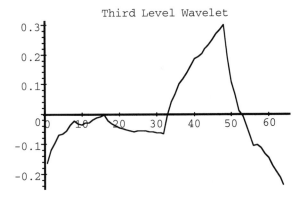

Engineering

In this, the last section of examples, we establish how Maple can help us tackle problems in electrical engineering, mechanical engineering, and thermodynamics. Yet again Maple's ability to manipulate unknowns and arrays easily will be used to great advantage.

Example E1: Circuit Analysis

A common problem encountered in electrical engineering is the analysis of circuits. An electric/electronic circuit can contain all or some of the following basic components: power sources, linear elements, nonlinear elements, passive elements, active elements, and signal sources. Once the appropriate models for the components have been developed, the circuit can be analyzed in various ways. One common technique often applied is nodal analysis. In this example, we demonstrate how Maple can help us apply this technique. The circuit we will be analyzing is shown in Figure 5.5.

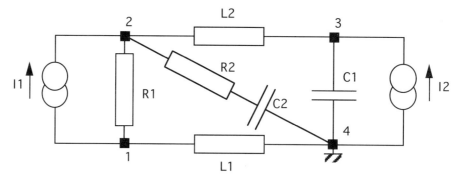

Figure 5.5 The Test Circuit

NODE ANALYSIS As we will use functions found in the linear algebra package, we "load" it using `with`.

```
> with(linalg):
Warning, new definition for norm
Warning, new definition for trace
```

Using functions, we define the impedance of a capacitor and an inductor in terms of the angular frequency ω.

```
> cap:=(c, omega)->1/(I*omega*c):
> ind:=(l, omega)->I*omega*l:
```

By applying Kirchoff's current law, we define the set of node equations for the test circuit as follows.

```
> n1:=v1/l1 + (v1 - v2)/r1 = -i1:
  n2:=v2/(r2 + c2) + (-v1 + v2)/r1 +
  (-v3 + v2)/l2=i1:
  n3:=(v3 - v2)/l2 + v3/c1=i2:
```

NODE ANALYSIS A popular way of representing the node equations is as a matrix. Here we use `genmatrix` to perform the transformation. By using the optional argument `flag`, we force Maple to form the augmented matrix automatically.

```
> mat :=
  genmatrix({ n1, n2, n3}, [ v1, v2, v3], flag);
```
mat :=

$$
\begin{bmatrix}
1/l1 + 1/r1 & -1/r1 & 0 & -i1 \\
-1/r1 & 1/r1 + 1/l2 + 1/(r2 + c2) & -1/l2 & i1 \\
0 & -1/i2 & 1/l2 + 1/c1 & l2
\end{bmatrix}
$$

This matrix is then manipulated to form the matrix equation **ax = b**. This is then solved using `linsolve`.

```
> ans:=linsolve(submatrix(mat,
  1..rowdim(mat), 1..coldim(mat)-1),
  submatrix(mat, 1..rowdim(mat),
  coldim(mat)..coldim(mat))):
```

Here the expression describing the voltage at node 1 is returned. The solutions obtained are all in terms of symbolic quantities that represent the circuit elements.

```
> ans[ 1, 1];
```

$$
-(-c1r2i2 - c1c2i2 + r2i1r1 + i1r1l2 + c2i1r1 + i1r1c1)l1/
$$
$$
(r2l1 + c1r1 + r1l2 + l2l1 + c2l1 + r2c1 + l2r2 + r1c2 +
$$
$$
c1l1 + c2c1 + l2c2 + r1r2)
$$

Here we substitute the component values into the symbolic solutions.

```
> subs(r1=5, r2=10, l1=ind(.5,omega),
  l2=ind(.5,omega), c1=cap(10^(-7), omega),
  c2=cap(10^(-7), omega), i1=exp(-t),
  i2=cos(omega*t), omega=1, eval(ans)):
```

Again, we return the expression for voltage at the first node.

```
> "[ 1, 1];
```

$$
(.1000000238 \times 10^{-19} + .5000000750 \times 10^{-14}\, I)
$$
$$
(100000000\, I \cos(t) + 100000000000000 \cos(t) + 50\, e^{-t}
$$
$$
- .999999975 \times 10^{8}\, I\, e^{-t})
$$

This converts the array of results into a single list.

```
> list_ans:=map(op, convert("", listlist)):
```

Here we extract the solution for the voltage v_3 and convert it into a function.

```
> f:=unapply(list_ans[ 3], t);
```

$$
f := t \rightarrow (.2000000475 \times 10^{-12} + .1000000150 \times 10^{-6}\, I)
$$
$$
(-.499999875 \times 10^{8}\, I \cos(t) + .1000004975 \times 10^{8} \cos(t)
$$
$$
- 50000000\, I\, e^{-t} + 50\, e^{-t})
$$

NODE ANALYSIS This plots the real component of the voltage v_3 against its imaginary one using `complexplot`.

```
> plots[ complexplot] (f(t), t=0..10,
    title=`Complex plot of f(t)`,
    labels=[ `Re`, `Im`]);
```

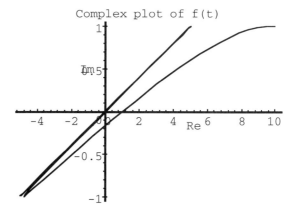

This plots $|f(t)|$.

```
> plot(abs(f(t)), t=0..10, title=`|f(t)|`);
```

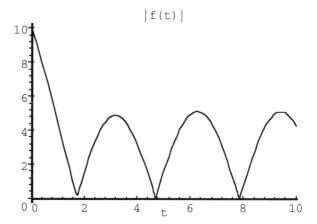

Example E2: A Continuously Distributed Force

In our second example, we use Maple to calculate the resultant force and its effective point of action for a continuously distributed load. The load is distributed as $\sin^2 x$ along a horizontal beam of length b. The resultant force is calculated by taking the integral of the force function over the limit $x = 0..b$ and the effective point of action of the force is then given by $\int_0^b x f(x)\, dx / \int_0^b f(x)\, dx$, where $f(x)$ is the force distribution along the beam.

RESULTANT FORCES By using Maple's `alias` facility, we are able to give the `int` function a more meaningful name in the context of the problem.

```
> alias(resultant=int);
```

$$I, resultant$$

The force distribution, as a function, is defined as shown.

```
> f:=x->sin(x)^2;
```

$$f := x \rightarrow \sin(x)^2$$

The resultant force acting on the beam is calculated using the aliased function as follows.

```
> resultant(f(t), t=0..b);
```

$$\frac{-\cos(b)\,\sin(b) + b}{2}$$

Here we define a function that returns the effective point of action of the resultant force. We use the type `uneval` to hold evaluation on the argument `fn` so that we are able to extract the variable of integration and use it, thus making the function more general.

```
> x[r]:=(fn::uneval, r)->
  int(op(fn)*eval(fn), r)/
  resultant(eval(fn), r):
```

Using the function defined before we calculate the effective point of action of the resultant force on the beam.

```
> x[r](f(t), t=0..b);
```

$$\frac{-1/2\, b \cos(b)\, \sin(b) + 1/4\, b^2 + 1/4\, \sin(b)^2}{-1/2\, \cos(b)\, \sin(b) + 1/2\, b}$$

Example E3: Finite Elements

In the third example, we obtain the temperature distribution across a plate using finite-element techniques. The boundary conditions are as follows: the lower side is at zero (reference), the left-hand side has a $sin^2 x$ temperature distribution, and the top and right-hand sides both have a $1 - e^{-y\tau}$ temperature distribution. The plate has unit sides with 10 nodes on each side.

The solution to this example has three distinct parts: initialization, building the mesh equations, and solving the mesh equations. When building the mesh, we make extensive use of Maple's array indexing function to automate the production of the mesh.

HEAT TRANSFER These definitions define the mesh parameters for the nodes labeled 0 to 9.

```
> nodesi:=10:
> nodesj:=10:
> Deltai:=1/(nodesi - 1):
> Deltaj:=1/(nodesj - 1):
```

This procedure constructs the finite-element mesh. The procedure takes the node number and returns the corresponding node equation. The number of nodes in the mesh is set globally. If the node is on the boundary, the appropriate value is returned; if not, the node name (an unknown value) is returned.

```
> u := proc(i, j)
    global nodesi, nodesj
    if j=0 then
    elif i=0 the
      evalf(100*sin(Pi*j/(nodesj - 1))^2)
    elif j=(nodesj - 1) then
      evalf(200*(1 - exp(-i/(nodesi - 1))))
    elif i=(nodesi - 1) then
      evalf(200*(1 - exp(-j/(nodesj - 1))))
    else U[i, j]
    fi
  end:
```

This procedure returns a material-dependent value for every node in the mesh. The internode spacing is set globally.

```
> g:=proc(i, j)
    global Deltai, Deltaj;
    local temp;
    temp:=i*Deltai*j*Deltaj;
    1000*exp(evalf(-4*Pi^2*temp))/275
  end:
```

The temperature at any node in the mesh is a function of the surrounding nodes' temperatures. This procedure returns the equation describing each node's value.

```
> node:= proc(i, j)
    global Deltai, Deltaj;
    (u(i + 1, j) - 2*u(i, j) + u(i - 1,
    j))/Deltai^2 + (u(i, j+1) - 2*u(i, j)
    + u(i, j-1))/Deltaj^2 + g(i, j) = 0
  end:
```

HEAT TRANSFER This defines the first index function that returns the node equation for the $(i, j)^{\text{th}}$ node.

```
> `index/make_nodes`:=proc(indices)
    node(op(indices)) end:
```

Using the preceding index function, we automatically create an array of the mesh equations.

```
> Plate:=array(make_nodes, 1..8, 1..8);
```

$$Plate := array(make\_nodes, 1..8, 1..8, [])$$

By accessing the preceding array, we can look at a single node equation. Nodes without a value are represented by unknowns of the form $U_{[i,\,j]}$.

```
> Plate[ 2, 2];
```

$$81\ U_{[3,\,2]} - 324\ U_{[2,\,2]} + 81\ U_{[1,\,2]} + 81\ U_{[2,\,3]} + 81\ U_{[2,\,1]}$$
$$+ .5175923552 = 0$$

The array of node equations needs to be converted into a set of equations before we can proceed.

```
> convert(map(op, convert(Plate,
    listlist)), set):
```

The set of node equations is interrogated to determine the unknowns. The unknowns are returned as a set.

```
> unknowns:=indets(");
```

$$unknowns := \{U_{[1,\,5]},\ U_{[3,\,1]},\ U_{[4,\,6]},\ U_{[4,\,7]},\ U_{[4,\,8]},$$
$$U_{[5,\,5]},\ U_{[5,\,6]},\ U_{[5,\,7]},\ U_{[5,\,8]},\ U_{[6,\,1]},\ U_{[3,\,2]},\ U_{[2,\,2]},$$
$$U_{[1,\,2]},\ U_{[2,\,3]},\ U_{[2,\,1]},\ U_{[4,\,4]},\ U_{[3,\,5]},\ U_{[5,\,1]},\ U_{[5,\,2]},$$
$$U_{[5,\,3]},\ U_{[5,\,4]},\ U_{[4,\,5]},\ U_{[3,\,4]},\ U_{[2,\,5]},\ U_{[4,\,1]},\ U_{[4,\,2]},$$
$$U_{[4,\,3]},\ U_{[3,\,3]},\ U_{[1,\,1]},\ U_{[1,\,3]},\ U_{[1,\,4]},\ U_{[2,\,4]},\ U_{[2,\,7]},$$
$$U_{[1,\,8]},\ U_{[2,\,8]},\ U_{[1,\,6]},\ U_{[2,\,6]},\ U_{[1,\,7]},\ U_{[6,\,2]},\ U_{[6,\,3]},$$
$$U_{[6,\,4]},\ U_{[6,\,5]},\ U_{[6,\,6]},\ U_{[6,\,7]},\ U_{[6,\,8]},\ U_{[7,\,1]},\ U_{[7,\,2]},$$
$$U_{[7,\,3]},\ U_{[7,\,4]},\ U_{[7,\,5]},\ U_{[7,\,6]},\ U_{[7,\,7]},\ U_{[7,\,8]},\ U_{[8,\,1]},$$
$$U_{[8,\,2]},\ U_{[8,\,3]},\ U_{[8,\,4]},\ U_{[8,\,5]},\ U_{[8,\,6]},\ U_{[8,\,7]},\ U_{[8,\,8]},$$
$$U_{[3,\,6]},\ U_{[3,\,7]},\ U_{[3,\,8]}\ \}$$

Using **solve**, we solve the mesh equations for the unknowns

```
> sols := solve("", unknowns):
```

HEAT TRANSFER This second indexing function automatically creates an array of nodes. If the node is on a boundary, the boundary value is returned; otherwise, the node name is returned.

```
> `index/make_plate`:=proc(indices)
    u(op(indices))
  end:
```

Using the second indexing function, we automatically generate the generic node array.

```
> array(make_plate, 0..9, 0..9):
```

This substitutes the node values calculated before into the generic node array and plots the resultant temperature distribution.

```
> plots[matrixplot](subs(sols,
  convert(", listlist)),
  title=`Heat distribution`,
  orientation=[0, 0], style=PATCHCONTOUR);
```

Heat distribution

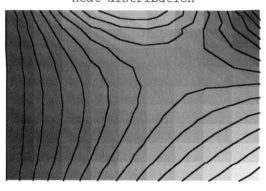

MORE HELP

`?indexfunction`

Returns the help page for making index functions for tables and arrays.

`linalg[indexfunc]`

This function will return the indexing function used in the creation of an array.
Example:
`linalg[indexfunc](array);`

NEW **FUNCTIONS** **AT A GLANCE**	`about( name )`	Find if any assumptions have been made about the symbol `name`.

`additionally( name, prop )` Make the additional assumption `prop` about the symbol `name`.

`alias( alias`$_1$`=name`$_1$`, alias`$_2$`=name`$_2$`, .., alias`$_n$`=name`$_n$
Alias the names `alias`$_i$ to the names `name`$_i$.

`arctan( y, x )` Calculate the arctangent $\tan^{-1}(y/x)$.

`assume( name, prop )` Make the assumption `prop` about the symbol `name`.

`augment( mat`$_1$`, mat`$_2$`, ..,mat`$_n$` )`
Join the matrices **mat**$_i$ together horizontally.

`AXESTICKS( [ ticks`$_x$`], [ ticks`$_y$`], [ ticks`$_z$`] )`
The axes ticks data structure used in plot structures.

`beta` The beta statistical distribution.

`blackscholes( price`$_1$`, t, price`$_2$`, sd, percent )`
Calculate the present value of a call option with an exercise price `price`$_1$ and a current price `price`$_2$ at time `t` to exercise date and having a standard deviation `sd` and a continuously compounded risk-free rate of interest of `percent`. The hedge ratio and option delta are also calculated.

`cdf` The cumulative density function.

`chisquare` The χ^2 test statistical distribution.

`denom( poly )` Return the denominator of `poly`.

`fit[ leastsquare[ vars, eqn, params]] ( data )`
`fit[ leastsquare[ vars, params]] ( data )`
`fit[ leastsquare[ vars]] ( data )`
Found in the statistics package, this computes the linear least-squares fit to `data` in `vars`. There is one list in `data` for every unknown in `vars`. If present, `Eqn` gives the fit equation. The optional argument `params` is used to specify symbolic quantities that are not variables.

NEW FUNCTIONS AT A GLANCE	`fratio`	The f ratio statistical distribution.
	`gamma`	The gamma statistical distribution.
	`inverse( mat )`	Found in the linear algebra package, this computes the inverse of the matrix `mat`.
	`isolate( eqn, term )`	This readlib-defined function is used to isolate `term` in `eqn`. Unlike `solve`, an equation of the form `term=…` is returned
	`listlist`	Keyword used by convert.
	`loglogplot( expr, range, opts)`	Found in the `plots` package, this plots `expr` over `range` on logarithmic axes. The optional arguments are the same as `plot`.
	`mean( data )`	Returns the mean of the statistical data.
	`mul( expr, range )`	Forms a sequence of `expr` given by `range` and returns its product.
	`normald`	The normal statistical distribution.
	`numer( poly )`	Returns the numerator of poly.
	`pdf`	The probability density function.
	`piecewise( eqn`$_1$`, eqn`$_2$`, .., eqn`$_n$`, default )`	Define a piecewise function using the Boolean relations `eqn`$_i$. The optional parameter `default` defines the function's value for all portions not defined by `eqn`$_i$.
	`random`	The statistics subpackage `random` for the production of random numbers.
	`rank( mat )`	Returns the rank of `mat`.
	`remove( patt, object, opts )`	Removes the elements corresponding to `patt` from `object`. The optional arguments are used by `patt` if it is a Boolean-valued function.

NEW FUNCTIONS AT A GLANCE

`rootlocus( oltf, var, range, opts )`

Found in the `plots` package, this will plot the rootlocus of the open-loop transfer function `oltf` in `var` over `range` of the forward path gain.

`semilogplot( expr, range, opts)`

Found in the `plots` package, this plots `expr` over `range` on semilogarithmic axes. The logarithmic axis is the ordinate axis. The optional arguments are the same as `plot`.

`skewness( data )`   Calculates the skewness of the statistical data.

`spacecurve( [pts], opts )`   Plots a space curve in three dimensions given by the triplets `pts`. The optional arguments `opts` are the same as for `plot3d`. `Spacecurve` is found in the `plots` package.

`specfunc`   Type specification.

`stack( elem`$_1$`, elem`$_2$`, .., elem`$_n$` )`

Stacks `elem`$_i$ to form a new matrix. The elements `elem`$_i$ can be either matrices or vectors.

`standarddeviation( data )`   Compute the standard deviation of the statistical data.

`statevalf[ func, dist ]( args )`

Found in the statistics package, this evaluates numerically the statistical function `func` having a distribution `dist` for `args`.

`studentst`   The student's T test statistical distribution.

`submatrix( mat, range`$_1$`, range`$_2$` )`

Isolates the submatrix of `mat` specified by `range`$_i$.

`variance( data )`   Calculates the variance of the statistical data.

FAQs 1: Can I use Maple's adaptive plotting algorithm to plot the numerical solutions returned by the dsolve function?

Yes, as the following example demonstrates. The procedure returned by Maple is assigned to a variable that is used as a function.

```
> Eqn:=diff(x(t), t, t) + diff(x(t), t)*2 + 100*x(t)=100*sin(5*t),
  x(0)=10, D(x)(0)=10:
  ans:=dsolve({Eqn}, x(t), numeric);

ans := proc(rkf45_x) ... end

> ans(0);
```

$$\left[t = 0, \ x(t) = 10., \ \frac{d}{dt}\,x(t) = 10.\right]$$

With reference to the previous output, we can see that it can be used to perform a substitution to get the value of either $x(t)$ or its first derivative at any time t. The simplest way of doing this is to define a function as shown.

```
> fn:=T -> subs(ans(T), x(t)):
```

This function can then be plotted. Note the use of the delayed evaluation quotes.

```
> plot('fn'(t), t=0..5, title=`System time response`);
```

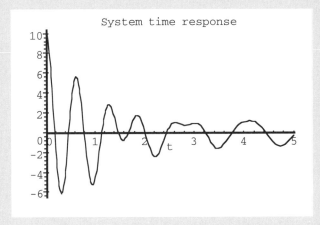

FAQs 2: Is it possible to turn off the tilde (~) tag for variables with assumptions?

Yes. In Maple Vr4 it is possible to turn off the tilde tagging mechanism by setting the interface variable `showassume` equal to 0.

```
> interface(showassume=0);
```

3: What happens if I leave off the hold evaluation quotes from around `rand`?

The function will be evaluated immediately so that the random number will "stick."

4: Why should I convert the data structure to an array at this point?

In this example, using the array structure to store the data makes for efficient data access and retrieval.

5: What happens if I chose a matrix instead of an array to store the signal data?

The FFT function will not work!

BEWARE 1: Maple Vr4 comes with a finance package; in older versions, the finance functions are readlib-defined.

2: The idea of subpackages was introduced in Release-3.

3: The function plots[semilog] is not available in releases before Vr4. The following code mimics its behavior by using the same technique as the plots[semilog] function to produce the logarithmic axis. First, we produce a dummy plot and remove the axis information from it.

```
> ff:=plots[ loglogplot] (f, f=0.1..10):
> xaxis:=op(1, op(select(type, [ op(ff)], specfunc(anything,
  AXESTICKS)))):
```

Then we produce a Bode plot with linear axes.

```
> Func:=10/(-w^2 + w*I + 4):
> p:=plot([ log10(w), 20*log10(abs(Func)), w=0.1..10]):
```

The final plot is then constructed from the various parts, as shown.

```
> plots[ display] (PLOT(op(subs(AXESTICKS(DEFAULT,DEFAULT)=
  AXESTICKS(xaxis, DEFAULT), [ op(p)]))), axes=FRAME, title=`The Gain
  Response`);
```

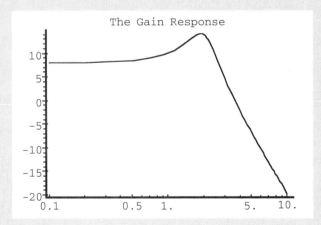

BEWARE 4: The piecewise function supported in versions older than Vr4 does not support compound logical relationships of the form condition$_1$ and/or condition$_2$. When using a version of Maple older than Vr4, the following code should be substituted for Maple code in the example.

```
> gain:=readlib(piecewise)(err(t)<-1, 1, err(t)>=1, 1,
  err(t)>=-1, s, 1):
```

5: The ability to perform arithmetic operations on a list element is not supported in Release 3 and older. For example, `[1, 2] - [a, b]` → `[1 - a, 2 - b]` is not possible.

6: Release 4 has a random-number subpackage. Be careful to use the correct random-number generator.

7: The `inttrans` package is new in Vr4 and groups together the *Laplace*, the continuous *Fourier* transform pairs, the *Heaviside* and *Dirac Delta* functions, all of which were readlib-defined, as well as additional transforms not present in earlier versions of Maple.

Maple Inside

The impact of computer algebra systems like Maple on the way we do mathematics has been quite dramatic. It is questionable whether the researchers and developers of the 1960s would have anticipated that 30 years into the future over 300,000 users, from finance to education, would be using these systems everyday. What is not so surprising is that increasing numbers of people using purely numerical analysis tools are demanding access to symbolical computations. Invariably they do not, at least to begin with, want to learn a brand new system (although Maple is easy to learn) just to do one or two symbolic computations. This demand has been addressed, at least in part, by some of the numerical software vendors. Most notable are: MathSoft with MathCad, The Math Works with the MATLAB Symbolics Toolbox, and Visual Numerics Inc., with PV-Wave and PV-Wave Advantage. All of these products use all or some Maple technology as a means of providing symbolic mathematics from inside of what has historically been a numerical tool. Using Maple technology to provide a mathematics engine is not the sole preserve of analysis tools. The ability to represent mathematical objects in documents has long been a nontrivial problem as T_EX, $L\!A\!T_EX$, Expressionist, and others bear witness. If we use the Maple engine and its ability to produce typeset output, we cannot only represent these quantities easily, but we also have the ability to manipulate them as well. In this second class, we have MathOffice for MS-Word, TCI's Scientific Word, and Scientific WorkPlace.

In this chapter, we take a brief look at using Maple when it is inside MATLAB, which is a well-regarded numerical analysis tool.

The Symbolics Toolbox

The Symbolics Toolbox, although not seamless, makes a good attempt at giving MATLAB users access to Maple and its symbolic mathematics without forcing them to learn Maple. The toolbox provides the interface between MATLAB and Maple through the `maplemex.mex` file interface. As far as MATLAB is concerned, the MATLAB version of the Maple kernel looks like a huge MEX file. MATLAB uses MEX files as a means of attaching external resources to itself. Provided that MATLAB can find the Maple library, you can, via the MEX-file interface, access some or all of Maple's functionality. The exact amount of the Maple system that is available to you is determined by the version of the toolbox that you are using. Although the interface is the same, there are three levels of toolbox functionality: Student, Standard, and Advanced; the Student version is the least powerful, but only just. The symbolic functionality provided by each toolbox is summarized in what follows. Emboldened **functions** are not available in the Student version; italicized *functions* are not available in the Standard version.

TOOLBOX	allvalues	factor	laplace	pretty	symop
FUNCTIONS	charpoly	finverse	latex	*procread*	sympow
	collect	fourier	linsolve	simple	symsize
	colspace	funtool	maple	simplify	symsub
	compose	horner	**mapleinit**	singvals	symsum
	cosint	int	**mfun**	**sinint**	symvar
	determ	inverse	**mfunlist**	solve	taylor
	diff	invfourier	**mhelp**	subs	transpose
	digits	invlaplace	**mpa**	sym	vpa
	dsolve	invztrans	nullspace	sym2poly	**zeta**
	eigensys	jacobian	numden	symadd	ztrans
	expand	jordan	numeric	symdiv	
	ezplot	**lambertw**	poly2sym	symmul	

In the following discussion it may appear that we consider the Standard and the Advanced Toolboxes separately, but this is not the case. The functions introduced in the section "The Standard Toolbox" are also available in the Advanced Toolbox. In the section "The Advanced Toolbox", we will concentrate on how we access more of Maple and how to use our own existing Maple functions.

Initializing the Maple Kernel

When the Maple system is first accessed by MATLAB it is initialized. During the initialization process, the location of the Maple library is set, the `linalg` package along with some additional functions is loaded, a number of aliases are defined, and the default number of significant digits is set to 16. By default MATLAB will look in its own directory structure and use the version of the Maple library shipped with the toolbox. However, it is possible to link to an existing Maple library if one is present. If you are first a Maple user and second a Symbolics Toolbox user, this allows you the option of maintaining only a single copy of the library on your machine. The location of the library to be used is held in the `mapleinit.m` file in the variable `maplelib`. By editing this variable, you can direct the MATLAB version of Maple to use your exiting library. If you are using a PC, you might want to set `maplelib` to 'C:\MAPLE\LIB'; if you are using a Macintosh, 'LENIN:MAPLE VR2:LIB' may be the path of your existing library; and, finally, if you are a UNIX user, '/USR/LOCAL/MAPLE/LIB' is an example of the library path.

MAPLEINIT.M ...

```
already_have_Maple = 0;
if (already_have_Maple)
   maplelib = '.....';
else
```

MAPLEINIT.M   % Find 'symbolic' or 'symbolic_lib' in the MATLAB path.
…

% Inform Maple of path to its library.
maplemex(maplelib,0);

% Load linear algebra package, load library routines, and set digits.
maplemex('with(linalg):');
maplemex('readlib(ifactor):');
maplemex('readlib(laplace):');
maplemex('readlib(fourier):');
maplemex('readlib(ztrans):');
maplemex('Digits := 16;');

% Establish aliases.
maplemex('alias(I=I, i=sqrt(-1), pi=Pi);');
maplemex('alias(log=ln, inf=infinity, Inf=infinity, fix=trunc);');
maplemex('alias(asin=arcsin, acos=arccos, atan=arctan);');
maplemex('alias(asinh=arcsinh, acosh=arccosh, atanh=arctanh);');
maplemex('alias(acsc=arccsc, asec=arcsec, acot=arccot);');
maplemex('alias(acsch=arccsch, asech=arcsech, acoth=arccoth);');
maplemex('alias(eye=&*());');

% Turn off "bytes used" and garbage collection messages.
maplemex('words(0);');
maplemex('gc(0);');

The Standard Symbolic Toolbox

The Standard Symbolic Toolbox provides us with 53 functions covering object definition, manipulation (expansion, factorization, symbolic substitution, conversion and so on), equation solving, basic calculus, arbitrary precision arithmetic, and special mathematical functions such as the sine and cosine integrals. Although at first glance this may seem limited, the functionality in this toolbox is more than adequate for the numerical analyst who wants to dabble in the symbolic realm.

Unlike Maple, MATLAB still uses a command-line style of interface. If you are experienced with using Maple, this may cause a few headaches to begin with. It also means that we are now unable to take full advantage of Maple's typesetting ability. All is not lost, however, as we shall see. Two other points to consider when using the toolbox are the syntax has been deliberately chosen to keep the MATLAB users comfortable and MATLAB makes far more assumptions about dependent and independent variables than Maple. This means that functions are defined slightly differently, and the order of the input arguments sometime seems odd. Despite all of this, using Maple from inside MATLAB is surprisingly easy, as we will see.

MAPLE This returns the general help page.   »help

INSIDE
```
HELP topics:

    matlab:general      -  General purpose commands.
    matlab:ops          -  Operators and special characters.
    matlab:lang         -  Language constructs and debugging.
    matlab:elmat        -  Elementary matrices and matrix manipulation.
    matlab:specmat      -  Specialized matrices.
    matlab:elfun        -  Elementary math functions.
    matlab:specfun      -  Specialized math functions.
    matlab:matfun       -  Matrix functions - numerical linear algebra.
    matlab:datafun      -  Data analysis and Fourier transform
                           functions.
    matlab:polyfun      -  Polynomial and interpolation functions.
    matlab:funfun       -  Function functions - nonlinear numerical
                           methods.
    matlab:sparfun      -  Sparse matrix functions.
    matlab:plotxy       -  Two dimensional graphics.
    matlab:plotxyz      -  Three dimensional graphics.
    matlab:graphics     -  General purpose graphics functions.
    matlab:color        -  Color control and lighting model functions.
    matlab:sounds       -  Sound processing functions.
    matlab:strfun       -  Character string functions.
    matlab:iofun        -  Low-level file I/O functions.
    matlab:demos        -  The MATLAB Expo and other demonstrations.
    Toolbox:local       -  Local function library.
    Toolbox:sigsys      -  Signals and Systems Toolbox.
    symbolic:lib        - (No table of contents file)
    Toolbox:symbolic    -  Symbolic Math Toolbox.
    Molotov:Student MATLAB - (No table of contents file)

For more help on directory/topic, type "help topic".
```

Here we get the help page for the   »help digits
function digits.

```
DIGITS Set Maple's Digits.
     The accuracy of Maple's numeric computations is determined by
     Digits.
     DIGITS, by itself, displays the current setting of Digits.
     DIGITS(D) sets Digits to D for subsequent calculations.
     D = DIGITS returns the current setting of Digits.

     See also VPA.
```

MAPLE INSIDE MATLAB represents symbolic variables and constants as strings. Here we define a symbolic constant to be the first five digits of π.

```
»sym_number = '3.1416'

sym_number =

3.1416
```

This tests the symbolic constant with the built-in quantity. We get an unexpected result because MATLAB first converts the string sym_number into a list of characters and subtracts their ASCII values from MATLAB's numerical approximation to π.

```
»pi-sym_number

ans =

  -47.8584   -42.8584   -45.8584   -48.8584
-45.8584   -50.8584
```

Here we repeat the previous operation after first converting the symbolic constant into a number quantity.

```
»pi-numeric(sym_number)

ans =

  -7.3464e-06
```

This assigns a symbolic quantity to the MATLAB variable ans.

```
»'This_is_a_symbol'

ans =

This_is_a_symbol
```

Here we test to see if ans is a string. This is a good test to see if a quantity could be symbolic. A "1" means true.

```
»isstr(ans)

ans =

     1
```

This assigns a symbolic quantity to the Matlab variable f.

```
»f='so_is_this'

f =

so_is_this
```

MAPLE INSIDE Here we define a 3-by-3 symbolic matrix. Note that the array syntax is MATLAB's and not Maple's.

```
»a_mat = sym('[ 1,2,3;a,b,c;4,5,6] ')

a_mat =

[ 1,  2,  3]
[ a,  b,  c]
[ 4,  5,  6]
```

This changes **a_mat$_{2,2}$** from *b* to *X*.

```
»a_mat = sym(a_mat,2,2,'X')

a_mat =

[ 1,  2,  3]
[ a,  X,  c]
[ 4,  5,  6]
```

Here we find the symbolic determinant of **a_mat**.

```
»determ(a_mat)

ans =

-6*X + 3*c + 3*a
```

Here we use MATLAB to calculate the answer to this numerical quantity.

```
»1/2/3/4/5/6/7/8/9

ans =

   2.7557e-06
```

This uses Maple's arbitrary precision arithmetic to calculate the answer to 16 significant digits.

```
»vpa('1/2/3/4/5/6/7/8/9')

ans =

2.755731922398589e-6
```

Here we get Maple to return the exact answer.

```
»symop('1/2/3/4/5/6/7/8/9')

ans =

1/362880
```

MAPLE INSIDE Here we build up a symbolic expression.

```
»symdiv(sympow('a', 'n'), 'a - n')

ans =

a^n/(a - n)
```

This returns the symbolic sum for $n = 0..3$.

```
»poly = symsum(ans, 'n', 0, 3)

poly =

1/a + a/(a - 1) + a^2/(a - 2) + a^3/(a - 3)
```

Here we ask MATLAB to find the simplest (least number of characters) form of the polynomial. MATLAB echoes the simplification techniques that it tries, along with the answer obtained.

```
»simple(poly)

simplify:

(-a^3 + 11*a - 6 - a^4 - 2*a^5 + a^6)/a/
(a - 1)/(a - 2)/(a - 3)

radsimp:

(-a^3 + 11*a - 6 - a^4 - 2*a^5 + a^6)/a/
(a - 1)/(a - 2)/(a - 3)

factor:

(-a^3 + 11*a - 6 - a^4 - 2*a^5 + a^6)/a/
(a - 1)/(a - 2)/(a - 3)

ans =

1/a + a/(a - 1) + a ^2/(a - 2) +
a^3/(a - 3)
```

This takes the symbolic derivative of the polynomial. The question that needs to be asked here is: How does MATLAB choose the independent variable?

```
»diff(poly)

ans =

-1/a^2 + 1/(a - 1) - a/(a - 1)^2 + 2*a/
(a - 2) - a^2/(a - 2)^2 + 3*a^2/(a - 3) -
a^3/(a - 3)^2
```

CHOOSING A VARIABLE

Here we ask for the independent variable of an empty string. MATLAB returns *x*.

```
»symvar('')

ans =

x
```

This repeats the process on the symbolic quantity *symbol*. Again MATLAB returns *x*.

```
»symvar('symbol')

ans =

x
```

Here we try using an object similar to our polynomial. This time the expected result is returned.

```
»symvar('(1 - t)/(1 + t)')

ans =

t
```

In our final test, MATLAB has two choices: *a* and *z*. It chooses *z*.

```
»symvar('(a - z)/(a + z)')

ans =
z
```

The reason for MATLAB's behavior is simple. Unless otherwise instructed, MATLAB looks for a single lowercase character in the symbolic quantity to use as the independent variable. If none is available, the default variable name x is used. If x has already been assigned, then t (if unassigned) is used. If multiple single-character names are present, the one closest to x is selected. If two are found that are equally spaced, then the lowest in lexicographic order is selected.

MAPLE INSIDE

If a function has both a symbolic and a numeric meaning, MATLAB tests for the presence of symbolic quantities in the arguments and chooses the function accordingly. Here we take the difference of the elements in the list and not its derivative.

```
»diff([ 1,2,3,4] )

ans =

    1       1       1
```

MAPLE
INSIDE

Although we cannot take advantage of Maple's standard typeset output, we can get an approximation. Here we use `pretty` on *poly*.

```
»pretty(poly)

                      2          3
        a            a          a
1/a + ----- + ----- + -----
      a - 1   a - 2   a - 3
```

Here we get the LATEX form of poly.

```
»latex(poly)

a^{-1} + {\frac {a}{a - 1}} + {\frac
{a^{2}}{a - 2}} + {\frac {a^{3}}{a - 3}}
```

Here we define the symbolic equations for a circle radius *r* centered on the origin and a line of unit slope and intercept *1/b*.

```
»quad='x^2 + y^2=r^2';line='y=x + 1/b';
```

This returns the exact solution for their points of intersection. The solution is exact. If the radius is unity and the intercept is 2, the coordinates of intersection are obtained as follows.

```
»solve(quad, line, 'x, y')

ans =

x=RootOf(2*_Z^2*b^2 + 2*_Z*b + 1 -
r^2*b^2), y=(RootOf(2*_Z^2*b^2 + 2*_Z*b + 1
- r^2*b^2)*b + 1)/b
```

First, we substitute for *r*.

```
»subs(x, 1, 'r')

ans =

RootOf(2*_Z^2*b^2 + 2*_Z*b + 1 - b^2)
```

Then we substitute for *b*.

```
»subs(ans, '1/2', 'b')

ans =

RootOf(1/2*_Z^2 + _Z + 3/4)
```

This computes the floating-point approximation to the previous exact answers. Thirty significant digits are used.

```
»vpa([ans], 30)

ans =

[ -1. + .707106781186547524400844362105* i]
[ -1. - .707106781186547524400844362105* i]
```

MAPLE INSIDE Here we take a look at solving the circuit example *E1* using Maple inside MATLAB. First, we enter the node equations.

```
»n1='v1/l1 + (v1 - v2)/r1 = -i1';
»n2='v2/(r2 + c2) + (-v1 + v2)/r1 +
(-v3+v2)/l2 = i1';
»n3='(v3 - v2)/l2 + v3/c1 = i2';
```

This solves the three simultaneous equations and assigns the answers to *v1*, *v2*, and *v3*, respectively.

```
»[ v1, v2, v3] = solve(n1, n2, n3, 'v1, v2,
v3')
```

```
v1 =

l1*(-r1*l2*i1 - c1*i1*r1 - r1*r2*i1 + c2*i2*c1 + r2*i2*c1r1*c2*i1)/
(c1*c2 + r1*l2 + l2*r2 + l1*l2 + c1*r1 + r1*c2 + l1*r2 + l1*c1 +
r1*r2 + l2*c2 + c1*r2 + l1*c2)

v2 =

(r1*c2*i2*c1 + r1*r2*i2*c1 + c2*l1*i2*c1 + r2*l1*i2*c1 + r1*i1*c1*c2
+ i1*r1*l2*r2 + i1*r1*l2*c2 + r1*i1*c1*r2)/(c1*c2 + r1*l2 + l2*r2 +
l1*l2 + c1*r1 + r1*c2 + l1*r2 + l1*c1 + r1*r2 + l2*c2 + c1*r2 +
l1*c2)

v3 =

(c2*l1*i2 + r2*l1*i2 + r1*r2*i1 + i2*l2*r1 + r1*c2*i1 + r1*r2*i2 +
r1*c2*i2 + r2*i2*l2 + c2*i2*l2 + i2*l2*l1)*c1/(c1*c2 + r1*l2 + l2*r2
+ l1*l2 + c1*r1 + r1*c2 + l1*r2 + l1*c1 + r1*r2 + l2*c2 + c1*r2 +
l1*c2)
```

Here we define the circuit component values.

```
»vals='r1=5, r2=10, l1=j/2, l2=j/2,
c1=-1/(j*10^(-7)), c2=-1/(j*10^(-7)),
i1=exp(-t), i2=cos(t)'
```

```
vals =

r1=5, r2=10, l1=j/2, l2=j/2, c1=-1/(j*10^(-7)), c2=-1/(j*10^(-7)),
i1=exp(-t), i2=cos(t)
```

MAPLE INSIDE Here we obtain the expression for *v3*. You will recall that in the previous example, we had to substitute for each unknown separately, which would prove tedious in this example. A solution is to make a call to the Maple `subs` routine directly.

```
»vpa(maple('subs', vals, v3), 3)
```

```
ans =
```

```
-1.00e7*(-1.00e7*cos(t) + 12.5*cos(t)*j + 50.*exp(-1.*t)- 5.00e7/j*
exp(-1.*t) - 5.00e7*cos(t)/j + .250*cos(t)*j^2)/j/(1.00e14/j^2 +
12.5*j + .250*j^2-2.00e8/j - 1.50e7)
```

We also can solve differential equations symbolically using Maple's ode solver. This solves an E-B field example previously done using Maple (see "Brief Tour": Chapter 1). Note the way in which the first and second derivatives are defined. In this example, we explicitly choose *t* as the independent variable.

```
»dsolve('D2Y = 1 - DX', 'D2X = DY', 't')
```

```
ans =
```

```
X(t) = C1+t+C4*sin(t)-C3*cos(t),
Y(t) = C2+C3*sin(t)+C4*cos(t)
```

In this example, we find the impulse response for an open-loop system with a time response 1-e^{-t} when negative unity-gain feedback is applied.

```
»sys = symadd(1, '-exp(-t)')
```

```
sys =
```

```
1-exp(-t)
```

This returns the Laplace transform of the open-loop system. Note the order of the arguments.

```
»oltf=laplace(sys, 's', 't')
```

```
oltf =
```

```
1/s/(s + 1)
```

MAPLE INSIDE   Here we find the closed-loop system's transfer function.

```
»cltf = symdiv(oltf, symadd(1, oltf))
cltf =
1/s/(s + 1)/(1 + 1/s/(s + 1))
```

Here we simplify the result using `simple`.

```
»simple(cltf)

 simplify:
 1/(s^2 + s + 1)
ans =
1/(s^2 + s + 1)
```

This finds the exact time response by taking the inverse Laplace transform of the impulse response.

```
»invlaplace(ans, 't', 's')
ans =

2/3*exp(-1/2*t)*sin(1/2*3^(1/2)*t)*3^(1/2)
```

MORE HELP

```
            help symbolic
```
Returns the help page for the Symbolics Toolbox.

```
    info@mathworks.com
```
The electronic mail address for the information server at The MathWorks.

```
     The MathWorks, Inc,
     24 Prime Park Way,
                Natick,
                MA 1760
```
The address, telephone, and fax numbers for The MathWorks.

```
 Phone: +(508) 653 1415
   FAX: +(508) 653 2997
```

The Advanced Symbolic Toolbox

The two operations that separate the Advanced Symbolic Toolbox from the Standard one are the ability to load Maple packages and functions, and the ability to load your own Maple functions and procedures into the current MATLAB session. This means that we now have access to the full power of Maple. We can now use all of Maple's functions, and more importantly, we can now develop our own specialized Maple functions in Maple and use them in a MATLAB session. Maple programming is not really recommended from within MATLAB. The following examples demonstrate the two important features unique to the Advanced Symbolic Toolbox.

MORE MAPLE   By using MATLAB's Maple assignment function, we define a simple function in the Maple workspace.

```
»mpa('test', '(x, y)->x^y');
```

MORE TO MAPLE We can make calls directly to Maple from within MATLAB with the `maple` keyword. This tests our new function by making a call directly to Maple to invoke it.

```
»maple('test', 's', '23')

ans =

s^23
```

Here we access the Maple print command directly to view our new function.

```
»maple('print(test)')

ans =

proc (x, y) options operator, arrow; x^y
end
```

A major advantage of using the Advanced Symbolic Toolbox is that we can gain access to all of Maple's functionality. This is made possible through the enabling of the `with` and `read-lib` commands. Here we "load" the Grobner Basis package.

```
»maple( 'with', 'grobner');

ans =

[ finduni, finite, gbasis, gsolve, leadmon,
normalf, solvable, spoly]
```

This defines two equations in the Maple workspace.

```
»mpa( 'eqns', ' x^2 + y^2 - r^2, y - x');
```

Here we use the `finite` function to determine whether a finite number of solutions exists for our system of equations. The result is false because Maple thinks that there are three unknowns.

```
»maple('finite([ eqns] )')

ans =

false
```

This calls the function again, using an alternate syntax. This time we explicitly tell Maple that the system of equations is in two unknowns: *x* and *y*.

```
»maple('finite', '[ eqns] ', '{ x,y} ')

ans =

true
```

MORE MAPLE Here we read one of our own Maple procedures into the current MATLAB session. The procedure is stored in the file *testproc.txt*. in plain text. During the reading of the file, all comments are removed.

```
»readproc('testproc.txt');
```

This calls our procedure with the argument $x + y$. We get the expected result.

```
»maple('testproc', 'x + y')

ans =

x^2+2*x*y+y^2
```

Here we print out the body of the procedure.

```
»maple('print(testproc)')

ans =

proc (x) expand(x^2) end
```

In addition to loading packages using `with`, we can also gain access to `readlib` defined functions. This "loads" `isolate`.

```
»maple('readlib', 'isolate')
```

```
ans =

proc (expr, x, n) local expr1, expr2, ito; option `Copyright 1992 by
the University of Waterloo`; if nargs < 2 or 3 < nargs or nargs = 3
and not type(n,integer) or not type(x,algebraic) or not
type(expr,{ `=`, `<`, `<=`, algebraic}) then ERROR(`invalid arguments
for isolate`) fi; if not has(expr,x) then if type(x,`^`) and
type(op(2,x),'rational') and 0 < op(2,x) then RETURN(x = 1/op(2,proc-
name(expr,1/x,args[ 3 .. nargs]))) fi; ERROR(expr, `does not
contain`,x) fi; if type(expr,relation) then expr1 := expr else expr1
:= expr = 0 fi; expr1 := subs(x = _XX,diff = _DIFF,int =
_INT,expr1); if nargs = 3 then ito := n else ito := 100000 fi;  to
ito while expr1 <> expr2 do expr2 := expr1; expr1 := traperror(iso-
late1(expr1)); if expr1 = lasterror then ERROR(`unable to isolate`,x)
fi; if 1 < nops([ expr1] ) then userinfo(1,isolate,`Warning: solutions
lost`); expr1 := expr1[ 1] fi od; subs(_XX = x,_DIFF = diff,_INT =
int,expr1); RETURN(") end
```

MORE functions. This "loads" isolate. **MAPLE** Because we can gain access to all of Maple, it is useful to look at Maple help pages. Here we look at the help page for Maple constants.

»mhelp('constants')

```
HELP FOR: Maple constants

SYNOPSIS:
- The numeric constants in Maple are integers, fractions, and
  floating-point numbers.

- The global variable constants is an expression sequence of all
  names which are initially known as symbolic constants in Maple.
  These are

                    false    gamma       infinity
                    true     Catalan     E
                    FAIL     I           Pi

- The user can define new symbolic constants by appending them to
  the constants variable.

- More generally, a Maple expression is of type constant if it is an
  unevaluated function with all arguments of type constant, or a
  sum, product, or power with all operands of type constant.

SEE ALSO: integer, fraction, float, type, type[constant]
```

NEW	`'expr'`	Defines a symbolic expression.
FUNCTIONS		
AT A GLANCE	`determ( mat )`	Calculates the symbolic determinant of `mat`.

`diff( expr )`
`diff( expr, var )`

Differentiates `expr`, if symbolic, or returns the difference, if numeric. The second form will differentiate `expr` with respect to `var`. If `var` is omitted, the independent variable is determined by `symvar`.

`dsolve( eqn`$_1$`, eqn`$_2$`, .., eqn`$_n$`, cond`$_1$`, cond`$_2$`, .., cond`$_n$`, var )`
`dsolve( eqn`$_1$`, eqn`$_2$`, .., eqn`$_n$`, cond`$_1$`, cond`$_2$`, .., cond`$_n$` )`
`dsolve( eqn`$_1$`, eqn`$_2$`, .., eqn`$_n$`, var )`
`dsolve( eqn`$_1$`, eqn`$_2$`, .., eqn`$_n$` )`

Solve symbolically the differential equations `eqn`$_i$ with respect to `var`. If the initial/boundary conditions `cond`$_i$ are omitted, the result will contain constants of integration. If `var` is omitted, the default variable x is used.

`invlaplace( expr, s, t )`

Find the inverse Laplace transform of the symbolic expression `expr` in `s`. The result will be an expression in `t`.

`isstr( expr )`

Test to see if `expr` is a string. A "1" is returned if true, a zero otherwise.

`help topic`
`help`

Returns the help page for `topic`. If no topic is selected, the general page is returned.

`i, j`

The complex constant.

`laplace( expr, t, s )`

Find the Laplace transform of the symbolic expression `expr` in `t`. The result will be an expression in `s`.

`latex( expr )`

Returns the LATEX form of `expr`.

`maple( func, arg`$_1$`, arg`$_2$`, .., arg`$_n$` )`

Call the Maple function `func` with arguments `arg`$_n$.

`mhelp( topic )`

Returns the Maple help page for `topic`.

`mpa( var, expr )`

Assigns `var` to `expr` in the Maple workspace.

`numeric( expr )`

Converts `expr` to a numeric quantity if possible.

NEW FUNCTIONS AT A GLANCE	`pretty( expr )`	Produces the pretty-print output form of `expr`.
	`procread( file )`	Reads a Maple procedure from the text file `file`.
	`simple( expr )`	Returns the simplest form of `expr`. The simplest form has the fewest characters.
	`simplify( expr )`	Simplifies `expr`.
	`solve( eqn`$_1$`, eqn`$_2$`, .., eqn`$_n$`, vars )` `solve( eqn`$_1$`, eqn`$_2$`, .., eqn`$_n$` )`	Solves symbolically the equations `eqn`$_i$ with respect to `vars`. If `vars` is omitted, the variables are determined by `symvar`.
	`subs( expr, value, var )` `subs( expr, value )`	Substitutes `value` for every occurrence of `var` in `expr`. If `var` is omitted, the variable is determined by `symvar`.
	`sym( row, col, mat, value )` `sym( mat )`	Create the symbolic matrix `mat`. If `row` and `col` are given, the specified element is replaced with `value`.
	`symadd( expr`$_1$`, expr`$_2$` )`	Add `expr`$_1$ to `expr`$_2$.
	`symop( arg`$_1$`, arg`$_2$`, .., arg`$_n$` )`	Concatenates `arg`$_i$ and returns the symbolic result.
	`sympow ( arg`$_1$`, arg`$_2$`, )`	Raises `arg`$_i$ to the power `arg`$_2$ and returns the symbolic result.
	`symsum( expr, var, range`$_1$`, range`$_2$` )`	Calculates the symbolic sum of `expr` in `var` for `var=range`$_1$`..range`$_2$.
	`symvar( expr )`	Returns the variable of `expr`.
	`vpa( expr, digits )` `vap( expr )`	Returns the numeric approximation of `expr` to `digits` significant digits. If `digits` is omitted, the current setting of `digits` is used.

Data File Listings

The following pages contain either full or partial listings (size-dependent) of the data files used in various exercises presented in Chapters 4 and 5. The files listed are also available, in their entirety, with the Maple Worksheets, containing all of the examples used in this book, on Prentice Hall's ftp and world wide web sites.

data1.txt

a_list := [[1,2,3],[a,b,c],[A,B,C]];
convert(a_list, matrix);

data2.txt

b_list:=[[1a, 2a, 3a], [aa, ba, ca], [Aa, Ba, Ca]];
op(op(1 2, b_list));

data3.dat

1 2 3 4 5
1 4 9 16 25
1 .5 .3 .25 .2
1.2 34 5.6 789 100

eigentst

This is a partial listing.

(*^

::[frontEndVersion = "Macintosh Mathematica Notebook Front End Version 2.1";
        macintoshStandardFontEncoding;
...
{1.782474995823492743, 1., −1.137283254638380886}
;[o]
{1.78247, 1., −1.13728}
^*)

usa.dat

This is a partial listing.

USA := [[[−117.11667, 32.533333], [−117.28333, 33.], [−117.28333, 33.], [−120.61667, 34.566667], [−122.48333, 37.516667], [−121.41667, 38.016667], [−123.70000, 38.933333], [−124.18333, 42.], [−124.18333, 42.], [−124.06667, 46.283333], [−124.06667, 46.283333], [−124.71667, 48.400000], [−122.75000, 48.166667],

...

[−141., 69.650000], [−141., 60.300000], [−135.46667, 59.800000], [−130.01667, 55.916667]], [[−155.81667, 20.266667], [−154.80000, 19.533333], [−155.66667, 18.916667], [−155.81667, 20.266667]], [[−153.26667, 58.], [−152.33333, 57.433333], [−154.80000, 57.350000], [−153.26667, 58.]]]:

sdata.dat

This is a partial listing.

data:=[[0.5175, 0.5253, 0.5533, 0.6396, 0.9244, 0.9914, 0.9931, 0.9690, 0.9927, 0.9931, 0.9744, 0.9261, 0.8672, 0.8582, 0.9073, 0.9504, 0.9632, 0.9742, 0.9944, 0.9948, 0.9929, 0.9913, 0.9912, 0.9944, 0.9323, 0.6362, 0.5571,

0.5340, 0.4809, 0.4848, 0.4515],
…
[0.5785, 0.5769, 0.5788, 0.5883, 0.6449,
0.5818, 0.2605, 0.1232, 0.1684,
0.2695, 0.1920, 0.2105, 0.2118, 0.1996,
0.1887, 0.2687, 0.5520, 0.5363,
0.6288, 0.4971, 0.4848, 0.5044, 0.5068,
0.5025, 0.5057, 0.5034, 0.5006,
0.4967, 0.4916, 0.4876, 0.4849]]:

pole.dat

This is a partial listing.

[[[−2, −2, 0.07443229275647868679], [−2,
−1.9, 0.08005138347854845721], [−2, −1.8,
0.08616603372611768704], [−2, −1.7,
0.09282570620387664895], [−2, −1.6,
0.1000851566514553019], [−2, −1.5,
0.1080046105452210741], [−2, −1.4,
0.1166495234274826645], [−2, −1.3,
0.1260895619445456836], [−2, −1.2,
…
0.1783742111259984578], [2., 1.5,
0.1648696210050418768], [2., 1.6,
0.1518706576618573568], [2.,
1.700000000000000001,
0.1395529707014143569], [2.,
1.800000000000000001,

0.1280263276403057258], [2.,
1.900000000000000001,
0.117345049270749424], [2., 2.,
0.1075206661140940714]]]:

vect.dat

0
.9453559925
.9381374240
.8786893259
.6884614320
.9666666666
.5884614320
.5453559926
.9381374240
.9453559925
−.6666666671e−1
−.6786893260
−1.004804091
−.6120226594
−.5884614321
−.7666666668
−.6551280988
−.5453559927
−1.071470757
−.7120226593
0

Procedure Listings

The following pages contain listings of the procedures referenced in Chapter 5. The procedures listed are also available, in their entirety, on Prentice Hall's ftp and world wide web sites.

make_TM

```
> make_TM:=proc(mat, n)
  # form the transformation matrices
  local temp, nn, nnn;
  with(linalg, [ matrix, augment, coldim, stack, submatrix] );
  if n>4 then
    temp[ 0] :=augment(mat,matrix([[ 0$(n - coldim(mat))],
    [ 0$(n - coldim(mat))]]])):
  else temp[ 0] :=mat
  fi:
  for nn to n/2 - 1 do
    temp[ nn] :=augment(submatrix(temp[ nn - 1], 1..2,
    coldim(temp[ 0] ) - 1..coldim(temp[ 0] )),
    submatrix(temp[ nn - 1], 1..2,1..coldim(temp[ 0] ) - 2));
  od:
  eval(stack(temp[ nnn] $nnn=0..nn - 1));
  end:
```

WaveletTF

```
> WaveletTF:=proc(mat, data)
  # mat is the matrix of coeffs, data is the matrix of samples
  # (power of 2)
  options `Copyright Coded by Dr. Steve Adams`;
  local sd, w, T, TM, len, n, nn, Data;
  with(linalg, [ transpose, matrix] );
  Data:=data;
  len:=coldim(data);
  # number of data points
  n:=4;
  while n<=len do
    # make TM matrices
    TM[ n] :=make_TM(mat, n);
    n:=2*n;
  od:
  n:=len:
  while n>=4 do
    # make data and coeffs
```

```
   T[ n] :=transpose(evalm(TM[ n]  &* transpose(Data)));
   sd[ n] :=[ seq(T[ n][ (1, 2*nn - 1)], nn=1..n/2)];
   w[ n] :=[ seq(T[ n][ 1, 2*nn], nn=1..n/2)];
   Data:=matrix([ sd[ n]] );
   n:=n/2;
 od;
 matrix([ map(op, [ sd[ 4], seq(w[ 2^nn], nn=2..sqrt(len))])] );
 end:
```

InvWaveletTF

```
> InvWaveletTF:=proc(mat, data)
  # mat is the matrix of coeffs, data is the matrix of wavelet data
  # (power of 2)
  options `Copyright Coded by Dr. Steve Adams`;
  local Coeffs, itf, TM, len, n, nn, temp;
  with(linalg, [ coldim, transpose, matrix, submatrix] );
  len:=coldim(data);
  # number of data points
  n:=4;
  while n<=len do
    # make TM matrices
    TM[ n] :=make_TM(mat, n);
    n:=2* n;
  od:
  n:=4:
  itf[ 4] :=transpose(evalm(transpose(TM[ 4] ) &*
  transpose(matrix([[ data[ 1, 1], data[ 1, 3], data[ 1, 2],
  data[ 1, 4]]] )))));
  # make first one manualy
  while n<len do
    # make rest of inverse data
    Coeffs[ n] :=submatrix(data, 1..1, n + 1..2*n);
    temp:=map(op, zip((x, y)->[ x, y], convert(convert(itf[ n],
    vector), list), convert(convert(Coeffs[ n], vector), list)));
    n:=n* 2;
    itf[ n] :=transpose(evalm(transpose(TM[ n] ) &*
    transpose(matrix([ temp] )))));
  od;
  eval(itf[ n] );
  end:
```

Index of FAQs
And Pitfalls

This index is organized by FAQ and Beware subject heading. Each entry in this index points to either an FAQ (?) or a Beware (!) entry. The format of each entry is: question and answer page (example page(s)). The plain text entries refer to FAQs while the **emboldened** entries point to a Beware entry. For example, a potential pitfall related to integer data types is highlighted on page 138 and put in context on page 117 - **integer**, 138 (117).

Data Transfer

Efficiency

Evaluation

Rules

Types